RUNNING WITH THE FOX

RUNNING WITH THE FOX

DAVID MACDONALD

Illustrations by
PRISCILLA BARRETT
Photographs by
DAVID AND JENNY MACDONALD

UNWIN HYMAN
LONDON · SYDNEY

For Jenny

ACKNOWLEDGEMENTS

Anyone who reads this book will soon realize that any success my research has achieved has been due, in large measure, to the many people who have helped me. My attempts to study foxes have led me into the company of an enriching diversity of people, and it has been my pleasure and privilege to be guided by them through many walks of life. These people have differed greatly – some have had little interest in foxes until they collided with my enthusiasms, others have had a lifetime of experience with them, and held varied, and sometimes strongly opposing views – yet they have gone to astounding lengths to help me, and to teach me, and have shown me the courtesy of listening to my ideas about fox behaviour. There are aspects of man's relationship with foxes that divide people, yet on all sides of these divides I have been greeted good-naturedly by those who were more sincere and honourable than their caricatures commonly suggest. I am heartily grateful to them all.

My students and assistants have helped with this project, contributing hard work and fresh insights. They are too many to name individually, but I single out for special thanks those whose fox-tracking efforts have won us notoriety as The Oxford Foxlot – Geoff Carr, Chris Dickman, Patrick Doncaster, Pall Hersteinsson, Heribert Hofer, Nick Hough, Gill Kerby, Ian Lindsay, Malcolm Newdick, Colin Pringle and Andrew Taber. In these people, and others in the Foxlot working on different animals, foxes have brought me close friends and fine companions. It is too often forgotten that people are only as good as those who support them, and therefore I owe a great debt to the skill of the University's technical staff – in particular, Dick Cheyne, Tony Price, Mike Dolan, Terry Barker and Dave Palmer.

I thank sincerely those organizations who have kept the fox research solvent, amongst them: Balliol College, the Ernest Cook Trust, the Ministry of Agriculture, Fisheries and Food, the Natural Environmental Research Council, the Nature Conservancy Council, the Nuffield Foundation, the Royal Society for the Prevention of Cruelty to Animals, the Science and Engineering Research Council, and the Wellcome Trust.

This book has been enlivened by Pricilla Barrett's drawings, and greatly improved by the staff at Unwin Hyman. John Haywood helped to draw the best quality out of some of my poorer photographs. I am grateful to the following for use of their photographs: Malcolm Newdick (pages 112, 183, 186, 187, 189, 193, 194, 199, 211); Nick Hough (page 191); Pall Hersteinsson (page 12) and Lary Shaffer (page 157). Friends and colleagues have plodded painstakingly through various drafts of the text, and their suggestions forestalled many errors. I have greatly valued critical comments from: Jo Bird, Pricilla Barrett, Colin Booty, Ian Coghill, Dr Wilma Crowther, the late Edwin Dargue, Dr Marion Dawkins, Dr Chris Dickman, Dr Patrick Doncaster, Dr Keith Eltringham, Mike Fenn, Erika Ison, John Gee, Dr Pall Hersteinsson, Dr Heribert Hofer, Nick Hough, Dr Alex Kacelnik, Dr Robert Kenward, Gill Kerby, Dr Hans Kruuk, Dr Erik Lindström, Gwyn Lloyd, Jenny Macdonald, Stephan Natynczuk, Dr Malcolm Newdick, Dr Dick Potts, Dr Jonathan Reynolds, Patricia Searle, Dr Lary Shaffer, Dr Stephen Tapper, Tom Tew, and Denis Voigt.

Above all, of course, I thank my wife for everything.

First published in Great Britain by Unwin Hyman, an imprint of Unwin Hyman Limited, 1987.

UNWIN HYMAN LIMITED
Denmark House, 37–39 Queen Elizabeth Street,
London SE1 2QB
and 40 Museum Street, London WC1A 1LU

Allen & Unwin Australia Pty Ltd
8 Napier Street, North Sydney, NSW 2060, Australia

Allen & Unwin New Zealand Ltd with the
Port Nicholson Press
60 Cambridge Terrace, Wellington, New Zealand

ISBN 0 04 440084 5

British Library Cataloguing in Publication Data
Macdonald, David W.
    Running with the Fox.
    1. Foxes
    I. Title
    599.74'442   QL737.C22

Designed by Colin Lewis
Printed in Italy by
New Interlitho S.P.A.

CONTENTS

1 | A BRUSH WITH FOXES

THROUGH BINOCULARS, I could see the fox's outline clearly: the sun sparkled on a cascade of dew-drops that sprang free as she moved slowly through the grass. Her coat was dark and spiky, saturated from a night of brushing through drizzle-soaked undergrowth. For my part, I could feel the dew percolating through my beard, and an unwelcome breeze squeezing icily between my muddy trousers and goose-pimpled skin. It had been a long night. Aided by a full moon, the vixen and I had tracked our quarries from dusk to dawn. Both of us had strained for sounds, whiffs of scent, and glimpses of our goals, she pursuing her prey; I pursuing her.

The first rays of sunlight struggled across the skyline to fringe the silhouette of her angular ears. The vixen stood soaking up the warmth. Stifling a yawn, she craned towards a noise which had caught her attention. Taking a tense, measured pace, she plunged her nose into the grass—in the stillness of the dawn I heard the vixen's teeth snap shut twice, before she swallowed the incautious beetle and resumed her yawn.

No longer could she be described as a beautiful fox; she was too lean and haggard for that. She was unusually marked. Her autumn-red mask and velvety, black-backed ears were conventional enough, but her neck verged on orange fading into a grey body broken by a tawny yellow, saddle-shaped mark across her back. Her lean brush, which bore no white tag, had a serrated appearance, due to the absence of large tufts of fur recently removed by exuberant cubs. The vixen's blotched appearance made her unmistakable and had led me, some months earlier, to name her Mottle. If the summer dawn was sunny, and if the cowman was not too raucous while gathering his milking herd, Mottle invari-

ably sought out that first patch of sunlight at the top corner of Back Field. Often, I had crouched nearby in the hedgerow, whispering into a dictaphone, willing the contrary breeze not to betray my whereabouts.

On this particular July morning in 1973, another fox trotted into view just as Mottle curled up to snooze in her pool of sunshine. This second vixen was slightly bigger than Mottle, with a flame-red coat and dark heavy brush. The newcomer walked slowly up one edge of the field, occasionally missing a pace with her right hind leg. When I had first seen Red Vixen in late spring, the limp had been severe and had enabled me to recognize her at a glance. At that time, her lower leg was swollen, and never touched the ground. Now the injury was almost healed and soon her vivid colour would be my only clue to her identity. Red Vixen disappeared behind a rise, but her progress along the field edge was charted by an apprehensive clucking of blackbirds. She reappeared, trotting into the sun where Mottle dozed.

As Red Vixen approached, Mottle's head jerked up, her ears flicking back, but almost at once she relaxed again. Red Vixen flattened her ears, though, and, with a rippling twitch running the length of her brush, momentarily quickened her pace. She crouched as she reached Mottle. The two vixens sniffed noses, then sat side by side. Behind them, a third fox stood up from a couch in the grass, stretched on the tips of its toes, with arched back and elevated tail, before dropping its forequarters to the grass with its haunches aloft. This was Other-Mottle. She shared Mottle's blotchy appearance, but the detail of her patterning was very different. She too moved into the crowded patch of sunshine.

A ratchet-like noise shattered the peace. The three vixens' heads swivelled as one, a blackbird exploded from the hedgerow and two fox cubs tumbled forth, engaged in noisy combat ending as unexpectedly as it had begun. A third cub wandered into view. These cubs were well grown, almost the size of small cats. Other-Mottle began to groom behind the ears of the cub nearest to her, whereupon it rolled onto its back. She groomed its underside, and nuzzled between the pads of its feet as it batted at her muzzle.

Red Vixen stood up. Two boisterous cubs lunged towards her and she broke into a run. After a short zig-zagging chase, Red Vixen wheeled around and faced the cubs. In one uncoordinated somersault, they crumpled to a rapid halt and flung themselves onto their sides, ears pasted back against their heads and tails thumping showers of dew from the grass. Red Vixen sniffed at them amicably enough, but the cubs' confidence had deserted them and their squalling wails rang out across the fields. As soon as the adult moved off, however, they were again dancing and jinking at her heels.

Time and again Red Vixen trotted from the squirming bundles at her feet, and each time they sped after her, only to collapse at the slightest hint of rebuff. Eventually, she too began to bounce with vulpine agility, darting first at the cubs, and then in pursuit of invisible adversaries hidden beneath the grass stalks, or lurking in the tip of her brush. Beside Red Vixen's gymnastics the cubs' antics palled to clumsy-footed legginess.

At last one cub sat down and Red Vixen began to groom it. In the meantime, another two cubs had appeared in Back Field. Mottle was still stretched out in the sun, unmoved by the antics of the cubs. Both she and Other-Mottle had a fuzz of dense, pinkish-grey fur growing back to hide their distended nipples. They had evidently nursed cubs, but which cub belonged to which mother I could not say.

It was 5.35am when a heavy-shouldered dog fox appeared at the southern corner of Back Field. He slipped through a gap in the paling fence, where the coarse wood was rubbed smooth and dark by the passage of generations of foxes. Foxes in the English lowlands may be a trifle slight besides their brethren in the Scottish highlands, but Big Ginger was a splendid fox by any standards. He trotted straight across the field towards the group of vixens and cubs, each jaunty stride exactly in front of the one before, leaving a straight line of padmarks punched into the wet grass like a string of beads. Big Ginger didn't throw the group of vixens a glance as he passed within ten metres of them. Each head turned to watch him disappear into the undergrowth; even Mottle was alert and staring. Five minutes later, another fox appeared from the same passageway through which Big Ginger had made his exit. This time it was Grey Vixen, and she was carrying a partly eaten crow.

Two of the cubs rushed to greet her; she dropped the food and the cubs fought furiously

for possession of the prize. Two other cubs sped from the far corner of the field, where they had been squabbling over a pigeon's feather. The dilapidated crow was pulled across the field in crab-like fashion, with a cub at each corner, all of them gekkering and snirking violently. The jostling, feather-bound mass of cubs lurched from sight into the woodland, but sounds of their fracas continued for a quarter of an hour or more. By then the adults had drifted from sight. It was 6.15am and my observations for the morning of 24th July were finished.

'Nobody could call Mr Tod nice,' wrote Beatrix Potter, 'for he was of a wandering habit, had foxy whiskers, and had half a dozen houses but was seldom at home.' The same rumours were rife among naturalists, who saw the red fox as a lonesome and anti-social roamer. Science had enshrined this solitary reputation as the basis for a theory which counterpoised the fox against the more obviously social wolf. In fact, these two species are quite close cousins (*see* Box 1, p. 10) and, in most parts of the world where wolves occur, live side by side—as they did in Britain until wolves were exterminated in 1740. Despite their dog-like appearance, and the similarities in some aspects of their behaviour, the two species were typecast as complete opposites as far as their social lives were concerned: wolves living in

1. WHAT ARE FOXES?

Foxes are carnivores. In zoological terms this, rather confusingly, can mean two things, and in the case of foxes it means both. First, foxes live a carnivorous, or meat-eating, lifestyle; second, they are members of the taxonomic Order Carnivora (not all meat-eaters are members of the Carnivora, nor are all members of the Order carnivorous—the giant panda eats bamboo and is therefore a vegetarian carnivore!). An order is a rather broad category or pigeonhole into which biologists group species whose similarities indicate a common ancestry in evolution. The Carnivora is one of 18 Orders into which mammals are split.

The Order Carnivora includes some 231 species which are grouped into finer subdivisions called families (there are seven of them: the cats (Felidae), dogs (Canidae), bears (Ursidae), raccoons (Procyonidae), weasels (Mustelidae), civets and mongooses (Viverridae), and hyaenas (Hyaenidae), and some people subdivide the procyonids to split off the pandas into a separate family (Ailuropodidae)). All these creatures share one, and only one, characteristic that uniquely qualifies them as members of the Carnivora and indicates their distant common ancestry some 50 million years ago: they all possess carnassial teeth. That is to say, their first lower molar and fourth upper premolars are adapted to have a cutting edge capable of shearing through

A timber wolf in Minnesota.

flesh. Foxes have carnassial teeth and are therefore carnivores. Foxes also have some other important traits—they have 42 teeth, long legs so designed that they walk on the four toes of each foot (a condition known as digitigrade), two wrist bones are fused (the scaphoid and lunar) and the front leg bones (radius and ulna) are locked to prevent rotation. All these features and others are indicative of a body designed for a swift, enduring, predatory lifestyle.

Foxes are one of 35 species that are bonded together by these traits to form the family Canidae; they are all descended from common ancestors that

highly sociable packs, foxes travelling alone. It was this difference that the theory sought to explain, and the argument revolved around the sizes of their prey: the contrast of moose and mouse.

Wolves hunt large prey; indeed, a moose may weigh 600 kg, ten-fold the weight of the largest wolf. Alone, the wolf would be little more than chaff to the moose's antlers. A pack, however, can muster the collective might of its members. Indeed, by working as a team they are transformed into a new creature, a super-predator whose summed capability exceeds the hunting prowess of the individuals involved. A fox, in contrast, is some 300 times heavier than a mouse. The vulpine hunt involves no lung-bursting marathon, no rip and rend, no sparring against hoofs. Rather, stealth, agility, a graceful leap and a precision nip seal the mouse's fate.

So, the logic ran, wolves have evolved a sociable lifestyle enabling them to hunt coopera-

tively for large prey; foxes, on the other hand, are solitary because their small prey do not merit such concerted effort. The idea is plausible enough. Wolves do seem to form the largest packs in areas where they hunt for the largest prey. Packs of seven or so are typical in the forests of Minnesota where they hunt white-tailed deer, and up to 20 are often found in the north of Alberta where they challenge wood buffalo or moose. Equally, foxes are generally seen alone and the prospect of half a dozen of them pooling their collective might to overwhelm a mouse would seem to be a doubtful recipe for social harmony when it comes to dividing the spoils.

However, within one hour at dawn on the 24th July 1973, crouched in a ditch and chilled to the marrow, I had just watched 11 foxes (five adults and the six cubs of two litters) interacting good naturedly. In these circumstances the pre-vailing wisdom on foxes as solitary animals

A silver-backed jackal in the Kalahari desert.

An African wild dog in Tanzania.

arose in North America in the Eocene 38 million years ago. So, foxes are carnivores and, more precisely, they are a type of wild dog. Their relatives include the coyotes, jackals, wolves, and the domestic wolf—the dog. However, the fox-like 'vulpes lineage' split off from the wolf-like canids in the Miocene (12 million years ago). Subsequently, they have diverged to the extent that, contrary to popular belief, fox-dog hybrids are an impossibility (this is because they have different numbers of chromosomes—red foxes have 34 to 38 pairs, domestic dogs have 78 pairs). The red fox has probably been a distinct species for about 5 million years. Apart from the anatomical clues to their relatedness, canids have some other traits in common. Most striking of these is their opportunistic and adaptable behaviour. In particular, their societies are complex and flexible. Once upon a time biologists thought in simple terms about these societies: wolves lived in packs and foxes lived solitarily. Nowadays, although we are still only scratching the surface of understanding, it is clear that all wild canids have complex social lives.

seemed less compelling than it had been in the library. On that morning I was still in the early days of a quest which has occupied me for almost 15 years—a quest to uncover and to understand the fox's social life.

Officially, the story began in 1972 when I was 20 years old and recently fledged from Oxford with a degree in Zoology. With enormous good fortune, I was given a grant from the Science Research Council to study for a doctorate in Professor Niko Tinbergen's Animal Behaviour Research Group at Oxford. Better still, my research was to be supervised by Dr Hans Kruuk, one of the finest field biologists.

The idea for my research project had come one evening that spring, while we struggled through a morass of revision for finals. A friend had suggested a break in the welcome form of an evening spent watching a litter of fox cubs he had found near the village of Islip. As we watched the earth, four adults emerged, accompanied by a frolicking bundle of nine variously sized cubs. I could hardly believe my eyes, but this sociable throng definitely jolted the notion that foxes were solitary.

The early seventies were exciting years in the field of animal behaviour—a new generation of field studies began to disclose how marvellously intricate were the societies of wild animals. People began to realize that explaining the social behaviour within these societies, especially among primates and carnivores, was one of the most challenging topics facing biologists. Closer inspection of the groups in which mammals live was beginning to reveal a network of subtle relationships ranging from cooperation to merciless power struggles. The wolf pack could no longer be dismissed as a harmonious gathering of like-minded and rather anonymous hunters, each sharing a common goal for the good of the pack (even less so for the good of the species). The well-being of the pack was not the purpose

2. HOW MANY SPECIES OF FOX ARE THERE?

There are approximately 21 species of fox around the world. The exact number is a matter of opinion (a species is defined rather imprecisely as a group of organisms that can potentially interbreed). The animals generally referred to as 'foxes' mostly belong to one of two categories: the 13 vulpine foxes (genus *Vulpes*) of the Northern Hemisphere, and the 7 Dusicyon foxes of South America. One species, the bat-eared fox (*Otocyon megalotis*) of African grasslands fits into neither group of species due to its larger number of teeth (46 to 50 in total) and an extra muscle attachment on their lower jaws—these are adaptations to its insectivorous lifestyle (termites can make up to 70 per cent of their diet). Members of the genus *Vulpes* span North America (and the north of South America), Europe, Africa and Asia. They are recognizable by their pointed muzzles, erect triangular ears, long bushy tails and, often, black triangular face marks between eyes and nose. Relative to dogs (genus *Canis*), they have flattened skulls (the brows formed by the frontal skull bone above and between the eyes of vulpine foxes are indented or dished, while those of dog-types are domed).

Because the red fox (*Vulpes vulpes*) is the most widespread and familiar species, it is often thought of as the 'typical' representative of vulpine foxes. In fact, as far as weights and measures go, it is the least typical for, apart from anything else, it is the biggest species. At the other extreme in size is the 1.5kg Fennec fox (*Vulpes zerda*, previously known as *Fennecus zerda*) of north African deserts. In terms of appearance the most distinct species is the Arctic fox (*Alopex lagopus*) which has dense fur and short extremities as adaptations to cold (Arctic foxes also occur in two strikingly different colour phases: white and 'blue'). Amongst the vulpine group of foxes the Indian fox (*Vulpes bengalensis*) is really the most average in dimensions; at between 2 and 3kg it is about half the weight of a red fox. The Cape fox (*Vulpes chama*), of Southern Africa is very like the Indian fox, and along the N–S arc that links these close relatives lie the distributions of four other related species. Three of them are small species adapted to desert environments: Ruppell's fox (*V. ruppelli*), the Fennec fox, and the Pale fox (*V. pallida*). The fourth species, Blanford's fox, is also small—1.5kg and seems to be adapted to mountainous habitats. Very little is known about the behaviour of most species of fox.

A Cape fox in the Kalahari dessert.

An Arctic fox in Iceland.

A bat-eared fox in the Serengeti Plains.

of its members, rather the pack was the product of their self-interest. It was more like a team of sportsmen, playing together because each individual does better than he would alone. Nonetheless, the team is made up of very distinct individuals, each with his own skills, weaknesses and aspirations—individual differences which, on the one hand, ensure that the team is more than the sum of its individual members, but, on the other, guarantee that it will be prone to rivalries and dissent.

It no longer made sense to think of the behaviour of an average wolf, any more than it makes sense to think of an average rugby player: a prop-forward and a fly-half are different, just as an old dominant male wolf has different abilities and expectations to a subordinate adolescent female. The functioning of the team, and the pack, are the products of these different traits, not their cause.

Where once it had seemed sufficient to describe a society as a pack or a herd, these labels now seemed woefully simplistic when applied to societies whose adaptations rendered most fantasies dull by comparison. Furthermore, it was becoming clear that social behaviour could be very flexible, so that individuals of the same species might behave quite differently in different places, adapting their social lives to suit local circumstances.

That evening, as we watched the foxes I thought I saw before me the perfect animal on which to explore the flexibility of social behaviour. After all, the red fox has the most expansive geographical range of any living carnivore, spanning most of the northern hemisphere, introduced to Australia, and embracing habitats ranging from desert to ice floe (*see* Boxes 3 and 4 on page 14). If ever a species provided scope for studying variations in behaviour, it seemed to me it was the red fox. What was more, before our very eyes, in a location no more exotic than the outskirts of an Oxfordshire village, foxes were breaking every rule in the behavioural textbook.

So transpired my proposal to Hans Kruuk for a study of fox behaviour. The central question was: how is fox society organized, and how and why does it vary between contrasting habitats? In this flush of enthusiasm it slipped past my notice that foxes are elusive to the point of invisibility; that they have been honed by evolution to avoid people and, most punishing of all, that they do not go to bed at night. Fifteen years later I am more than acutely aware of these little practicalities.

If the official story began in 1972, the seed of the unofficial version was sown long before, in the unlikely setting of a golf course at St George's Hill in Surrey. At ten years old I had grave misgivings about my human peers. Their roughness upset Hamish, the pride of my guinea pig herd, their shouting frightened Mealie, my hand-tamed robin, they were insensitive to Theodore the tortoise and mocked my Scottish pronunciation. No, other children had little to commend them. Quite frankly, I preferred the company of characters to be found in the pages of Jack London's *Call of the Wild* and *White Fang*—those silent, skilful backwoodsmen who could read every sign of the wilderness.

Above all, I developed a fascination for wolves. Wolves were fleet of foot, enduring of power and purpose, they were the self-contained essence of wildness and, according to Jack London, they had beautiful amber eyes. At ten years old, more than anything else, I wanted to be like a wolf, and it was the desire to practise lupine skills which led me to the golf course. Weekend after weekend, while my father and his chums stalked birdies, I stalked them, a shadow in the rhododendrons. It was here that I first encountered foxes, or rather their tracks which concentrated in bunkers. It is an abiding mystery to me why foxes should favour bunkers for a frolic, but they do. Aided by my medical father, and looting his supply of plaster of Paris originally destined to repair fractured limbs, I began a collection of plaster casts of their footprints.

A swift sortie in a wonderful book called *String Lug the Fox* and I was converted. What Surrey lacked in wolves, it more than made up in their small red cousins. The plaster cast collection grew and soon secured me a prize at Wallop, my inauspiciously but all too aptly named prep school. This upturn in what had been a mightily undistinguished scholastic career convinced me that I should immediately write a book on foxes. This, at the age of 11, I proceeded to do. Today, reading again the resulting 16-page mutilation of the English language, I really wonder how much closer I am now to getting inside the fox's skin. If those painstaking pages count as the first draft of this book, then it has taken me 25 years to get it published!

Two further events completed my intoxication with foxes. First, when I was about 12 years old, I discovered an earth amply trampled with fox footprints in the woods beside the 16th hole. Nothing would dissuade me from the intention to watch this den at night. So, during one afternoon, my mother and I manhandled branches and bracken into a wigwam-like structure about 20 metres from the earth. There, my mother and I sat, peering expectantly into the darkness until dawn. We saw nothing, but for me the mysterious sounds of four-legged footfalls on the leafy floor were enough. Naturally, it never crossed my mind as unusual that my mother was prepared to sit in the woods night after night, under circumstances in which I now know we had no chance of seeing a fox.

The second event occurred a few weeks after the nocturnal sojourn in the woods. A friend of my father's had lured a fox into taking scraps of food from his garden. So, when my parents went to a cocktail party at his house I, too, was invited to see the fox. At length, the lights were dimmed

3. WHERE ARE FOXES FOUND?

Red foxes have the most expansive geographical distribution of any wild carnivore. They are found throughout almost all of the Northern Hemisphere, as well as in Australia. In North America they span the continent from the Aleutian Islands to Newfoundland. In the Old World they stretch from Ireland to the Bering Sea, spanning the huge landmass of Europe and Asia, known collectively as the Palaearctic region. In the north of America on Ellesmere Island at 76°N, red foxes are well within the Arctic Circle. In the south they are almost in sight of the Tropics when they reach the Caribbean coast of Texas (30°N). Between these extremes they are found coast to coast, with the exception of Arizona, southern Florida and a sliver of land running north-south from Alberta in Canada to Mexico.

Individuals of the same species that haunt copse and pasture of the traditional English landscape are just as much at home in the deserts of the Middle East or Spanish Sahara with scarcely 80mm of annual rainfall, or in Arctic tundra (where they only begin to shiver at -13°C), or on Alpine passes at over 4,000 metres, or in the concrete jungles of Central London.

4. HOW DID FOXES REACH AUSTRALIA?

British expatriates, homesick for the traditions of rural England, formed hunt clubs and transported foxes to the colonies. The most far-reaching effect of fox hunting has been to promote a colossal expansion of the fox's natural geographical range. In Australia the first known release of English foxes was in 1845, on the property of one T.H. Pyke near Keilor, Melbourne, Victoria. These colonial foxes were newsworthy. The arrival of two dog foxes in 1855 was reported in the Sydney Echo. In the Australasian of 25th April 1868 there is an account of one dog fox and two vixens which arrived in 1864 on the ship Suffolk and were released by the Melbourne Hunt Club.

It is generally believed that these early introductions did not become established, and that Australia's modern fox population stemmed from two subsequent shipments liberated in Victoria. In 1871, Dr King ('a well known sportsman and acclimatizer') released a pair 20km from Ballarat. In the early 1870s Mr T. Chirnside released several more on Point Cook. The descendants of these foxes flourished and their spread from property to property was recorded. By 1880 they had reached the north shore of Corio Bay, and shortly afterwards linked up with descendants of these released by Dr King.

In less than a decade the descendants of a handful of English red foxes had colonized some 13,000sq km of Victoria. It is uncertain to what extent their subsequent spread was aided by transportation (possibly to control rabbits), but by 1893 they were so numerous that the first fox bounty schemes were introduced. That year they were seen near Yarrawanga on the Murray River, and a few months later the first fox was shot in New South Wales. By 1911 they were established in southern Queensland, by 1920 one was seen at Long Reach, 1600km north of Melbourne, and by 1933, Julia Creek, a further 320km north-west. In the meantime, they had crossed the desert to arrive in Western Australia in 1911. From 1929–60 they were under bounty in Western Australia, and some 893,000 descendants of the original foxes were killed. Today they occur throughout mainland Australia, except in the northerly parts of Queensland and Northern Territory. A pair of foxes imported for hunting to Tasmania by two British army officers in 1890 were destroyed, and Tasmania remains free of foxes today, as does New Zealand (where an act of 1867 prohibited their importation). The effect of the red fox on Australia's native fauna is uncertain, but it is held partly responsible for the decline of the Brush-tailed rock wallaby, the crescent nail-tailed wallaby, and the melee fowl.

and some food thrown out for the fox. Minutes passed and feet began to shuffle, clearly not all the gathered assembly felt the same enthusiasm for this vigil as I did. Then the fox came. For five or ten seconds a fleeting shadow moved eerily about the garden. Its sudden departure was heralded by a surprisingly loud hissing noise as a box of matches in my father's trouser pocket burst into spontaneous combustion. The ensuing dowsing of the flames with a soda-water siphon emblazoned the already momentous occasion all the more vividly in my memory.

Fate had many strands to her web as I stumbled towards a 'career' as a foxologist. One such strand concerned rabies, a dreadful and incurable disease in man. Since the beginning of recorded history, people have dreaded hydrophobia, that awful symptom causing rabid patients agonizing spasms and terror even at the sight of water. Rabies is a viral disease of the nervous system that affects all mammals, but foxes are especially susceptible. Excepting a few islands, including the British Isles, red foxes are burdened as both the victim and vector of this disease throughout most of the northern hemisphere. Attempts to eradicate rabies have prompted governments to authorize massacres of hundreds of thousands of foxes. Yet the disease has shown little sign of abating in wildlife.

From a biologist's perspective, this regrettable state of affairs was unsurprising, since plans were laid for the management of rabies among foxes on the basis of almost no knowledge of how foxes behaved. In particular, since rabies outbreaks behave differently in different places, and since foxes more than likely behave differently in different habitats, it seemed probable that variation in the one explained variation in the other. Therefore, I thought, unravelling the intricacies of fox behaviour could be not only interesting, it could also be useful.

People often ask why I chose to work with foxes. Generally I reply that this species offers the best of many worlds: the thrill of observing behaviour rarely seen before, the satisfaction of the intellectual wrestle to explain why evolution has worked each nuance of design into these remarkable creatures, and the conviction that this new knowledge will be useful, contributing to the solutions of problems as grand as rabies and as small (but annoying) as the beheading of a barnyard fowl. This reply is honest, and the arguments underlying it are robust. However, to give another answer, no less important: I study foxes because I am still awed by their extraordinary beauty, because they outwit me, because they keep the wind and rain on my face, and because they lead me to the satisfying solitude of the countryside; all of which is to say—because it's fun.

2 | FIRST FIND YOUR FOX!

OUTWITTING FOXES HAS stretched man's ingenuity for at least 2,000 years. In the 16th century, one George Tubervile wrote his solution: 'Take a skin of bacon, and lay it on a gridiron, and when it is well boiled and hot, then dip it and puddle it in the source that is within the pot, and make a train therewith, and you shall see that if there be a fox near to any place where the train is drawn, he will follow it. But he which maketh the train must rub the soles of his shoes with cows dung, lest the fox vent his footing. And thus you may train a fox to a standing, and kill him in an evening with a crossbow.' An elaborate concoction, perhaps, but no more eccentric than the modern-day recipe recommended by one of my farming friends. The ultimate lure for a fox, he assured me, was a dead cat, soaked in fox urine, and left to ripen.

Back in 1972 my interest was soon heightened in any such concoction that would bring me into contact with foxes. It had not taken me long to discover that not only do foxes do what they do by night, but that they are extraordinarily secretive about it. And who would not be secretive under the circumstances? As long ago as 2000 BC, Alexander the Great mounted Nisaean horses and led his Medes and Persians in pursuit of foxes, and doubtless he was not the first to hunt them. In the intervening years (*see* Box 6, p. 20) nothing has happened to improve the fox's view of humanity. In my experience it's easier to find places where almost everybody is trying to kill foxes than it is to find places where nobody wants to harm them. It is more than likely that this vendetta has had far-reaching effects on fox behaviour.

It is well documented that only a few dozen generations of soot-stained industrial landscapes have exerted sufficient selective pressure for evolution to change the camouflage of peppered moths from white to black (the first black mutant was caught in Manchester in 1848, but they were at such an advantage in escaping birds that by 1895 98 per cent of peppered moths were black).

Perhaps then, thousands of generations of persecution (especially when the opposition resorts to dirty tricks like marinading cats in urine) have fashioned foxes with their almost uncanny abilities to avoid man and his devices. I had, it seemed, chosen for my detailed study of social behaviour, a creature that had been finely honed by evolution to avoid biologists, and anybody else for that matter. The only solution lay in finding a way to study foxes without disturbing them, and that meant keeping well out of sight and scent.

For millennia, people have been trying to sneak up on wild creatures. Yet, even with the most knowledgeable fieldcraft, generations of countrymen have been thwarted by chance gusts of wind betraying their scent, or by stony ground refusing to yield the tell-tale imprints of passing paws. As far as shy, nocturnal foxes are concerned, traditional fieldcraft can only yield glimpses into a few facets of their private lives. True, some trappers had a treasure trove of foxlore gleaned from a lifetime of pitted wits. Others knew every trick of a fox running before hounds, and yet others had been thrilled by many an hour of watching cubs at play. But these vivid insights were no more than fragments of the story—the remainder was hidden in the darkness that cloaks the night of the fox. To penetrate that darkness, to trace the patterns that make up the fox's life history, required a revolution. That revolution came in the early 1960s with the development of radio-tracking—electronic surveillance at a distance, a technique that has transformed field biology (*see* Box 5) and an invention that ranks with binoculars in importance. All at once it became possible not only to keep constant contact with one's subject, but also to remove the disruptive presence of the biologist to a safe distance. In theory the device sounds good, but in practice things are not so straightforward—first, you must catch your fox.

In October 1972 I moved to Cumnor village on the outskirts of Oxford, where I found lodgings at Denman's Farm, the property of John and Pamela Gee. This move turned out to be an enormous stroke of luck. The Gees were skilled at all those things at which I was unpractised. It was John who taught me how to operate a JCB digger, how to handle an arc-welder and how, by scuffing one's wellies together at every pace, it was possible to walk across ploughed fields less encumbered by manacles of sticky clay.

When I moved to Denman's Farm it had not been my intention to study foxes on the farm. Rather, I began work in the near-by Wytham Estate. This estate, owned by Oxford University, spans some 800 hectares of beautiful woodland and park. It is a biologist's dream, not least because of the wealth of background information available. More doctoral theses have probably been written on the natural history of that woodland than on any other piece of countryside.

During those early months I stalked, waited and watched in Wytham Woods for seemingly interminable hours, but never saw a single fox. The woodlands thronged with wildlife including, according to the gamekeeper, all too many foxes. My failure to watch them nourished a disheartening fear that I had bitten off more than I could chew. What I did not realize then was that the dense plantations and lush understory that made Wytham a sanctuary for foxes also made it an exceptionally difficult place to study them.

At the Gees', however, I learnt more, and more quickly, than in any other period of my life. As it happened, John Gee was the organizer of the neighbourhood fox drive—an annual onslaught on foxes by a group of the local farmers. Invited by John on these outings, I found myself thrown in with the company of men who had not only had their hands on many more foxes than I, but also had been taught from the cradle that the best sort of fox was a dead one. In these circum-

stances, it was a remarkable gesture when John's sympathy for my frustration led him to suggest that I transfer my floundering efforts from Wytham Woods to his farm.

Soon I was ensconced in the farm's workshop, an Aladdin's cave of spanners, wrenches, oil and grease. In a few days, sheets of heavy gauge weldmesh and Dexion bars were snipped, bolted, and hammered into the shape of six large box-traps. A drop door was suspended on a pin through which one end of a string was threaded. The other end of the string was trailed into the depths of the trap and, there, entwined around a hopefully irresistible mass of chickens' entrails. These six monuments to my naïvety were positioned strategically about the farm and left for a week to bed-in.

The big night arrived. All the traps were baited and set. At midnight I began my rounds to inspect my catch, with a bag full of prototype radio-collars. Undaunted by an initial round of empty traps, I made a second round of the traps at dawn. Still nothing. My optimism was slightly less pristine when I had fruitlessly completed this twice-nightly trek during every night of three months during the early winter of 1972–3.

I had woefully underestimated my adversary. With hindsight I know that the traps were too small, badly designed, poorly sited and incorrectly baited, but at the time I was reluctant to abandon them. I tried various antics to turn the sow's ear to silk: some traps I moved frequently, others I left in place; some opened into the field, others into the hedgerow; in some I sprinkled urine collected from foxes killed by cars, in others I hung rotting cats as the recipe dictated. The local foxes were intrigued by these traps. They circled them, urinated on them, dug under and climbed on top of them, defaecated into them, even pawed through the mesh to extract the bait from within. The one thing that they never did was to enter.

January found me in the doldrums. Time was ticking away, my grant diminishing, and although I was learning some important, if painful, lessons about field research, the frontiers of scientific discovery remained steadfastly unmoved. During one forlorn conversation about what was tactfully referred to as my progress, Hans Kruuk suggested that the solution must lie in Ravenglass, a coastal nature reserve in West-

5. HOW DOES RADIO-TRACKING WORK?

Where is it? This is a very simple question for a biologist to ask about an animal, and a very important one. Not only do you need to know your subject's whereabouts in order to observe it, but the patterns of its movements and those of its companions and rivals can reveal much about its lifestyle. Yet, because of their nocturnal, secretive habits, this simplest of questions was unanswerable for most mammals until the early 1960s. It was then that two Americans, Cochran and Lord, published the circuitry for the first radio transmitter suitable for use on wild animals. Perhaps it is a measure of their greater than average desperation that it was biologists working on foxes and wolves who most eagerly embraced the technique. Less than two decades later, radio-tracking must be the lynchpin of a thousand studies around the world.

The technique works as follows: the subject to be tracked is fitted with a battery powered, miniature transmitter (a 'bleeper' in the jargon), generally attached to a collar, harness or some suitable protuberance (e.g. glued to a feather and imped into a hawk's tail, or sunk into a hole drilled in a rhino's horn!). This transmitter emits a pulsed signal (a bleep) via a broadcasting antenna, which may be a loop around the neck, a whip of wire, or a coil of copper wire around a ferrite rod. The signal is inaudible to the subject and is commonly on a high frequency (generally VHF, i.e. more than 100 MHz). Some distance away (in the case of my transmitters 1km or more), the biologist is equipped with a receiving antenna which has reciprocal properties to the transmitting antenna and so picks up the signal and feeds it into a receiver. Inside the receiver, some electronic wizardry (specifically, a Beat Frequency Oscillator) transforms the received signal into sound. The whole system operates just like a household radio. The only difference is that whereas the householder tunes into the BBC, I tune into one of several foxes, each broadcasting on slightly different, and therefore recognizable, frequencies.

The receiving antenna can be wired up so that it has directional properties. That is to say, the signal volume will be louder or quieter depending on whether the receiving antenna is pointing at or away from the transmitter. At this point the tracker can answer the question 'Where is it?' with 'It's that way', but cannot specify how far. However, by repeating the direction-finding procedure and taking a second bearing on the subject from another vantage point, the transmitter's location is revealed as the spot where the two bearings cross. This process, called triangulation, is known in the jargon as taking 'a fix' on the animal.

In theory it is simple. In practice it is nightmarishly prone to a host of seductive errors. Fundamental, but unwarranted, assumptions in the above summary are that the animal has not moved between taking two successive bearings (ideally, two people track in

morland. Not only had Hans done the research for his own doctoral thesis there, but reading the daily chronicle of footprints in the sands of Ravenglass had inspired Niko Tinbergen's book on *Animal Tracks and Signs*, wherein intricate tales of fox behaviour were reconstructed with beautiful photographs of their tracks. It was decided that we would spend three days at Ravenglass with a view to relocating my project there.

The dunes of Ravenglass were stunningly beautiful, but devoid of foxes. Dawn of the third day found us perched on the tail-gate of the Land Rover chewing a shared rasher of raw bacon, staring disconsolately at the wheeling, black-headed gulls. Perhaps, Hans mused, foxes were simply too difficult for a doctoral project. If I wanted to change to any other topic of my choice he would support me. Had not pig-headed pride prevented me from devoting even a split second of rational thought to this generous offer, I might not have dismissed it with such peremptory haste. As things turned out, I am deeply grateful to Hans for granting me the privilege to make my own mistakes.

I hastened back to Oxford, with firm resolve, only to find that on the coming weekend the local farmers were foregathering at Denman's Farm for a pheasant shoot. My heart sank at the prospect that they might shoot the foxes I had struggled so vainly to capture. Early on Saturday, men and dogs began to arrive. There was Eric Wastie, gently stroking the lovely blued Damascus barrels of the aged shotgun with which he was a crackshot; Pat Boothe (who later taught me much about deer) was there with his German pointer; the big Barnett brothers were joking in quiet Warwickshire tones, and there was George Apsalam. Old George and Mrs George, as I came to know them, had, between them, ploughed a lifetime of furrows as managers of the neighbouring Red House Farm. Old George, who wore a

synchrony), that the signal really is coming from where it seems to come from (radio signals ricochet hither and thither where they collide with trees, wire fences, cliff faces and electric pylons), and that the biologist knows his own location (remembering that tracking is normally done in the dead of night, in dense vegetation, and under cold and wet conditions). There is also the assumption that the transmitter and subject are still wedded (show me a radio-tracker and I'll show you somebody who has spent hours stalking up on a transmitter shed into the most thorny undergrowth by its erstwhile bearer). Last, and by far the worst, is the problem of no signal at all, which might mean that the subject is elsewhere, but probably means that its batteries have failed.

There are solutions to all these problems, but I mention them to emphasize that radio-tracking is both the most wonderful and the most frustrating innovation in the modern history of field biology. There is an appealing irony in this: the modern naturalist prowls the darkness entwined in a tangle of leads and bedecked with the trinkets of a high technology which, at first, seems antipathetic to traditional fieldcraft. Yet with these aids today's biologists are realizing the dreams of generations of naturalists. With their advantages of keen senses and swiftness of limb, our subjects still have the edge on us, but radio-tracking is levelling the odds.

belt of baling twine and leggings of cut-off fertilizer bags, had hands like spades and a bull-neck etched in crows' feet creases through which had run a generation of rain and sweat. These farmers were clearly a good bunch, but if they were deeply suspicious of me, I was scared stiff of them! One had heard that I was going to breed foxes; another that I planned to move in foxes from other areas and release them; another that I wanted to have foxes protected by law. My disclaimers of these rumours went unheeded. I explained the truth of my plans and motives for the project, but even to me I sounded plaintive. John joked me through it when the going got tough, but Old George slowly shook his head and snarled intermittently under his breath the words 'Forkses ... forkses!'. I was beginning to learn that there are few other creatures on earth about which, one way or another, people feel as strong.

We beat through Denman's Wood. In the absence of much by way of pheasants, for which I and my foxes were held responsible, the men turned their attention to ribald jokes about boffins, townies and the like. However, enduring a cold wind and dripping noses together does wonders for breaking barriers. By the afternoon, hostility was ebbing away, leaving a large residue of incredulity at the idea of putting radio-collars on foxes. We had made our way through The Bog and into Shaddles Wood when Old George drew level with me, shook his head in disbelief, growled 'Forkses' and delivered such an unexpected, if well-intentioned, slap to the middle of my back that I was knocked forward. Over I toppled, providing final proof of my idiocy.

Moments later, just ahead of us, a fox leapt from cover and sprung in bounds over the tangled brambles, dashing towards us to break through the line beside me. I had never seen a fox

6. A HISTORY OF PERSECUTION

Men have killed foxes since time immemorial. There are, and probably always have been, three views of the fox which motivate this: first, the fox is perceived as vermin (a predator of stock or game, or a health hazard) and killed in an attempt to limit depredations (or at least to avenge them). In the second and third views the fox is perceived as a resource, as either a quarry or a furbearer, producing either recreation or a valuable pelt. For whichever motive, or combination of motives, the hunting of foxes has had a remarkable influence on human history.

In the 14th century BC, the Assyrians and Persians hunted for sport as a training for war. The earliest specific references to fox hunting are in the 4th century BC. Alexander the Great certainly hunted foxes, and a seal dated 350 BC depicts a Persian horseman about to spear a fox. Of the Greeks, Xenophon regarded hunting as part of a cultured man's education, and killed foxes as pests which distracted hounds from hares. Aristotle saw hunting as one of the gods' gifts to man: nature made nothing useless, so if she made animals suitable for hunting, nature plainly intended that they should be hunted. By AD 80 the Romans were hunting foxes.

By the Dark Ages hunting was a major element of European culture, an importance emphasized by a quote from 11th-century France: 'the first son of the Lord is a fighter, the second a hunter, the third a farmer, and the fourth a stock-raiser'. Initially the fox was a secondary quarry, but gradually it gained importance. In 18th-century Germany a new variant— fox tossing—became fashionable. Foxes were persuaded to run over narrow slings of webbing, of which one end was held by a gentleman, the other by a lady. The 'players' tossed the fox as it walked the tightrope—a good toss being up to 24 feet high. Augustus the Strong of Saxony was an enthusiastic fox-tosser and is reputed to have tossed to death some 687 foxes in one session (although how so many foxes were acquired is a mystery).

In England, the 9th-century Saxon, Alfred the Great, was a skilled horseman and passionate hunter. Two centuries later his Viking successor King Canute, who failed to influence the tides, had a major impact on legislation, enacting many hunting laws and classing foxes as Beasts of the Chase, a lower category of quarry than Beasts of Venery. In the Middle Ages, hunting was a part of daily life and a whole culture and vocabulary—the Terms of the Art of Venery—surrounded hunting. Many of these terms were in Norman French: 'il est hault il est hault' has metamorphosed into 'Tally ho!' In the 12th century, Richard I blinded and castrated poachers (when murderers could escape with a fine). Gradually the fox was hunted less as vermin and more as a Beast of the Chase until, by the late 13th century, Edward I had a royal pack of foxhounds and a fox huntsman. Increasingly foxes were hunted above ground by hounds rather than below ground with terriers. In 1338 the first treatise on hunting was published in Normandy—*Le Livre de Roy Modus*—which concerned ten beasts of venery, five sweet or red (e.g. deer and hare) and five foul or black (including the fox). By 1420 when Edward, Second Duke of York, published *The Master of Game*, the fox was slowly climbing the ladder of merit as a quarry. Edward also recorded foxes scavenging around villages (*see* Chapter Ten) and eating 'foul worms' (*see* Chapter 6).

Soon foxhunting was undertaken as a noble amusement for its own interest and excitement and by the Renaissance, hunting was an indispensable part of a polite man's attainments. In each age it has had its opponents—of the Greek philosophers, the Sophists, of Renaissance men, Thomas More's Utopians. In the time of James I it was said that hunting was the 'sole almost and ordinary sport of all our noblemen . . . 'tis all their study, their exercise, ordinary business, all their talk; . . . they can do nothing else, discourse of nought else.' The destruction of deer and deer parks during the English Civil War is said to have turned attention increasingly to foxhunting. By the mid-17th century, Britain began to be divided into foxhunting territories and soon foxhunting clubs formed (the first was the Charlton Hunt Club of 1737). In the 18th century foxhunting exploded in popularity.

The British took foxes and their style of hunting on horseback around the world (*see* Box 4, p.14). American colonists regularly imported foxhounds (the first pack being shipped to Maryland in 1650). By the 18th century the grey fox was the principal game species of Virginia, with George Washington its most famous practitioner. The southward expansion of red foxes, and displacement of grey foxes (*see* Box 13, p.84), was no doubt speeded up by the Virginian tobacco merchants who imported red foxes from Britain. Today foxes are hunted in the general sense (with dog and gun) almost everywhere, but even the mounted 'English' style of hunting is widespread— there are packs of foxhounds from Mexico to Kenya.

Hunting foxes for sport greatly affected society,

livestock and the countryside. Rising costs of keeping hounds led to them being 'trencher fed' (i.e. maintained by tenants who were obliged by their leases to keep hounds). An astonishing tradition of horse and hound breeding developed—the genealogies of today's foxhounds can be traced in staggering detail to famous ancestors such as Brocklesby Ringwood, the 'stallion' hound immortalized by Stubbs in 1788. In 1880 a Belvoir hound called Weathergauge 'lined' 300 bitches, and each one of these liaisons, and their fruits, are documented, as are most of their descendants to the present day. An extraordinary history is recorded of notorious foxes (in 1775 a fox known as Old Caesar reputedly led hounds a 50-mile chase) and foxhunters (such as the Duke of Northumberland who defied at least half of Oscar Wilde's 'unspeakable in full pursuit of the uneatable' remark by eating a fox's head, devilled for dinner, after it had given him a good run).

The impact of foxhunting on the English countryside is remarkable: Henry VIII nominated large areas of London as parks in order that he could hunt close to home—St James', Hyde and Regent's Parks were among them. In those days foxes ranked a poor second to quarry such as stag and hare, but had the virtue of continuing between January and March when no other game was hunted. By the 18th century, foxes were a prime quarry. The 2nd Duke of Bolton grew tired of the long hack via London Bridge from his London home north of the Thames to his hunting grounds to the south, and so led the parliamentary lobbying for the new Westminster Bridge opened in 1750.

Between 1760 and 1797 there were 1,539 Enclosure Acts which took common land out of small-holdings and converted it to parks and grazing land ideal for foxhunting. Coverts were planted to hold foxes, and between 1800 and 1850 it is said that the area of gorse in Leicestershire was doubled in an attempt to create favourable fox habitat. The foxhunters viewed foxes as a quarry and not a pest, so they planted more coverts to foster more foxes to sustain more hunting days. However, they were killed by farmers as vermin. Hunts paid farmers to spare breeding earths on their land, and often checked their hounds to spare the fox for another day. Where numbers ran short foxes were bought and released (such 'bagged' foxes sold for 10 shillings at the Leadenhall Market in 1845 and included a brisk trade in imports from the Continent). Overharvesting was deplored (the famous 18th century hound breeder Hugo Meynell said 'Murder of foxes is a most absurd prodigality'). However, just as the late 18th century saw great changes in the landscape, partly caused by, and great y benefiting, foxhunting and foxes, it also saw two other new factors. First came pheasant shooting and with it the conflict between the foxhunter, who wanted many foxes, and the gamekeeper who wanted none. The *impasse* was summarized by a noted foxhunter of the day, Capt. Percy Williams, who concluded that pheasants 'have brought in their train envy, hatred, and malice, have dispossessed the fox, and demoralized the country'. Secondly, farming changed, bringing more spring clover, too easily damaged by hooves, and more stock to be contained by wire fences too dangerous to jump. In 1882 barbed wire arrived, ending the golden age of English foxhunting and presaging an era of intensive agriculture that may yet finish it altogether.

The fox as a furbearer has had no lesser effect on modern history. Trade in furs in general, and foxes in particular, large y determined the European settlement of Canada and Alaska. In 1534 the French explorer Jacques Cartier sailed up the St Lawrence Seaway, and soon French fur trappers and traders were sent to establish settlements. Britains followed too, and in 1670 the Hudson's Bay company was chartered to ship furs to England. Between 1689 and 1763 the French and the British were frequently at war over the trapping territories. By 1760 more than 2,000 fox skins were being exported from North America annually. The settlement, the economy and the culture of Canada were all based on fur trapping, much of it by Highland Scots, and much of it in pursuit of foxes. The harvest of fox furs remains a large, and highly controlled, business in North America. In Ontario in the 1940s 50,000 to 60,000 foxes were trapped for their skins annually (the number has fallen to between 12,000 and 20,000 now due largely to rabies). In the 1970s, fox fur came back into fashion. In 1979, the Ontario Trappers Association published record prices averaging £92 ($203) per red fox pelt, with top prices of £220 ($486). In 1976–7 US trappers caught 356,249 red foxes (average price $48). The same boom gave the lower quality British and Irish fox pelts a significant market value—numbers traded increased 15-fold in the late 70s, and probably peaked at between 50,000 and 100,000 pelts.

leap and jink like that before. I was ecstatic with excitement; there was a thundering bang as Pat Boothe's gun discharged beside me, and the fox dropped dead not ten paces ahead. To these fellows, nothing could have been more inconsequential; nobody paused, nobody checked what sex it was, or looked at the wear on its teeth. There was no big deal, only one less vermin on the land. My dreams collapsed into a spattering of blood on that lovely ginger pelt. For a moment, that fox became the only fox I had been striving to catch, and with its death my project seemed to be destroyed. However, as the farmers dispersed at the end of the day, Old George lumbered over and placed a mighty, gnarled hand on my shoulder. 'Forkses', he said, and smiled.

In the meantime, Hans and I had started to develop a bit of technical wizardry aimed at solving the problem of capturing foxes. The idea sprang from the frustrating fact that gamekeepers using neck snares seemed able to catch foxes with relative ease, although at mortal danger to the captive. These nooses of pliable, braided wire, are set inconspicuously on well-trodden fox paths at fox-nose height. Since, in stark contrast to the gamekeeper's job, my priority had to be the fox's safety, there seemed no way for us to copy their success. Quite apart from concern for the foxes' well-being, this reluctance to take risks had a very practical aspect: in a study of fox society, it would be pointless if fatalities were continually disrupting the social milieu. However, I learnt from gamekeepers that foxes could be caught alive in snares as long as they were only set in 'safe places' and fitted with a 'stop'—a block to prevent the loop closing any tighter than the diameter of a fox's neck. Stopped snares could be set safely on fox paths that were both well away from possible entanglements, such as fenceposts on which the noose might corkscrew tight, and well shrouded with lush vegetation as camouflage.

It sounded straightforward, but in Oxfordshire, safe sites are few and far between—fox paths tend to congregate in places where entanglements abound. Indeed, only one or two per cent of the trapping sites that would suit a gamekeeper's purpose were safe enough for mine. There were several solutions to this. One was to trick the foxes into using the path I wanted; for example, drive across a field of grass, whereupon foxes crossing thereafter would use the 'tramlines' of the tyre tracks, rather than blaze their own trails. However, we decided on a different tactic. Where a well-used fox path led from one field to the next we staked a long wire into the ground, fixing one end near the hedge and the other well into the open field. At the field end we built a clip into the wire. Onto this 'running wire' we also threaded a curtain ring of just the right diameter so that it could pass onto, but not over, the clip. In turn, we affixed the snare to the curtain ring. With this apparatus a fox could be caught in the hedge, but would be free to run into the field, drawing its curtain ring along the running wire until the ring snapped into the clip, apprehending the fox well away from dangerous hedgerow entanglements.

Making these running snares was a very fiddly job, and setting them was worse. However, a score or more were soon in position. To minimize inconvenience to the foxes, I checked the traps every three hours during the night. Such frequent disturbances doubtless contributed to the weeks of failure that ensued. Then, at about 8 pm one February evening in 1973 it happened: a dog fox was caught. Theory and practice came together perfectly: the curtain ring was caught by the clip, and the fox was secured, no more damaged than a dog on a lead.

With beginner's luck I had landed a prime specimen. Broad head, thick neck cloaked in a deep red mane of winter fur, and burning yellow eyes that stopped me in my tracks—eyes, the like of which I've seldom seen since. Apprehensive of my inexperience, John grabbed the fox before it could grab me. With John's help my first radio-transmitter, neatly riveted to a dog's leather collar, was strapped in place. It was February, and for four months I had toiled for that instant. From then on I would know every movement made by 'Denman's Dog'. I released my grip and he bounded away. Beside me the receiver relayed the bleeps from his radio-collar. Forty metres off he stopped, his remarkable eyes burning back along the torchbeam. In the same instant the bleeps at my side slowed, became erratic, and stopped. Denman's Dog turned and trotted off up the field, and not so much as a crackle ever emanated from his transmitter again. So much for beginner's luck.

A week later John Gee did a remarkable thing. Despite a poor season's shooting, and with lambing approaching, he issued a dictum that no further foxes were to be shot on his land while my efforts continued. Since I had barely begun to appreciate the depth of feeling that permeates the anti-vulpine culture of the countryside, I didn't realize the magnitude of the schism he was driving between himself and his friends for my benefit. Next, John led me to a surprisingly

inconspicuous earth that had traditionally housed cubs since his father's day, and sure enough there were signs of occupation. The plan was laid to bolt the fox into a net, and for this we needed a dog with a special personality: I was about to get my first taste of yet another new and engrossingly complex aspect of the rural under-world—the culture of the terrier-man.

My first reaction to the proposal of using a terrier to bolt the fox from its retreat was one of horror. Surely one of these belligerent, lop-eared little dogs would injure the fox. But no, it transpired that there are terriers and terriers, and horses for courses. There are indeed 'hard' dogs that would weigh into a fox, but there are others, the so-called 'baiters', who don't have the nerve for tooth-to-tooth encounters. Instead, having sniffed out the fox, they stay just out of fang's reach, yapping incessantly until either they chivvy the fox into bolting, or somebody digs down to them. Really reliable baiters are a rare commodity, but Bob Dibble had a prized speci-men called Jock.

On the 11th February 1973, cajoled into this improbable escapade by John, Bob brought Jock to the scene. I stood by expectantly with a radio-collar. We examined a clear set of tracks which led into, but not out of, the hole, and our spirits rose. Jock's lead was slipped and with neither a glance to left or right and with tail quivering he almost flew underground, as if drawn by a vortex of vulpine magnetism. A net was draped over the entrance and we crouched silently, lest any trace of our presence should dissuade the fox from bolting. Almost at once Jock landed on the fox. A volley of oddly disembodied barks drifted from the entrance. Pressing our ears to the ploughed earth, we could locate the precise point below where Jock was haranguing his new acquaintance. Long minutes passed filled with excited expectation tinged with dread that, despite Jock's benign reputation, one or other of them might get hurt.

By the time Jock's barking had settled into a gentle rhythm, it was clear that the fox had no intention of making life simple for us. We began to dig—I rapidly learnt that this is skilled work. Down and down through dark, heavy clay. Closer and closer we homed in on the beacon of Jock's yaps, but each time we got close, he and the fox shifted position and we had to bend our tunnel in backbreaking pursuit.

After a couple of hours of digging there were no more jokes, no more chatter, only hard graft. We broke through into a subterranean tunnel. Holding Bob's feet and lowering him head first into our excavation, he could see Jock's stumpy tail bobbing about. A glorious rank smell of wet fox suffused the air. Bob pulled Jock out in the hope that in his absence the fox would shift to a more accessible position. The once white dog was now yellow with mud and writhing with enthusiasm to get back into the hole. A genetic mania has been instilled in the Jack Russell Terrier by man, surpassing such trifling achievements of selective breeding as the dairy cow. Terriers alone in the animal kingdom struggle to seek out conditions least conducive to their survival.

A flash of red sped past our peep-hole in the burrow. The fox had shifted and Jock was allowed back in pursuit. Soon his barking became mysteriously distant. Slowly it dawned on us that the fox's burrow led into a field drain. Not to be defeated, John fetched his JCB mechanical digger, and he began to excavate. Again, my spirits sank—surely the immensely heavy mechanical giant would cave in the soil, squashing the fox? Again, I was wrong. With deft use of the controls John cautiously pared off layers of soil. Soon the drain was exposed and Jock removed. Two reflecting beads gazed unwelcomingly into my face. Offering the fox a sack to chew, Bob grabbed it by the scruff. In a trice the radio was buckled on, tested, and Denman's Vixen was released. This time the transmitter did not fail.

My education now began in earnest. As dusk began to fall between 6.00 and 7.00pm, Denman's Vixen would stir from her day-time lair. She slept in secluded spots, often under a thorny tangle of scrub at the junction of four hedgerows. Hidden in hedgerows or ditches, I would be lurking somewhere downwind, hoping to glimpse her before the light failed, but always in contact through the bleeps in my headphones. In fact, I saw little of Denman's Vixen, but the change in note of her bleeps (a fortuitous result of poor design in the transmitter's circuitry), betrayed her awakening.

She began each evening by meandering around her resting place, sniffing the breeze, stretching, grooming. Then she would shake, as if taking a reluctant decision to throw off her drowsiness and change gear. With sharpened movements and purpose in her demeanour, she would set off at a trot. Within an hour of darkness she was travelling the hedgerows. During late February and early March in 1973, each night's activity continued almost unabated until she bedded down once again between 5.30 and 6.00am.

By night, I tried to get an accurate fix on the fox at least every quarter of an hour between dusk and dawn. Much of the tracking was done by car, with the heavy antenna mounted on a bracket on the roof. The routine was to drive rapidly between vantage points that could readily be found on a map, such as field junctions or gates. There, I would leap out of the car and rotate the antenna until the signal strength allowed me to draw a bead on the fox's direction, and then speed on to the next vantage point to secure the cross-bearing. Of course, if the fox was moving in the meantime, my triangulation point would become slurred. Thus each night passed in

a race against time to minimize the inaccuracy caused by a delay between bearings.

In what little daylight remained after sleeping for most of the short winter's days, I tried to reconstruct, on foot, the vixen's trail during the previous night. Sometimes I found a scattering of chewed pigeon feathers, or sometimes a fresh dropping perched atop a mole hill, or the pleasing bouquet of fox urine. As my eye became practised, a network of previously invisible tracks and trails was unveiled across the farm.

Fragments of a pattern emerged as the nights passed. As Denman's Vixen moved south through her range, heading towards Cumnor village, she invariably chose a route which crisscrossed through the wood before intersecting with a badger path that led her into a field of blackcurrant bushes. From there, she trotted along the tractor tracks running beside a line of cypress trees, before swinging south again through a well-trodden hedgerow passage that

led to the particular furrow which she preferred for travelling around the perimeter of the adjoining wheat field. Bit by bit, these fragments of pattern merged until each nook and cranny on the farm took on vulpine significance in my mind's eye—I was losing sight of the wood and beginning to see the trees.

As it happened, a large section of Denman's Farm fell within a triangle bounded on two sides by minor roads, and on the third, by a farm track. Denman's Vixen's nightly travels took me everywhere within that triangle, but it soon became clear that she treated these roads as the borders of her range. This patch measured 230 hectares, and embraced a patchwork of pasture, plough, woodland, orchard and a smattering of houses and gardens.

Denman's Vixen was not alone in this neighbourhood for during February and March the countryside around Denman's Farm was alive with the hoarse, strangulated shrieks of foxes—

wild haunting sounds that echoed through ice-clad winter nights. On one still night in mid-March I could hear five different foxes with voices as distinct as those in any human conversation (*see* Box 7, p. 28).

Staring down the arm of the radio antenna towards Denman's Vixen I could hear her, or another fox close beside her, calling from the marshy area north of the farmhouse. An answering cry came from Shaddles Wood, another from The Bog. Two minutes later, another volley was exchanged, this time including a fox calling from the bottom of Wytham Wood, across the valley two kilometres distant, followed by another cry from my vixen, and then another from a fox in Smith Hill Wood to the west. Their wails wafted back and forth across the frost-furred countryside for ten minutes or more. In the darkness, there was a sadness to the beauty of these voices from another world.

The rise and fall of the land around Denman's Farm was such that I was often thwarted for lack of a good vantage point from which to pinpoint the vixen's radio signal. John Gee had

the answer: we would convert the disused wind-pump, standing ten metres tall on the highest promontory of the farm, into an elevated antenna mast. The plan was to remove the sails from the pump, and in their place hoist the antenna aloft the pylon frame, above 7.5cm water piping.

This proved to be easier said than done. The wind sails could be reached only from a small and derelict wooden platform, from which most planks were missing. Access to the platform itself required scaling a badly rusted ladder built into the pylon's framework. Up this ladder, and onto the platform, we gingerly hauled an oxy-acetylene cutter. The weight of the gas bottle threatened to topple the platform, so we had to keep it counterbalanced by our own weight perched on the other end of the plank. John began to cut through the central joist on which the sails pivoted. As the last millimetres of metal sheared, the cartwheel-shaped sails rolled onto the platform alongside us and the cutting gear. Then, defying the effect of gravity on which our whole plan had depended, the cartwheel began to roll around the platform, chasing us from one

rusty handhold to the next, before it finally succumbed and crashed to the ground.

A further day's strenuous jiggery-pokery saw 20 metres of irrigation piping inserted up the middle of the pylon, on top of which the antenna swayed perilously. Handles made from more piping allowed the antenna to be rotated either from the crow's-nest platform or from the ground. With this extra height, there was nowhere in her range that I could not pick up the vixen's signal to an accuracy of better than three degrees.

It was becoming clear that a field biologist must be a chimaera, combining qualities not normally found together. On the one hand, he must be fit for bookworming and relish the critical thought required to tease out the questions that are worth asking. On the other, to put hard-won ideas into practice, he must be an amateur engineer and an accomplished navvy.

During the first weeks of March, Denman's Vixen focused her movements on the seven earths that were scattered around the farm. Each morning a fresh heap of soil lay outside those that she had refurbished by night. To my surprise, she re-excavated, and often used, the earth at which we had originally caught her. One morning in early March, the radio signal came loud and clear from the direction of Webb's Barn. Careful cross-bearings left no doubt: the fox was inside. With the image of Denman's Vixen caught slaughtering chickens and now riddled with shot and hung up in the barn to lure me into a confrontation with Mr Webb, I nervously knocked at the farmer's door. No, Mrs Webb could not recall her husband seeing a fox recently and, yes, I was still welcome to wander around the farm. In the corner of the dimly lit barn I found a spoil heap of freshly dug soil. Denman's Vixen was throwing caution to the winds in her choice of den sites! Over the following days she laid up several times beneath the barn. Then, on the 15th March she spent the day in Rochester Corner, a patch of marshy ground near the centre of her range.

That night it seemed that disaster must have struck since the vixen did not stir as dusk fell. Tracking on foot with a hand-held antenna, I

7. WHAT DO FOXES' CALLS MEAN?

Foxes produce a wide array of different sounds which grade into each other and span five octaves. In a classic study of animal vocalizations, Gunther Tembrock categorized more than 40 fox sounds into 28 recognizable groups. My impression is that the majority of these can be grouped into two groups— 'contact' calls and 'interaction' calls. Contact calls vary with distance whereas interaction calls vary with aggression.

The most familiar fox sound is the 'wow wow wow' call—a sort of bark involving three to five syllables (of which the last is the most protracted and highest pitched) heard most frequently from December to February (when it can be confused with the territorial calls of tawny owls). Protracted 'wow wow wow' 'conversations' often ricochet back and forth between two or more widely spaced foxes. I have made sonograms (voice-prints) of this call, confirming that individuals have characteristically different voices. Indeed, Tembrock showed that his tame dog fox responded to tape recordings of its mate's contact calls, but not to those of other vixens. The 'wow wow wow' call is often made by two foxes as they move towards each other, and I think it is the long distance version of the 'contact' calls which translate loosely as 'Here I am, where are you?' When two foxes draw close together it grades into a trisyllabic greeting warble not dissimilar to a chicken clucking. Adults greet cubs with the quietest version—a gruff 'huffing' noise. When we quietly say 'hmmf hmmf hmmf' to our hand-reared cubs they respond with rapturous tail-lashing, ears flat and lips drawn back as they pant loudly. The circumstances in which the contact call is heard are similar to 'hello'—one might shout 'hello' when lost in a wood, or mutter it as a preamble to shaking hands.

The second group, the 'interaction' calls, are heard when foxes are interacting at close quarters. Fox greetings sometimes involve a high-pitched whine, voiced especially by the more submissive individual. If a dominant fox advances on a subordinate this whine can become a ululating siren-like shriek. If the two begin to spar, or if an encounter is aggressive, the whine grades into staccato, rasping clicks. In a fight this stuttering, throaty noise (c-c-c-c-) sounds like a football fan's ratchet, or a stick being rattled on a paling fence. I call this noise gekkering, an anglicized version of Tembrock's German *keckern*. Sometimes one or two syllables of this explosive sound will be spat out, and I call this snirking. While eating, a cub will wheel around and snirk if a sibling passes too close. Gekkering is most frequently heard during the courting season (or when cubs are at play),

when the sounds emanate from rival dog foxes or from vixens rebutting too forward a suitor. Country people often term the call, and the fox's breeding season, clicketing.

A call which fits into neither of these categories is the long drawn-out monosyllabic wail (waaaaah). This eerie and magnificent sound is the one which I think most people have in mind when they talk of 'a vixen's scream'. It may indeed normally be the vixen's prerogative, but I have seen dog foxes make it. I have very occasionally seen foxes screaming, and they have always been on the move, pausing only for long enough to throw their whole body into the effort of the call. At the same time I have seen nearby foxes show no visible sign of interest. Since this wail is much more common during the breeding season it is widely assumed, but far from proven, to be a vixen on heat summoning dog foxes to compete for her.

Another monosyllabic call, sometimes not dissimilar to the scream, is the alarm bark. This is generally given by an adult of either sex to warn cubs of danger. At close quarters it is a muffled cough. At longer range it is a sharp bark. Cubs dive for cover at this noise. The cubs themselves make a tuneful, warbling whimper while nursing, which is much louder when they are dissatisfied. They are generally silent when alone. At about 19 days old their whimpers become more rhythmic and develop into a piercing version of the adult 'wow wow wow' bark, which signifies that they want attention.

The interplay between the roles of sound and scent in fox communication is a fascinating and unexplored topic. I have the impression that foxes are more vocal in some areas than others. If so, then this may reflect local differences in ecology. For example, under circumstances where foxes are less likely to meet in person or to encounter a scent mark, vocalizations might be more frequent.

skirted around and around her position. By dawn my heart was sinking; there had been not so much as a quaver in the pulsed signal to indicate movement. The next two nights dragged past without sign of life. By sunrise on the 18th I was convinced that, at best, the vixen had slipped her collar. At worst, she was dead.

Rochester Corner was a glorious oasis among the barren cereal fields. Although no more than a hectare in area, a jungle of brambles and bullrushes cloaked a shimmering duckpond. Splashing through ankle-deep water, I tracked the position of the transmitter down to a few tussocks of reed standing amidst a watery bed of decaying rushes. I unplugged the antenna and still picked up a loud signal, confirming that I was within about ten metres of the transmitter yet, clearly, Denman's Vixen was not there. Back and forth I waded, probing the mud and tussocks of reed with my feet. The fact that we had had a fox in our grasp, and then voluntarily released it, had so inflamed elements of the anti-fox lobby that it was far from absurd to suspect that somebody had sought out and killed the fox, then thrown the radio-collar into the water in an attempt to avoid detection. So, sloshing about on hands and knees, I felt beneath the water's surface, kneading the detrital mulch for the transmitter. John Gee brought his old collie bitch, Growler, to sniff through the area, but she too was nonplussed. Wet, dejected, and facing the bleak prospect of a return to square one, we started back for home. Barely five paces from where we had been searching, Growler thrust her nose into a tussock of reeds. From beneath her paws, Denman's Vixen sprang into the air and, like a pebble skiffing the surface, splashed at full speed through the deepest water.

Nestling cosily in the dry tussock, in a couch just above the water's surface and swaddled by thick reeds, lay five mole-grey coloured newborn cubs. We left at once, harangued by the staccato barking of the alarmed vixen. Almost immediately she returned to the cubs and remained with them until nightfall. Then, at 9.15pm, and hidden downwind, I watched her shadowy figure in the moonlight as she carried them, one by one in her jaws, to one of the other earths she had prepared. The new earth was about 100 metres from Rochester Corner, and dug into the bank of a ditch. She remained there, within the immediate vicinity of the earth, until the 21st March when, for the first time in six days, she made a single, 20-minute excursion of about 150 metres. During the next three nights she made slightly longer excursions, but otherwise re-

mained inactive at the den. On the 25th March, ten days after the birth of her cubs, Denman's Vixen began to make longer sorties throughout her home range. Nevertheless, the bulk of her time continued to be spent near the cubs. Only when they reached three weeks, and had begun to eat meat, did her movements return to their previous pattern.

A huge oak tree stood over her earth. Sometimes, instead of radio-tracking, I crept to this tree before dusk, and climbed above the den. When darkness came I could hear the mewings of the cubs below, and I caught occasional glimpses of their mother as she melted in and out of the moon's shadows. I heard the gurgling slurps as they nursed from her, and heard her whimper as pinprick teeth tugged her teats. Perhaps it was because of their rough treatment that, by day, she soon took to lying a few metres from the earth.

Twice I saw another fox visit the earth and greet Denman's Vixen, but in the poor light I could discern little of what passed between them and nor could I confirm my suspicion that it was Denman's Dog. On one of these occasions I

heard the sound of crunching bones and thus suspected that the visitor had brought food for the vixen. However, I never saw any other foxes at the den, and all the indications were that Denman's Vixen shared her range only with her mate. My early expectations of finding large teams of social foxes began to seem unfounded for this family at least.

I continued to track Denman's Vixen night by night until the 20th April that year, when I decided to take a night off. The next day she was in the earth with her cubs and, to my surprise, did not move as dusk settled. I spent that night listening to an extraordinary cacophony of fox calls. These were not the prolonged, monosyllabic screams of midwinter, but staccato 'wow-wow-wow' barks. I followed on foot as a fox (I suspected it was Denman's Vixen's mate) toured almost the entire border of her range, barking as he went, and pausing twice for prolonged shouting matches with neighbouring foxes. By the next morning the vixen had still not moved and I went to investigate. The earth had been dug in and gassed. The whole family was dead.

3 | REYNARD'S FOX

CREEPING INTO THE wind, hidden amongst the silhouettes of a line of gorse bushes, the radio-bleeps grew louder in my headphones. Not far ahead was Snowflake, a young vixen with an uncommonly fluffy, white-tipped brush. I was armed with the 'hot-eye', a pair of infra-red binoculars that had revolutionized my fieldwork. On even the darkest night these remarkable binoculars allow the user to see, while remaining discreetly unseen. A 32-watt, infra-red beam illuminates the scene with a light invisible to human, and vulpine, eyes. A cathode ray tube in the binoculars converts the reflected infra-red light into a visible image. Through the eyepieces, the viewer sees the world in an eery mono-chromatic green. Now, as I scanned ahead, ten luminous green dots wavered in the distance, five pairs of eyes whose owners' bodies were, at 150 metres, dim shadows faintly discernible as rabbits at the furthest range of the hot-eye.

A sixth pair of eyes flitted into my field of view, and began to slide towards the five which, after momentary bobbing, sped away leaving a zigzag of luminous trails across my viewfinder. Only the sixth pair of eyes remained; they blinked, flashed open, and glided away through the hedge. It is surprising what you can learn from the motion of a pair of eyes: those that bounce along like besotted pingpong balls belong to rabbits, those that are low slung, rather dim and rock jauntily from side to side are badgers', whereas the ghoulish gliders are foxes'.

Although the sound of Snowflake's radio signal was thumping in my ears, the fox that had just fluffed its stalking of the five rabbits was not her: in the light of the hot-eye she was easily recognizable by virtue of the circles of reflecting tape fixed to the sides of her radio-collar, giving the impression of a four-eyed fox.

Moments later, I glimpsed Snowflake at the bottom of a long garden beside the rabbit-infested gorse bushes. I searched in vain for a gap in the garden fence. Cursing the din of my boots crunching on the roadside grit, I tip-toed to the neighbouring garden. Bedecked like a human Christmas tree in coaxial cable, battery packs and a tangle of wires, I risked a slippery vault over the metal railings. Landing unscathed and with my wiring intact, I flinched as the antenna swung back and clattered against the railings with a metallic clunk. Standing stock still, I counted slowly to 100. Mercifully, the bleep in the next garden seemed unaffected. I slunk across the lawn and, peering over the fence, focused the hot-eye on two more green dots. Snowflake was so close that every detail of her fur, rain-raked into spiky runnels, was visible. For ten minutes (a very long time when one is trying to breathe quietly), she chomped noisily on windfall apples.

The following night, Snowflake's radio signal led me to the same garden. I assumed that she was feasting on apples again, but when I crept close I saw that, in fact, she was criss-crossing the lawn and picking up beetles. The next evening she was again in the same garden, where we both faced the added hazard of dodging high-spirited party-goers. Within a stone's throw of thumping bass notes and gales of laughter, I pinpointed Snowflake's signal, but this time I could not see her. Scan as I might, no tell-tale green eyes flashed through my view-finder. Then I saw her, beneath the apple tree, curled up and sound asleep. While I crouched nearby shivering for well over two hours, Snowflake's slumbers were unbroken by the noisy revelry.

I mention these observations on Snowflake because they illustrate the weakness of radio-

8. WHO IS REYNARD THE FOX?

Reynard is a fox who has had a greater influence upon European culture and perceptions than any other wild creature. He adorns the spandrels of mediaeval churches from Birmingham to Bucharest, leers from the pages of psalters, and has triumphed as an evil genius in more than a millennium of epic poems and bestiaries. He thrives in contemporary children's stories and has infiltrated our languages and thus our perception of his wild cousins: there is hardly a language in Europe in which the word 'foxy' is not synonymous with trickery and deceit.

Reynard, then known as Reinardus, first took his name in 1150 in a Latin poem about a wolf—*Ysengrimus*. Previously his unnamed ancestors had connived their way through about 2,000 years of fables. Initially, Aesop, who was probably a slave in the 6th century BC, used the fox rather benevolently to show the folly of being too clever by half. However, by the 2nd century BC prejudice had hardened—a natural history book, the *Physiologus*, depicted foxes as crafty personifications of the Devil, and quoted God as referring to Herod as 'that fox'. In 1175 the modern Reynard emerged as the central villain in Pierre Saint Cloud's *Roman de Renard*. In the Middle Ages he took Europe by storm, emerging as Reinhart in Germany, Rainardo in Italy, Reinaerde in Flanders. He crossed the English channel in 1250, but skulked in low profile until his dramatic appearance in Chaucer's *Nun's Priest's Tale* in 1390. In 1481, William Caxton published the history of *Reynard the Fox*. As they are told, retold and metamorphosed, one strand unites the many different Reynard stories: his invariable treachery, vindictiveness, rebelliousness and sublime ingenuity. He is also a loner.

Reynard conducted his devious business in the Kingdom of Noble the lion. There, he flattered Chantecleer the cockerel into singing with his eyes closed, tricked Tibert the cat into castrating a clergyman, duped Bruin the bear into being a stooge (getting him flayed alive), and all too often betrayed the friendship of Grimbert the badger. He behaves true to character when he cajoles Hersent the she-wolf into an adulterous affair. Revelling in this amorous success he scornfully urinates on Hersent's whelps, who dejectedly tell their father, Isengrin, who is enraged. Hersent pleads, untruthfully, that Reynard raped her, so the two wolves race off to catch the fox. Reynard leads them a merry chase, before dashing into a burrow. Hersent follows and becomes firmly stuck, her hindquarters protruding, undignified, from the entrance. Reynard emerges from another exit and this time he gleefully rapes Hersent in full view of

---

tracking: the vixen's locations were identical on each of these nights, yet observations revealed that she was occupied very differently on the three occasions. The sophisticated technology of radio-tracking is a wonderful complement to traditional fieldcraft, but no substitute for it. Having found where the animal is, one wants to know what it is doing there, and with whom it is doing it.

I had been watching Snowflake on Boar's Hill, only four kilometres from Denman's Farm but a world away in fox terms. Not long after the death of Denman's Vixen I had spent a melancholy evening with Hans Kruuk, who lived on Boar's Hill. It arose in conversation that he was puzzled by the disappearance of scraps from his bird-table during the night, and as the night wore on it suited our darkened mood to switch off the lights and mount vigil until the thief disclosed his hand. Shortly before midnight not one, but three adult foxes trotted confidently into the garden and proceeded to clean up every last morsel of the bread crusts, bacon rinds and fat provided for the birds. The next day, we scoured the surrounding fields and found fox highways stippled with pad marks from a thousand footfalls. In one afternoon I found almost 20 piles of droppings. Chance had led me to the perfect study area, and in the coming years my nightly prowlings on Boar's Hill were to yield almost 10,000 radio fixes on the local foxes.

The district includes the last straggling houses of Oxford's more affluent suburbia, spanning two ridges and scattered with such auspicious place names as Foxcombe Hill, Foxcombe Lane, Foxfields and Badger Lane. This enclave of rural-suburbia sandwiched between town and farmland is typified by large detached houses and spacious gardens. Strands of residential property are linked by unmanaged wood, scrub and orchard, and weave amongst cereal fields and pasture. Much of the woodland is deciduous, including oak, beech, ash and sycamore. Large parts of many of the gardens are delightfully derelict. Overgrown orchards are swathed in understories of bramble and dog's mercury.

Isengrin as he runs to the rescue. Reynard makes good his escape, leaving the enraged Isengrin to pull his wife from the hole by her tail. Reynard's crimes are recounted to King Noble's Court and Reynard is brought from his castle, Maupertuis, and sentenced to hang. But he pleads with such eloquence that Noble believes him reformed. Reynard is pardoned, dons a pilgrim's habit and staff, and sets off to the Holy Land. No sooner is he out of Noble's sight when he clubs Couard the hare with his staff and escapes to his castle.

Reynard's adventures are compelling because they are so nearly right, yet so very wrong. Many doubtless stem from rural observation—the enmity between wolf and fox is real (see Box 13, p. 84), as is the importance of urine, the fox's adaptability and, doubtless, the chaos in the poultryhouse of which Pinte the hen dreamed. Even Aesop (and Salome, in the *Song of Songs*) is accurate in portraying the fox's taste for grapes, as is the 12th-century French version of the story where the grapes are replaced by blackberries. Other stories probably have a basis in fact: Reynard is often portrayed as a clergyman preaching to a congregation of ducks or geese. Since these and other birds often mob foxes, one could easily imagine that the portrayal stemmed from watching a seemingly eager congregation of fowl as they harassed a fox.

Today's stories continue the tradition. In *The Sly Fox and Little Red Hen*, the fox captures a hen to feed his family. Carrying it home in a sack (slung over his shoulder as illustrated in all mediaeval depictions), he pauses to rest. The hen escapes and loads the sack with boulders. On arrival at his lair the sly young fox greets his mother and empties the sack into the cooking pot. 'The boiling water splashed all over the sly young fox and his mother. They were both killed at once.' So reads the 'happy' ending of a moralizing book for seven-year-olds. By coincidence, Hans Kruuk's small daughter, Loeske, had just read this story when we took her to watch foxes. We spotted a fox and for a moment she was overjoyed, before guiltily asking 'Daddy, is it alright to like foxes?' The Sly Fox carries the legacy of the opening lines of Rutebeuf's 12th-century poem, *Reynard the Corrupt*: 'Reynard is dead, Reynard is alive; Reynard is foul, Reynard is vile; and Reynard reigns.' By unveiling some of his secrets perhaps I have helped give a voice to Reynard's reply.

Until the scourge of Dutch elm disease in the mid-seventies, tall hedgerows supported stately stands of elm. To the north lies Oxford City, to the west, farmland—Denman's Vixen's range and, eventually, Wytham Woods. To the east, Boar's Hill is bordered by Bagley Wood, with large tracts of oak amidst plantations of Norway spruce, larch and Scots pine.

Some 500 metres across the fields from Hans Kruuk's house lies Hamels, a wooden Kentish barn rebuilt into a house by an eccentric 19th-century actress, and standing in six hectares of overgrown garden and paddock. Tracking the pawprints from Hans' garden, they led me to Hamels. There, a spaghetti junction of fox trails converged beside an almost impenetrable dome of scrub. Hacking my way through I found a long-disused tennis court. Weeds grew through the tarmac, a dilapidated summerhouse, curtained in convolvulus, stood to one side, and at the far end a large heap of freshly dug soil spilled out from a bushy tangle of broom and briar. I crept into the summerhouse in the late afternoon of 20th May and waited for foxes to emerge.

At 8.30pm a fox appeared near the earth. In appearance she was undistinguished in every respect, save that her full brush was swathed in a heavy cloak of black guard hairs. I recognized her from Hans' garden as Blackfringe Vixen. She paused, standing warily in the server's square of the court, a field vole's stubby tail hanging cigarette-like from her lips. Tensing, one foreleg raised like a setter pointing game, the vixen stared straight at the summerhouse. At that moment, maddeningly, a horsefly plunged its proboscis into my unblinking eyelid. Blackfringe's paw was replaced on the ground; she relaxed and I risked screwing my eye shut.

Blackfringe lowered her head and uttered a low, warbling version of the 'wow-wow-wow' call. Like greyhounds from the trap, five cubs launched from the earth, barging and shoving towards the vixen. She dropped the vole, and all five cubs fell on it in an uproar of squealing and gekkering. The scrum toppled forward, each cub tripping in its effort both to pull the vole free

from the others, and to slam aggressively into them with sideways-barges. At the same time, they were lashing their tails from side to side and whimpering greetings to Blackfringe who was nuzzling them with a tenderness that seemed out of place in the snarling throng. Somehow, one kitten-sized demon secured the vole, sped across the tennis court and, managing to hold the others at bay by energetic hip-slamming, chewed down its furry trophy. Then the cubs scampered back to Blackfringe, all animosity between them gone, and threw themselves into writhing greetings.

Blackfringe stood still while all five cubs nursed from her. Four were identical in size, but the fifth cub was much smaller, and fared poorly in the ensuing rough and tumble. Two or three others would fall on the little one, one springing on him while others bit and shook at the base of his chubby little tail. At 8.45pm, Blackfringe left the tennis court, but the cubs continued to play amongst themselves and, as the light faded, began to scamper and probe in the vegetation around the court. At 9.30pm, another adult fox trotted into centre court and warbled a summons to the cubs. This too was a vixen in milk, her well-sucked teats protruding from the almost pinkish-grey underfur of her belly. She was Down-White Vixen, identifiable by the unusual white fur of her left hind leg. The white fur stretched up to about three centimetres below her hock where, at a sharply drawn border, and as if she had stood in a paint pot, the fur became typical reddish-brown.

Down-White stood with legs stolidly splayed, ears flicking back, mouth slightly agape, and winced and twitched while the cubs pulled enthusiastically at her teats. Once she cried out and tried to spring aside, but they anchored her like the guy ropes of a tent. Seven minutes after her arrival, Down-White finally shook the cubs free and immediately trotted from the scene.

The cubs had not long resumed their unsupervised play when Equal-White arrived. She was a slighter vixen, with a blaze of white up her left hind leg to a point level with the hock. She neither brought food, nor nursed the cubs, but they greeted her enthusiastically and, in a somewhat detached and adult manner, she joined in their play. The tumbling led them out of sight into the thick vegetation, and then there was silence. Half an hour later I slipped away. This had been my first substantial observation of fox family life, and my head was spinning with ideas about their society—hunches gleaned in a few minutes of observation, but to prove them right took a further four years.

Hans began to put scraps out in the garden, and also mounted a dim light outside. When Jane Kruuk invited me to spend a night peering into the garden from their darkened sitting room, she could hardly have anticipated that I would continue to do so on most nights for two years. Jane

9. WHAT ARE THE FOXES' VITAL STATISTICS?

Latin name: Vulpes vulpes
Family: Canidae

UK dimensions
Adult weight: male 6.5kg; female 5.5kg
Head-body length: male 57–77 (67) cm; female
   56–74 (63) cm
Tail length: male 35–49 (43) cm; female 28–49
   (40) cm

North American dimensions
   Wide regional variation, approx. average head-
   body length 60 cm; weight 4.5 kg. Southern forms
   2.5 kg, northern forms up to 9 kg.

Sexual dimorphism: male about 15% heavier

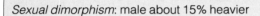

——————— 50mm

Male spermatogenesis: November–February
Female oestrus: 3 days during mating period
Mating period: January–February (earlier south, later
   north)
Gestation: 52–53 days
Peak cubbing season: March–April
Birth weights: 100gm
Mean litter size: mostly 4–5

Eyes first open: 11–14 days
Sexual maturity: 9–10 months

Trotting speed: 6–13km per hour
Max. speed: 50km per hour

Forefoot print: length 60mm; width 45mm
Hindfoot print: length 55mm; width 38mm

Tracks:

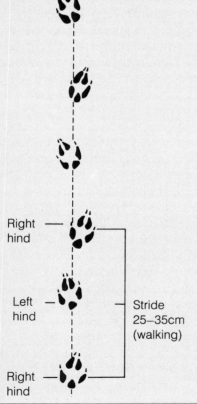

Right hind

Left hind

Stride
25–35cm
(walking)

Right hind

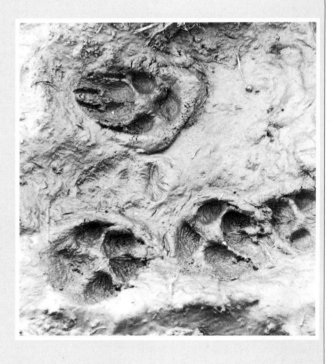

withstood this nightly intrusion with good grace, only baulking when Hans and I began to draw up plans for building an observation platform on their bedroom window-ledge.

The stage in front of the sitting-room window measured little more than ten metres across. It was visited almost every night by four adult vixens. Blackfringe, Down-White, Equal-White, Up-White, and one dog fox, Sampson. In the early days, we provided the foxes with scraps such as crusts of bread and bacon rind. Then we secured several dozen dead mice, confident that the foxes would be delighted at this upturn in their fortunes. We scattered a handful of mice among the normal scraps. When the nightly visitors arrived they were far from pleased at the new cuisine. They shrank fearfully from the mice until the bravest fox summoned up the courage to dash between them and snatch up the crusts of bread. The fox's guard against the unfamiliar, enhanced by centuries of poisoned baits and devious traps, is seldom relaxed: by morning not a single mouse had been eaten, but every crust was gone. Several nights passed before Blackfringe and her companions accepted this novel fare, gathering bread and mouse together in a most wholesome-looking sandwich.

The foxes visiting Hans' garden seemed friendly enough amongst themselves, and it was clear from my observations at the tennis court that their lives were thoroughly entwined. The idea of sociable foxes began to gain renewed credence, and all the more so once the results of my radio-tracking began to take shape.

The first surprising find was that these foxes were travelling over very small areas: the average adult fox on Boar's Hill seldom ventured outside an area of 40 hectares. The largest stable home range was 72 hectares, while the smallest was little more than 10 hectares (an area so small that a fox might canter across it in much less than a minute). What was more remarkable, was that such small ranges housed not one or two, but several adult foxes.

Radio-tracking had revealed patterns of movement, but to explore further the private life of the fox I would have to become better at watching them, better at those backwoodsman's skills I had revered for so long. Soon my nocturnal antics attracted a deal of notoriety. One night, as I skulked beside a boundary hedge, I heard the noisy footfall of three evacuees from the pub (fortuitously named *The Fox*), as they wobbled down the lane. My car, draped in wires and sporting a rooftop antenna, was parked near by. One man, seemingly a stranger in the district, exclaimed to his companion, 'What on earth is that?' 'That's just the Foxman', came the reply. Then, sensing the questioner's incomprehension, he added, 'Just some silly idiot who sticks microphones on foxes and sleeps rough in hedges so he can write some sort of book about it.' This, I felt, was as good an epithet as any for my endeavours to produce a doctoral thesis.

At first, I had struggled to find fox droppings and to spot the pinprick holes of their claws in the mud. But all at once, almost overnight, I found that I could not help but see signs everywhere. It was a joy to anticipate finding signs of foxes, even before finding them there. A sixth sense told that here is the sort of place where an earth will be dug, that there is a likely point for a fox to jump the ditch, and here a good spot to find scats. Reading the morning newspaper of events trodden in the mud was exciting, and the biggest thrill of all was to guess what the fox would do next and, at least sometimes, to be right.

Musing on the difficulties of getting inside somebody else's skin, the Austrian philosopher Wittgenstein, pointed out that even if an Englishman could become fluent in every nuance of the French language, he would never know what it was like to be a Frenchman. Of course, it is even more difficult, not to say impossible, to see the world through a fox's eyes. Nonetheless, trying to do so certainly changed my perception of the countryside in a most gratifying way. On Boar's Hill in the winter of 1973, there was a neatly combed parting through the frost-bitten grass in the top corner of Aubrey's Field. This path, one footfall wide, led under a gorse bush before curving around a rotting fencepost. One side of the post had a faint grey lustre about 25 centimetres above the ground and, just below, the rust-pitted surface of a twisted strand of wire was smoothed with a powder of dry clay. The grass had been parted by a fox. That fox had ducked below the overhanging gorse bough, dodged around the fencepost, brushing it with its shoulder as it broke its stride to slip over the bottom strand of wire, across which on wet nights its mud-soaked brush painted a fresh veneer of clay.

In 1986, 13 years later, the path was still there, although a bramble sucker now formed an arcade to its entrance and the fencepost had begun to rot into jagged splinters. Both of these rasping surfaces now carried fine and twisting, almost woolly, red hairs. These hairs are more likely to glint red if a slight breeze makes them shimmer, or if you blow on them. Thirteen winters after the frosts of 1973, the field-edge furrow still often bears paired slashes where a clawed rear foot has slithered in the rain. A brittle clump of corn stalks lanced by the combine but never fully buried by the plough, like its predecessors often bears a dropping. Nearby, the gorse bush droops almost to ground level now. In the summer the tips of its lowest bough push out new leaves, which by late winter have already been burnt brown and begun to bleach a speckled yellow. Foxes are born and foxes die, but as the years pass, that branch smells afresh of fox urine week in and week out.

When I first stood on this hillside overlooking Aubrey's Field, the woodlands behind it and the scattered farm buildings and horse-grazed meadows, I saw a whole landscape in a pattern of greens and browns; now when I look across that view I cannot but pick out all its myriad parts. I see the histories of a host of foxes, and my own history too. I see the urine-marked gorse bush and dozens of places like it, each with its well-trodden path. I see the slack ground running below a low hillock, through which a fox will certainly slink undetected and out of the wind.

From a distance, the ploughed land seems ringed by a chain of semi-circles which the tyre tracks left as the tractor turned at the end of each sweep of the plough. I know that the outermost chain of these semi-circles will be linked into one curving path, padded smooth by the tracks of foxes who prefer this prepared route to striking out across the sticky, pad-clogging clay. There are the earths, the resting places, the good mousing grounds. I see also the gardens which must be avoided because the dogs bite, the tree in which I was sitting during the winter's night when the skin of my thumb, moistened by damp breath, froze painfully to the metal of the hot-eye, and the spot where I caught the vixen who, upon release, grabbed my cap and sprinted off with it across the field.

After three years of intensive radio-tracking, the results turned the prevailing notion of fox behaviour squarely on its head. Some 20 adult foxes were resident in slightly over two square

kilometres of the study area. The tiny home ranges were shared by a group of foxes, each of whom travelled within roughly the same borders. Here it seemed that the fox's social unit was some sort of group, in which case my general enquiry into their sociology could be focussed into a logical series of questions.

First, how big were the groups and what was their composition? My estimates indicated that each group included between four and six adults and almost always contained only one adult male. True, these foxes seldom travelled together, and never operated as a pack, but they did meet fleetingly during their wanderings and doubtless scent and sound kept them in contact even when they were far apart. What is more, whereas the movements of foxes within each such group overlapped widely, those of neighbouring groups overlapped remarkably little, an arrangement that smacked of territoriality between the groups, that is to say, of orderly spacing out of home ranges (*see* Box 16, p. 117).

The best evidence that the Boar's Hill foxes were territorial came from radio-tracking. There were some areas where the distinction between two neighbouring ranges was hazy. For example, members of two groups laid up by day in the dense plantations of Bagley Wood and while members of each group seemed to keep to their own dens, their movements within the wood often overlapped. Similarly, the paths leading to the earths of another two neighbouring groups criss-crossed each other in Dixieland Wood. The situation was quite different in the vicinity of houses and gardens: there the borders were drawn with uncanny precision. Not long after beginning to radio-track foxes on Boar's Hill, I remember standing night after night at a junction of two narrow lanes in the village of Bayworth. As I turned the tuning knob on my radio-receiver, a harmony of different signals wafted into the headphones. On the north side of the road the signals told that two vixens, Blackfringe and Equal-White, were at the feeding site in Hans' garden. Not 40 metres to the east a vixen called Ethol (short for Ethology) was on the other side of the road, padding about in the farmyard. I never found any of these vixens on the 'wrong' side of the road. Later, when Toothypeg Vixen and her group members were equipped with radios, they frequented the caravan site only a stone's throw to the north, and well within reach of the whiff of scraps provided nightly in Hans' garden, yet for months on end there was no evidence that they trespassed. To the south, and within 100 metres of the spot where I had stood on the road between Blackfringe and Ethol, Blackears Dog would glean rich pickings from a small-holding which I never knew his neighbours to visit.

It seemed that borders were sharply defined and meticulously observed where key foraging areas were at stake. In contrast, deep in the sanctuary of the woods, used mainly for sleep by day, there was more latitude and neighbourly tolerance.

A framework of fox society on Boar's Hill had begun to take shape. But what sort of social life was entailed by this basic structure? The simultaneous radio-tracking of several foxes revealed that any two members of a group might, on average, be within 30 metres of each other for as little as four minutes during the ten hours of a winter's night, a total that was made up, moreover, of several fleeting encounters. Against these odds, being in the right place at the right time to watch important social exchanges was a daunting task. In a morbid moment I calculated

10. HOW TO TRACK FOXES?

Above: This field corner is rife with signs of fox. On the narrow, well-trodden path, patches of mud carry the traces of paw-prints. The prints are dog-like (especially like a sheepdog's), but more oval, with fur showing between the pads, and the two front claws, close together, making clear pin-prick impressions. This path, like many others, divides at the field corner to exit in two directions through the fence. The two routes are marked by the slight partings in the curtain of vegetation. Foxes travelling these routes squeeze between the bottom and middle strands of the fence, and the barbed wire has snagged tightly wound balls of coarse red guard hairs and thin, crinkly, grey underfur that glint in the sunlight. The bottom strand of wire is coated in a sheath of dried soil, where it has been repeatedly wiped by the foxes' mud-drenched brushes, and the wire is rusting faster in these places. Just to the right of the right hand passage a bramble stem catches a few more hairs, but the thorns have been broken and the bark polished smooth by the countless passings of vulpine flanks. The dog fox is cocking his leg to leave a token urine mark on a tussock of grass (in the snow he would betray his sex because the sprinkled urine would be projected forward of his rear paws, whereas that of a vixen, even if she cocked her leg, would tend to be projected rearwards or downwards).

Aside from the pleasing smell of fox urine on the tussock, the alert tracker would doubtless detect a yellowing of the grass leaves due to repeated dousings with these scent messages. The boulder to the right may also smell of fox urine, and perhaps also the more acrid adour of anal sac secretions that may daub the droppings neatly positioned aloft. The droppings will contain visible traces of undigested fox food, such as blackberry pips, some feather quills or the undigested glistening black fragments of beetle elytra. If the fox has eaten mammals such as rodents or rabbits there is a greater likelihood that the droppings will have the twirled ends often said to be characteristic of foxes, and composed of a mat of undigested fur. Nearby some feathers show where a fox carrying a pigeon paused. There are not sufficient feathers to indicate that the fox ate the entire pigeon there, but it did chew through a few wing feathers, as indicated by the bitten ends of the larger quill. Had the predator been a hawk, these feathers would be plucked, not chewed. Beside the trail a dead shrew lies uneaten, its body crushed by the fox's weight as it pounced, and its fur moist from saliva during a brief mouthing before it was discarded as inedible due to its unsavoury scent glands. The fox may even have sprinkled the shrew with an epitaph of urine.

Opposite: The vicinity of a breeding earth is littered with debris from the cubs' antics. In the foreground lies the skin of a hedgehog, its spines no protection as it was carefully eaten from the underside. Nearby there are other remains, the paired wings of a pheasant poult still bearing the wing tag that identifies it as a pen-reared bird. The lower hind-leg of a rabbit has been skilfully skinned, the skin peeled back towards the foot like an elegant evening glove, the leg bones chewed through, and engraved with the gnaw-marks of fox teeth. Even rural foxes feed a lot on human waste, and at the earth lies the remains of a plastic bag that once contained a chicken's giblets. Bone chips are clearly visible in some of the fox droppings around the den, and if the contents of these droppings are examined carefully any presence of bone chips in the absence of appropriate fur or feather is circumstantial evidence that they were eaten from human refuse.

The cubs themselves are playing with a mole. Foxes tend not to relish moles, so it is not uncommon for cubs to discard them at the earth having used them simply as playthings. Moles used as 'toys' are punctured by numerous pin-sharp cub teeth; sometimes the haemorrhaging associated with these bites indicates that the mole was still alive when the parent fox gave it to the cubs. Indeed, some countrymen believe that foxes deliberately take live moles to their cubs to play with. The items outside a fox family's earth are not likely to be representative of what the foxes have eaten—rather the debris consists largely of bits of prey too large or indigestible to eat, or remains of prey that are unpopular on the menu—fox's relish meadow voles, yet it is rare to find such prey at a den simply because they are all eaten whole! The earth itself is dug into the well-drained soil of a sandy bank and would, characteristically, have two or three entrances. The freshly worked spoil heap is well studded with paw-prints of both adults and cubs. The fact that the nearby vegetation has been flattened indicates that the cubs are old enough to be frolicking above ground. The entrances to two fox paths lead off through the tall grass to the left, and adult 'feetings' show another approach route just to the left of the hedgehog's skin.

11. WHAT DOES THE FOX'S BODY LANGUAGE MEAN?

With humans, tiny movements convey a wealth of information—a raised eyebrow versus a frown, a smile versus a grimace—and the same is true of foxes. In particular, movements of the ears, the tail, and the mouth are laden with meaning, as is the body posture. The body markings accentuate these signals: the tail often has a conspicuous white tag, and the inner edge of the black-backed ears are trimmed with cream fur. Certain postures are characteristic of dominant or aggressive individuals, others are characteristic of subordinate or fearful ones. Many postures blend the two, producing what is to me (but surely not to the foxes) a bewildering and rapid changing of expressions.

So, in the picture, and starting from the top, the first fox is uneasily sniffing the wind (the ears are often rotated, and flicking while sniffing), the second is in a playful mood, ears perked, and rearing on its hind legs (possibly leaning a forepaw on its companion's back) to solicit play. The third fox might be trotting back after successfully evicting an intruder, or might be a dog fox consorting with a vixen on heat.

On the opposite page, bottom left, a fearful fox grins in submission, its back arched and body curved, legs crouched. Its tail beats back and forth, and its ears are flush against its skull and pointing backwards. Submission need not be tinged with

that, of the hours I stalked on foot with the hot-eye, I had foxes in sight for only five per cent of the time. On the bright side, and at my best, I reckoned at least, to glimpse a fox on just over a third of the occasions on which I stalked them. These glimpses were my only chance to answer the next question on my list. What are the social relationships amongst members of a group of foxes?

One July evening in 1973, shortly before dusk, I had the opportunity of making one such observation. I lay hidden in the ditch at Hamels. In the overgrown pasture I could see the vixens Down-White and Equal-White. Through my headphones I could hear Blackfringe's stationary radio signal, still deep in Bagley Wood at her day-time resting place in a stand of spruce. Hamels' paddock was divided into halves by an east–west ditch, thickly vegetated with sedges and rushes. The northern half of the paddock rose up to the woodland's edge. At 9.40pm, and for no obvious reason, Equal-White sped up the ridge, hotly pursued by Down-White. The ground was pock-marked by ant hills and tussocks, and both foxes dodged wildly, leaping high into the air and springing from side to side, as a hunted fox jinks ahead of closing hounds. But this chase was not in earnest: catching up with Equal-White, Down-

fearfulness—it is often a relaxed expression of the *status quo*. If this fox had been merely submissive, and less fearful, its back would not have been arched, nor its body curved; its approach would have been direct and its posture low, so that its muzzle was reaching up to greet the dominant.

Bottom right: two reasonably well-matched foxes locked in a sideways-barging stalemate, each pushing its flanks against the other's. These two might have been approaching the same scrap of food, and moved sideways or backwards towards each other, their heads turned away, each slamming its haunches into the other in a series of blocking moves. Both foxes betray a mixture of aggression and fear: tails lash, bodies arch but do not crouch, ears are back but not flattened. Such interactions would be accompanied by a cacophony of gekkering (*see* Box 7, p.28)

Top right: a fox launching an attack. In attack there is often a bewildering blend of aggressive and fearful signals, but in this case the fox is rather confident: the attack is direct (not sideways or backwards, as a subordinate might attack a dominant approaching its food), the ears are rotated and flattened to the side, not backwards, and the tail is aloft.

White cut her off with a leftward swerve, and swung around to barge with her shoulder. With Equal-White still struggling to retrieve her balance, Down-White sped back down the ridge. Within seconds, Equal-White was in pursuit, and the roles reversed. Then, as if an invisible force had blown a whistle, both vixens stopped and nosed each other, ears twitching sensitively with each sniff at the other's face. Equal-White flopped to the ground and Down-White circled her, reaching forward timidly with her forepaws to prod at the prostrate body. Down-White's prodding evoked no response until, with ears perked, she sprang high into the air, hung motionless at the zenith of her leap, and plunged down, feet first, squarely onto Equal-White's ribs. Crouched beneath the blackthorn 20 metres away, I heard the wind rush from Equal-White's buffeted lungs. Down-White's hind legs never touched the ground from that jump, for she sprang in one lithe cartwheeling movement across Equal-White's body, and was running fast up the hill within the split second that it took Equal-White to reach her feet, gaping, ears back, and spluttering a muffled gekker. An instant later and Equal-White's ears were forward and, with brush coyly arched, she sped after Down-White. They continued, chasing back and forth, leaping

in the air and cavorting in a blur of feints and parries for 30 minutes.

At 10.10pm, as colours faded and shadows grew, the two vixens tired of play and began to forage. They seemed to ignore each other as their paths wove back and forth through fox shoulder-high vegetation. Sometimes they almost touched, and for the most part they were within five to ten metres of each other. Whispering into a pocket dictaphone, I tried to document every detail of their foraging. Their prey were beetles, and they caught several each minute. The vixens appeared to detect these crunchy morsels by ear. Each vixen plodded between the ant hills, then froze in position, often with a front leg raised, before moving quickly forward with mincing pace to plunge her snout into the grass.

So absorbed was I by this theatre that it was with a jolt I became conscious of the thundering bleeps in my headphones. Blackfringe must have been standing within a stone's throw of me. I peered around the blackthorn, and was just in time to glimpse Blackfringe jumping the ditch

into Hamels from the adjacent field. She paused within the hedge, the wind carrying her scent towards the other two foxes. Down-White was quick to notice her presence.

Down-White wheeled around and stood diagonal to the wind, ears flicking, back legs partly crouched and tail curved in an arc to her side. She charged the 40 metres that separated her from Blackfringe and buffeted into her with a sideways barge. With mouths agape and snirking loudly, the two foxes spiralled around each other, flinging their rear quarters into thumping contact as they circled. Blackfringe broke from the stalemate first, and sped into the field with Down-White in close pursuit. A sprint of 20 metres and Down-White stopped. Almost at once, Blackfringe stopped too. Without more ado, Down-White trotted up the ridge to the spot where she had been foraging before Blackfringe's arrival. Blackfringe crouched slightly, her gaze fixed on Down-White. A beetle caught Down-White's attention, and she snapped it up. Thirty metres away Blackfringe began to forage. During the next ten minutes the three vixens wove intricate paths through the southern corner of the field, all of them within metres of each other, and no more than 30 metres from me.

Blackfringe cocked her head, hearing a beetle almost ten metres away; she loped to it, brushing past Down-White without a glance. Whatever tension had provoked their earlier squabble was clearly defused for the time being. Munching the beetle, Blackfringe trotted on past Equal-White, at whom she cast a sideways glance. Under Blackfringe's gaze, Equal-White curled towards the ground, legs limp, ears plastered flat back, and mouth agape as she gave a shrill whine. Oblivious, Blackfringe trotted on, and Equal-White, her body curved awkwardly, half-crawled and half-galloped after her, with brush lashing feverishly and shrieks echoing through the wood. As if swept by a surge of contrition, Equal-White flung herself in front of Blackfringe. Blackfringe, seemingly unmoved by the writhing form at her feet, trotted on. Again Equal-White swerved ahead of Blackfringe, throwing herself on her back and pushing her forelegs up into Blackfringe's chest and chin. This time Blackfringe deigned to notice, and bounced backwards, legs stiff and straight. At once the two vixens began to play. For the next three minutes they threw themselves into an exuberant game of 'tag', chasing back and forth in flamboyant arcs across the field. Even in their play, status was not forgotten: it was Equal-White, and not Blackfringe, who, at the end of every lap, flung herself, rolling and squealing, to the ground beside her companion. Meanwhile, as they whirled around her, Down-White continued to forage. Once, Equal-White raced in a tight circle which brought her right up to my hiding place where she almost somersaulted to a halt in order to snatch a beetle from a stalk of grass just in front of me. She stared in my direction, cocking her head, and seemed to be on the verge of realization when her attention was jerked away from that unpleasant reality by Blackfringe charging playfully towards her.

In total, I saw 14 interactions in the open fields involving Down-White, Equal-White and Blackfringe, and of these the only instance of aggression was Down-White's attack on Blackfringe that I have just described. They were more often playful than antagonistic. Having said that,

attempting to categorize the mood and outcome of fox interactions is not always straightforward. In particular, the observer is bedevilled by the superficial similarity of aggression and play. The problem is that fighting in play has the same behavioural ingredients as fighting in earnest, except for the paradox that nobody gets injured. In the field one sensed that the fickle, jaunty movements and capricious changes in the combatants' roles during a burst of rough and tumble were playful rather than ferocious. The scientific mind, however, senses danger at trying to describe something that is so ill-defined and subjective. My 14 precious observations created an overall impression that relations were amicable among the adult foxes in the group.

At the feeding site in Hans' garden, though, the impression was slightly less harmonious. There, in the presence of tasty scraps, the edges of the foxes' relationships were sharpened and minor squabbles were common (indeed there were 20 serious fights out of 68 interactions observed). If there is one thing in fox society that is 'not done', it is to approach somebody who is eating. In this respect, the old contrast with wolves holds true: wolves sometimes feed from a kill side by side in relative harmony; foxes generally do everything possible to avoid even being seen with food and, if the worst comes to the worst, will at least turn their backs to each other while eating. This contrast is especially marked among youngsters: fox cubs invariably fight with astonishing savagery over food and can inflict serious injury, wolf pups are much more tolerant. Of course, as with every other generalization about foxes, there are exceptions to the rule: dog foxes feed their vixens and adults feed cubs.

There were major changes in the White-legged group during the period that I knew them. Up-White had disappeared early in 1973; Equal-White died of pneumonia in February 1974 (aged 8 years) and, later that year, Sampson was killed by a car near the northern border of their range. When he died, Sampson was 5 years old and the biggest fox I've ever handled, weighing 8.8kg. By then I had seen a great change in the relationship between Blackfringe and Down-White. Until late May, Blackfringe had been conspicuously dominant to Down-White. Perhaps it was more than chance that Blackfringe's

downfall coincided with the weaning of the cubs at the summerhouse in May 1973. Whatever the trigger for these events, the fact is that Blackfringe toppled from her dominant position and Down-White stepped into her shoes. Before this reversal of fortunes the two vixens had often visited the feeding site together. Afterwards, Blackfringe rarely appeared until Down-White had gone, and if she caught a scent on the wind of Down-White's imminent return, Blackfringe sped for safety. However, Down-White's supremacy was short-lived, and by early 1975, of the adults I had first met two years earlier, Blackfringe was the only one which still visited the feeding site, and by then she was accompanied by a new group of adults.

Who were these new foxes? Circumstantial evidence suggested that they were cubs born into the group during previous springs. However, as none was easily recognizable I could not be sure.

Blackfringe was once again dominant, but what was the significance of these changes in status? With so many questions piling up, it was with regret that we had to discontinue the feeding site because the Kruuks moved to Scotland. Nonetheless, it was already clear that the vixens within a group varied in their status. What is more, there were signs that these differences in status were somehow associated with reproduction.

The biggest group of foxes on Boar's Hill was the six-strong band to which Mottle belonged. They tended to spend the day in a patch of scrub called the Preservation. At twilight they often strolled from that secluded wilderness of gorse to relax nearby in the surrounding pastures, so I was able to lie in wait with a fair chance of seeing them. In this way I clocked up a total of 114 separate observations of recognizable adult members of the group. However, when it came to

analysing their social interactions, and after dis-allowing the cases where I could not see the outcome of the encounter, or where I was not fully confident of one participant's identity, I was left with a sample of only 18 completely documented interactions between the six adults.

Was a pecking order operating amongst these five vixens, as it seemed to amongst vixens in the White-legged group? One telling observation of the Mottle group was made soon after dawn in mid-August '73, when I spotted Grey Vixen foraging in High Gate Field. She paused and sat down, staring into the hedge towards a point 50 metres away. Nearly five minutes passed before Paleface Vixen emerged from the hedge, showing by her demeanour that she was well aware of Grey Vixen's presence. Sphinx-like, Grey Vixen sat stock-still, her head held high and ears perked. Paleface crouched as she ran forward and then around Grey Vixen, with her ears held back and tail lashing. Having edged around Grey Vixen, Paleface ran on 40 metres to the south before she slowed to a walking pace and

began foraging for beetles. Grey Vixen remained seated, only turning her head to watch Paleface.

On the previous occasion when I had seen Grey Vixen it had been her turn to play the supplicant to Mottle. Both foxes had been foraging close together for 20 minutes and both were catching beetles in the rye grass of Back Field. At one point, Mottle approached Grey Vixen who immediately flopped onto her side. Mottle pawed at her, and there was a brief skirmish after which the two vixens lay on the ground facing each other. Then, like mirror images, they sat up, still staring into each other's eyes, but now with playful stance. Mottle wheeled and cantered off across the field, but every few paces she stopped to look back at Grey Vixen who remained seated. Mottle turned and ran towards Grey Vixen at full pelt, only swerving to miss her at the last second. This taunting game of 'chicken' was repeated several times, but Grey Vixen sat her ground against the charges. Then, Grey Vixen suddenly sprang to her feet and sped up the field, and soon they were chasing each other back and forth.

Observations like these gradually built up the impression that social relationships between vixens in a group were complex, varied, tolerably amicable, and sometimes incomprehensible. Nonetheless, shimmering through the confusion was one generalization: vixens' social lives were organized within a hierarchy. Whenever two female group members met there was almost always some sign, however discreet, that one was socially dominant to the other. This observation led me on to a further question. If their social relationships were hierarchical, what then of their genetic relationships?

Blood, so they say, is thicker than water, and this certainly seemed to apply to the Boar's Hill foxes. Three adult vixens within one group had patches of white on roughly the same place on their left hind legs. Aside from these three, none of the other foxes I examined on Boar's Hill shared this trait. Similarly, two vixens from the most easterly territory in the study area shared another unusual trait: both Tan-Toes and Brown-Paws had brown feet, rather than the typical black stockings. Also, Mottle and Other-Mottle shared their odd piebald patterning. A more subjective, but to me a compelling example, nonetheless, was the facial similarity of vixens in Toothypeg's group. On the first of five occasions on which I caught this ancient vixen, I wrote in my notebook that she had an unusually blunt snout, giving a thick-set, dog-like breadth to her face. When I caught another fox in almost exactly the same spot, I saw the same blunt muzzle and wide cheeks and, in the torchlight mistook it for Toothypeg. In fact, this turned out to be another elderly fox who came to be known as Four-Ten Vixen, after her channel on the radio-receiver. Over a year later I radio-collared a third vixen in that range, and the same facial features reminded me of the broad-faced Arctic sledge dogs and led to her being named Husky Vixen.

It was evidence of this sort that convinced me that the groups of vixens which shared their home ranges on Boar's Hill were at least partly composed of relatives. Whether or not they were exclusively composed of relatives is impossible to say. Certainly, we have tagged vixen cubs which eventually grew up to become adult members of their parents' group. On the other hand, I once radio-tracked an adult vixen during the time she was failing in an attempt to join an established group, and I have never found evidence of vixens successfully emigrating into an existing group. Therefore, if one was to risk a generalization, vixens which share their home range are probably blood relatives.

What then of the *status quo* between vixens and dog foxes? In mid-April I watched Joyce and Whitetip Vixen as they cavorted back and forth in exuberant play chases, wheeling in wide arcs, colliding and tumbling over each other. Joyce must have swallowed the wrong way in her excitement, as she fell into a dreadful fit of coughing. The game was adjourned, with Whitetip standing by, splay-legged with expectation. More play followed, and another chase along the length of the field, culminating in a mock fight. Whitetip lay down, panting, and Joyce stood beside her with head cocked, watching a badger ambling about near by in search of earthworms.

Losing interest in the badger, Joyce trotted towards a group of trees which harboured a well-used earth. She paused about ten metres away, staring at the earth and Roger emerged from the den. These two foxes were the exceptions to my rule of using descriptive names, being called after Roger Bigland and his wife. The human Roger, terrier man at the Heythrop Hunt, knew as much about foxes as anybody I have met. The vulpine Roger was patriarch of what was arguably the richest territory on Boar's Hill. Now, as the two foxes stood side by side, I was taken aback at how bulky he appeared beside her. Joyce's neck was slender and elegant, Roger's stout and bullish. Roger moved towards the vixen at a trot and, as he passed her, threw a glance in her direction. Immediately, she crouched, shimmying towards him, with tail curled and lashing, ears well back. Roger paused and both Joyce and Whitetip ran to him, sniffing his flank as they sank low to the ground. Roger trotted on, giving no hint of reaction to the vixens.

He had covered no more than ten metres when both vixens catapulted after him. Again he paused, staring into the distance as the two threw themselves into paroxysms of squirming, and he trotted on without any outward acknowledgement of their existence. Half a minute later, Roger disappeared from sight as he entered the scrub, and almost immediately two short, loud screams came from his direction. Joyce and

Whitetip stared after him for nearly four minutes, until a furore of aggressive gekkering broke out from the direction of the screams and continued for well over a minute. What had prompted this voluble encounter? Was Roger involved? It is typical of the frustration of studying foxes that I could not witness the climax of this and many other potentially revealing vignettes.

Although my observations were incomplete, at least I could answer a confident but qualified 'yes' to the question of do foxes live in groups. Clearly, at least some foxes, or foxes in some areas, had a more gregarious social life than had been widely believed. In my study area, these complexities involved hierarchies among vixens and the general domination by the dog fox over his group. These small discoveries, however, served only to swell the flood of unanswered questions. Why do some foxes live in groups and others not? What was the consequence of the hierarchy among the vixens in each group? What are the pros and cons of larger or smaller groups?

While I struggled for observations that would shed light on these and other questions, fate had a trick up her sleeve regarding my own group size. One July evening in 1973 I had slunk into position on the little wooden bridge that spanned the ditch dividing Back Field and Preservation Side Field. From that vantage point, and effectively shrouded in brambles, there was a good view of both fields, and also of High Gate Field to the south. In previous days this had proved an especially good vantage point from which to observe Mottle's group at twilight, and so I had great expectations as dusk settled. Then, where the footpath emerged at the far corner of Back Field, a human figure appeared. To my annoyance, a young woman began to stroll towards the very spot from which I had hoped Mottle and her companions would emerge. The evening's observations were ruined, I was fuming. Continuing her circuit of the field, the woman seemed intent on heading for my hiding place, presumably to cross into the neighbouring field where she would further spread the odour of human scent which was doubtless already stinging Mottle's nostrils. I shrank back into the vegetation in the hope of avoiding detection. When she was 30 paces off she faltered: in the half-light a bearded, green-clad man crouching in the hedgerow seemed to make her uneasy. She

made as if to turn back, thought better of it and to my further irritation continued towards me so that I had to acknowledge her. With only rudimentary civility, I answered her questions about the route of the footpath. To her query about what I was doing, I muttered a curt response about watching owls, having found that unwary mention of foxes tended to bring out people with shotguns. Realizing at once that she had probably disturbed my subjects, and to avoid making matters worse by continuing on her way, the girl, whose name was Jenny, offered to stay put for a while – a generous offer considering she was already shivering in the cool evening. Moments later, Mottle's family tumbled into view and cavorted riotously as we watched. Their antics continued as the last glimmer of light had faded until, in darkness, we stood listening to excited gekkerings and the occasional footfall as a fox padded nearby. With so memorable an introduction there was no looking back.

Our romance was slightly unorthodox since I was generally asleep by day and foxing by night. Those few moments of daylight we shared were spent scouring the fields in the attempt to fulfil my self-imposed requirement to collect 100 fox droppings for diet analysis each month. So it came about that in the middle of the night, standing in a ploughed field called Honeyhill near the border between Blackears' and Scar Nose's territory, I proposed. Had Jenny not accepted, much of this story could never have been written.

So far, apart from discussing the relevance of boundaries, I have concentrated on the social behaviour within groups. But what of relations between neighbouring groups? Just after 1.00am one night in mid-May, I watched Whitetip Vixen foraging in Sands Field. The eastern edge of Sands Field was bordered by a 30-metre thick belt of conifers and scrub which, on the evidence of radio-tracking, constituted the boundary with the neighbouring Mottle group. As I watched her greenish image through the hot-eye, Whitetip meandered down that border and was momentarily lost from my sight. Seconds later a furore of gekkering shattered the night: it came from precisely the spot where I had last seen Whitetip. It was a cold night; infuriatingly my breath steamed the lenses of the hot-eye. For several desperate seconds I could see nothing, while the

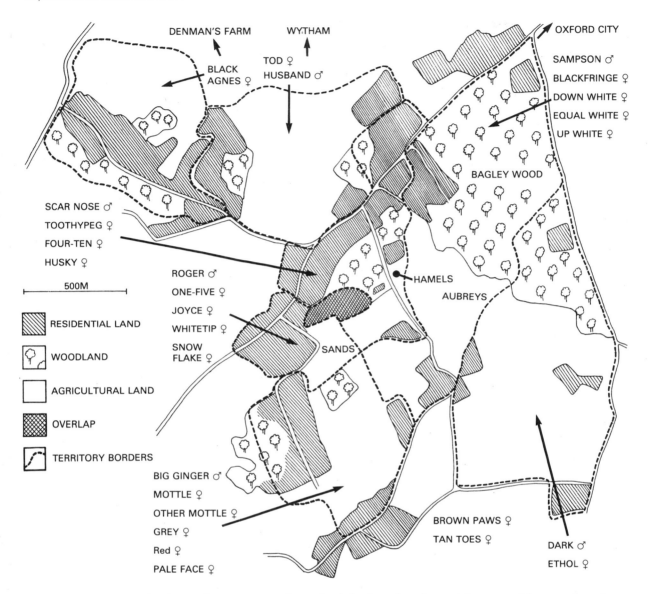

BLACK AGNES ♀
TOD ♀
HUSBAND ♂

DENMAN'S FARM
WY.THAM

OXFORD CITY

SAMPSON ♂
BLACKFRINGE ♀
DOWN WHITE ♀
EQUAL WHITE ♀
UP WHITE ♀

BAGLEY WOOD

SCAR NOSE ♂
TOOTHYPEG ♀
FOUR-TEN ♀
HUSKY ♀

500M

RESIDENTIAL LAND

WOODLAND

AGRICULTURAL LAND

OVERLAP

TERRITORY BORDERS

ROGER ♂
ONE-FIVE ♀
JOYCE ♀
WHITETIP ♀
SNOW FLAKE ♀

HAMELS
AUBREYS

SANDS

BIG GINGER ♂
MOTTLE ♀
OTHER MOTTLE ♀
GREY ♀
Red ♀
PALE FACE ♀

BROWN PAWS ♀
TAN TOES ♀

DARK ♂
ETHOL ♀

fracas raged; then the fogged eye-pieces cleared and I saw Whitetip Vixen and a stranger rolling over and over. For 20 seconds they repeatedly sideways barged each other, their tails arched, bodies contorted and corkscrewed as they parried fang with fang. Whitetip Vixen stumbled and gave ground. Leaping aside, she fled with the stranger in pursuit. The chase was fierce. Again and again the stranger overhauled Whitetip and the two foxes tumbled together, before running on. They raced across South Sands, into the neighbouring field and out of sight, then back in a wide loop almost to their starting point. Again the stranger overhauled Whitetip and for 45 seconds they buffeted and

jolted each other with more sideways barging.

More than one minute after the start of this second fight the intensity of their gekkering and screams had reached an extraordinary pitch. By then I had manœuvred into a small spinney in the middle of the field, and could hardly believe my luck as the rolling ball of teeth and fur careered to within a few metres of me, their bodies more than filling the hot-eye's field of view. At that moment I heard galloping footfalls and cast around in time to catch a glimpse of Roger hurtling across the field from the west. I knew from the radio signal that only minutes earlier he had been several hundred metres away in the gardens on the far side of the group's

ping it at his feet. The urgency seemed to have gone out of his mood as suddenly as it had arrived, and he stood tall, looking around him, craning for a clear view through the grass stalks. He began to sniff the half-eaten rabbit and to lick the flesh around its severed spine. Then he ate, bite by bite, sawing down the remains of the backbone to the pelvis, and crunching into the tops of the heavy leg bones. When he finally stood up, all that remained of the rabbit were the back paws and tail, attached to the pelt which had been neatly peeled off the back. Snipey sprinkled a few drops of urine on the remnants, and moved slowly away to rejoin the main path. He found a patch of shorter grass peppered with the conical depressions which told of another fox's earlier probings. Snipey took great interest in these, before trotting on as the final glimmers of daylight were extinguished.

The thrill of witnessing snippets of fox behaviour such as this one never palls, but neither does the frustration of having no way to link one such snippet to the next. That rabbit might have made all the difference to Snipey: who knows what the consequences of one square meal might have been on his behaviour that night. It might have changed the course of his life. Yet seeing a fox uncover a cache is no proof that the same fox provisioned the larder which furnished his meal. Many a countryman has found a fox's cache, their attention sometimes drawn by a leg or feather protruding indiscreetly from the hidden grave. Few people have seen foxes making their caches, while fewer have seen foxes excavating titbits just as Snipey had done. However, I could find nobody who had reasonable evidence as to whether foxes remembered where they had left these treasure troves. Perhaps they merely looked in likely places (as grey squirrels reputedly do) until they unearth a cache that might, or might not, be of their own making.

The problem was that to answer such questions required more than fleeting glimpses, more than jumbled fragments of the jigsaw puzzle. Time and again I was frustrated in this way. I would see the beginning of an interaction, but not the outcome; I would see a fox trotting past with food in its mouth, and then disappearing from sight leaving me none the wiser as to what happened next; I would see a fox cock its leg on a fencepost, and on the next in line, and on the

next, but then I might wait for ever for another fox to arrive and read the perfumed message.

Slowly an idea began to gel. I began by musing on the thought that if, night after night, I trailed after one fox it would eventually come to tolerate me close at hand. Happily, before too much time was wasted, my flirtation with this scheme was quelled by a sharp dose of reality. On deeper reflection, the sad fact is that most rural foxes are so nervous of humans that winning their confidence is generally a non-starter. Then came the idea of a spy in the opposition's camp: I would hand-rear a fox cub, win its trust, accustom it to as natural a life as possible in my company, and then go with it into the world of its wild cousins. My spy would seek out scent marks for me, unearth caches, and perhaps even befriend wild foxes, while I would be its silent, note-taking shadow.

I began to seek out people who had kept foxes. I soon saw how unsuitable they were as pets, and what an enormous task it would be to rear a cub (*see* Box 12, p. 56). However, I was not looking for a pet: far from it, since what I had in mind was a fox who would behave naturally in all respects save one, namely that it would tolerate me. I consulted widely and, equally widely, was warned off this hare-brained scheme. Despite this, probably due to the chronic lack of sleep that limited my capacity to think anything through, I determined to go ahead. A friend with two captive foxes arranged a mating between them, and in March 1974 the cubs made their entry into the world.

As I negotiated the one-way systems of Guildford's suburbs, every turn of the wheel triggered a renewed, breathless sobbing. In the passenger's seat was my friend Mike Woolridge, and it was from the region of his left armpit that the muffled cries emanated. There, snuggled in the folds of his pullover, was a tiny vixen, *en route* to an academic career at Oxford. Her infant eyelids were still sealed and her mahogany-coloured fur stood out like a fluffy powder-puff. I clearly remember that Mike's pullover was navy blue, as the colour clashed so strikingly with the milky-white vomit in which it was soon drenched.

I had moved into Swinford Farm with a rabble of zoologists. There, at the foot of my bed, I had prepared an ex-army wooden kit box to

12. ARE FOXES GOOD PETS?

Foxes are generally unsuitable as pets. Every spring a large number of supposedly abandoned or orphaned fox cubs are 'rescued' by well-intentioned people. In fact it is almost unheard of for vixens to desert their cubs, and few of the rescued cubs are genuine orphans. Most have been making a short sortie from a nearby earth, or may have been in transit with their mother between earths when they were startled (perhaps by the arrival of the would-be rescuer).

There are few things as enchanting as a fox cub, so the temptation to rear one as a pet is great. Nonetheless, the great majority of 'rescues' come to a sad end for all concerned. Most people have no idea of the time, dedication, facilities, skill and, above all, tolerance required to rear a fox. As sucklings they require milk at four hour intervals day and night, but this is a trifling difficulty compared with their behaviour once weaned: every fox cub I have known has had a passion for both leather and electric cables. The former results in destruction of wallets, handbags, shoes, suede or sheepskin coats, the latter wreaks havoc with household wiring. I have always rather liked the lingering smell of fox urine, but it is noteworthy that one landlady was unable to find another tenant for several months after my fox and I vacated the property.

Every spring I am besieged by desperate people begging me to help them with rescued cubs, foxes that wrecked their homes (the best one was the complete destruction of a new and expensive stereo system within one night). Every zoo and welfare society in the country is probably being offered a dozen such foxes each week of the summer. Many of these foxes end up being destroyed or confined to unsuitable or squalid cages. Almost all of this is avoidable. If you find a cub that seems to be lost, leave it alone in the hope that the vixen will retrieve it. If she has not done so by the next day, or if you are sure she has died, then it is better to provide the orphans with food in the wild (where they may also be fed by their father and other members of the family) than to take them home. If, as a last resort, you do adopt a cub, then feed it on puppy milk substitute for a small dog. Later, once it is weaned to fur and feather (you can pick up road kills or visit game dealers for natural food), find an outhouse bordering on a suitably undisturbed habitat (farm, wood or park) and make it fox-proof. Keep the fox there until September, then leave the shed open while continuing to feed the fox daily. Ideally, it will explore from the safety of the shed, buffered from hardship by the food you provide. Never leave a collar on a fox cub; if you do it will probably escape and strangle. Foxes reared in this way will doubtlessly suffer heavy mortality when they return to the wild, and truly wild foxes suffer heavy mortality too. If you are not in a position to take all this trouble, and you find nobody else willing to do so (farmers are in the very best position to help), it is probably better for all concerned if a vet destroys the cub at the outset.

receive the cub. Two small, wired windows were cut into the lurid tank-green box, and a cosy carpet of shredded newspapers lined its floor. On our first evening together the cub dined rather stickily on Lactol puppy milk, before I filled her hot water bottle and tenderly put her to bed. As I climbed into my own bed she began to warble. Warbling, as I now know, is what fox cubs do when they are lonely. For one so small and frail it is a powerfully expressive sound which, even after a short period of repetition, induces a great muscular tension in the chest of the listener. I lifted the waif into bed with me, achieving instant silence as she squirmed and nudged her way into the crevice between my collar bone and neck. It was an enchanting moment, and no less memorable than the succeeding one in which the warble exploded within an inch of my eardrum. It seemed to be a very long time indeed before the piercing cries gradually subsided to a murmur on the pillow, and the little fox finally fell asleep with her nose thrust as deeply as it would go into my ear. Little did I know that this was to be where she would insist on sleeping for the next five months. After this first night spent in sleepless fear of crushing her or, almost as bad, waking her, however, I had a small inkling of the rigours that lay ahead.

The days and nights which followed were punctuated all too frequently by the mixing and administration of puppy milk. The vixen developed a marked antipathy for her green box, and determined to centre her life upon my bed. The somewhat herbal smell which soon permeated my pillow led to her being named Niff. She continued to warble, but could now be soothed readily, especially by access to an ear in which to snuffle. Eye-dropperful after eye-dropperful of puppy milk was eagerly sucked up until her tummy was tight with milk, and a curtain of sleep would gradually fall as she murmured contentedly. When she awoke, it was time for simulated licking of her rear-end, by gentle massage with a warm sponge. Without this treatment her infant bladder could not release its contents. At 12 days old her hazy blue eyes began to open and soon she was staggering blearily about the bed.

Throughout Niff's infancy I was faced with a great dilemma. If she was to help fill the gaps in my knowledge of fox behaviour, then she must behave like a wild fox, despite her unconventional upbringing. However, for me to learn from her behaviour, I would have to watch from close quarters and she, therefore, would have to be very tame. The two requirements, naturalness and tameness, seemed incompatible, yet if they could not be reconciled I faced the unnerving prospect of wasting months, if not years, of effort. I reasoned that if Niff was the slightest bit perturbed by me, then the whole venture was doomed, and so I resolved that our friendly relationship was the top priority. To that end I determined that we would do everything together, living on top of one another. However, within the realms of practicality, I would do nothing to curb Niff's foxiness: she should behave as she wished, without reward, punishment or training, and as soon as possible I would introduce her to the wilds of the countryside. To aspire to a relationship like this might not seem too exacting to the uninitiated, but anyone tempted to conclude that Niff was a 'pet' would be woefully misled (see Box 12, p. 56). At the time, the whole adventure was a nerve-racking, time-consuming gamble, with far too much to lose. Mercifully, I was wrong in my fear that Niff would grow up de-foxed by my companionship. In fact, ours was to become a thrilling, professional relationship, with her the active partner and I the passive onlooker. My emphasis on our working arrangements is not to discount or devalue the sentimental involvement, but merely to explain that my relationship with Niff was a privilege granted on vulpine terms, and not

imposed on human ones. She was but the first of more than 20 hand-reared foxes that would become my fondest teachers.

Several more days passed with ever increasing quantities of puppy milk being converted into scampering fox. Although Niff's eyes were still cloudy, they were fully open and serrations had begun to perforate her gums. I arranged a supply of doomed male chicks from the local hatchery, and from them I extracted the soft livers which Niff greedily licked from my fingers. By now she had started to greet me with household-waking raucous squeals and convulsions of tail-lashing that shook her off balance. For much of the night she stayed at home, while I trailed the fields in pursuit of her wild brethren. In the morning she nuzzled into my ears as I tried to sleep, and in the afternoon she accompanied me in the car as I drove around to check the sleeping sites of my radio foxes. On these journeys, while she was still small, Niff scrambled into the space between my shoulders and the back of the driver's seat. This site had the dual advantages of affording her access to my ears, and a good view of other motorists who looked askance at the animated stole draped along my shoulders. When she was older, Niff opted instead for sitting on the seat between my legs, her nose level with the top of the steering wheel, from where she cast withering glances at dogs, which she had feared from the outset.

Then came the day when I learned one of the fundamentals of fox etiquette: never, but never, touch somebody else's meat. It had been a long night of radio-tracking and Niff and I were snuggled up in bed. I was intent upon sleep, but she was determined to practise her developing coordination by digging holes in my scalp. Thinking that some food might distract her, I stretched out for one of the day's quota of dead chicks in the adjacent chest of drawers. Still half-asleep, I drowsily proferred my feathery gift and was heartened that the digging stopped, and was replaced by some lusty sniffing. An instant later, Niff had locked her infant jaws around both the chick and my thumb. This, of course, was more her fault than mine, but despite the rectitude of my protest, she construed my reaction as an attempt to poach her prize. The final veils of sleepy confusion were cleared from my head by the ominous throaty screech that presaged what

was to become the first of many experiences of the fox's two-stage bite: the first pressure of molars on your finger, sufficient to prompt mild alarm, is relaxed with a slight movement of the lower jaw relative to the upper, following which, in a moment of ill-founded relief on your part, comes the final, grinding and unrelenting crunch. So it was with finger and chick impaled side by side in a brotherhood of their mixed blood that I learned the rule of rules—the mores of fox society dictate that there is no friendship so deep as to countenance even thinking about somebody else's food.

Even in those early days, when my main aim was to keep Niff alive and well, I learnt a lot from her. By the time she was one month old she not only fiercely defended meat, but was already a compulsive maker of caches. In every corner and crevice of my room she would scratch and scrabble, her mouth bulging with some trophy, ready to spit and gekker if anybody approached. Then she would nudge the remains into position with her nose and, using her nose again, sweep any near-by debris, such as my notebooks, over the hoard to hide it from view. Most households have frustratingly few diggable surfaces, so Niff was forever hiding and re-hiding the same item in different crannies. It was not long before she hit upon the idea of caching prey in the bed-clothes. The discovery of a disembodied chick under the pillow strained my resolution not to interfere with Niff's natural behaviour. Our divergent opinions about the pillow's function reached crisis point, though, when Niff drew the unwarranted conclusion that my approach to the pillow represented an attempt to loot her cache. Both of us endured some uneasily sleepless periods as we eyed each other distrustfully. I was intrigued to see that when Niff thought, often wrongly, that I had guessed the whereabouts of a

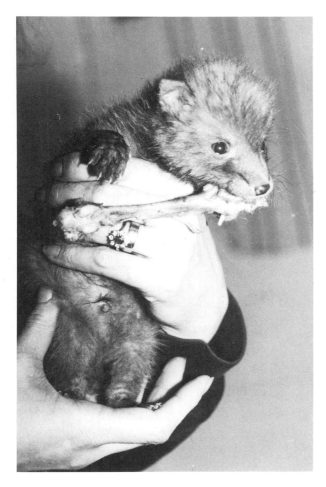

help me to understand the caching behaviour of wild foxes. It would be untrue to pretend there were not moments when our relationship was strained. Indeed, Niff's presence also had an increasing impact on the other zoologists who shared the house, not only because of the unusual, but to me pleasingly 'natural', aroma that permeated the building, but also due to her occasional forays out of my room and into nearby quarters. Her capital with Linda Partridge, who lived upstairs, plummeted to an all-time low when Linda was putting the last hurried touches to her preparations for attending a summer ball. It seems that both Niff and Linda realized at the same instant that her tights were injudiciously hung within the fox's reach, but it was Niff who moved the faster. There was a shriek of despair, a scamper of clawed paws on the uncarpeted stairs, and a thudding of ill-aimed missiles. The house was so constructed that if the appropriate combination of doors were open a circular course could be run from room to room. It was around this route that I caught slapstick glimpses of the vixen, tangling and stumbling over the trailing tights, hotly pursued by an enraged Linda in her ball gown.

I confess, too, that my own patience was tried during those months of Niff's frivolous adolescence. The root of the problem often lay in our different sleeping habits: I would spend the night away, radio-tracking, and on my return would be cold and tired. On arrival I would find yet more holes chewed in the upholstery, more paper stripped from the walls, another book chewed, an old treasure devastated. Nonetheless, Niff's ecstatic greeting would have been ample recompense had it not been for her unrelenting demand for play.

For weeks on end I was averaging four hours of sleep each day, and it was those four hours that Niff was determined to erode. The crunch came with her invention of the 'hair game'. That night had started well: I'd clambered into bed and found Niff asleep there. At first she snuggled on the pillow, as always her tongue probing addictively in my ear, her brush cloaked over the pillow. Nothing could have been more peaceful, and I sank into a deep and welcoming sleep. Then Niff awoke and, to attract my attention, she raked her claws painfully through my hair. I burrowed deeper in the blankets, but the idea of

cache, she would quietly unearth it and re-bury the contents elsewhere. Indeed, even when she was adult, I could provoke her to transplant a cache simply by staring at her as she put the finishing touches to its concealment.

Wild foxes are just as self-conscious about their caches. For example, I once watched a vixen as she cached some food in a pasture on Boar's Hill. After she had disappeared from view another fox strolled past the spot where the cache was hidden. Half an hour later the original vixen returned and clearly caught the scent of the passer-by. She followed the line of the second fox then returned to excavate her hoard, and move its contents to a new cache 30 metres away. Presumably, she had decided that the risk of looting was too great at the original site.

The parallels between wild foxes and Niff's protective enthusiasm for her bedroom caches boded well for my hope that one day she would

digging in my hair had gripped her. In easy leaps she bounced from the floor, dug three or four furrows in my scalp, bounced onto the dresser, back to the floor, and back again to my head. Again and again Niff leapt and dug and leapt and dug, in the highest of high spirits. Make no mistake, even a playful fox draws blood in these games. Deeper and deeper I tried to retreat, and as my temper fought through fatigue I flailed aimlessly at her. Niff dodged, sped along the mantelshelf cannoning my books onto the floor along with a cup of cold coffee. Then onto the sideboard, a dig at my hair, onto the floor, a dig at my hair. Nothing would stop her. Suddenly, I snapped. I was up in bed, pinning Niff with my left hand, my right fist clenched. In the same instant I came fully awake to see the blow I was unleashing onto my cherished fox. I locked every muscle in my body stopping my fist as it touched her. One of my gritted teeth fractured and snapped off. Perhaps it illustrates the difference between fox and dog, of wild and tame, of 4,000 years of domestic breeding, if I tell you that Niff immediately resumed her game. But, reflecting on her sensitivity to my moods in later years, perhaps it merely showed that adolescent foxes, like people, cannot resist the temptation to provoke.

Niff's early walks were helter-skelter affairs. She was eight weeks old when I first fitted her with a tiny dog's collar, attached to a three-metre length of orange baling twine. She was still puppy-plump and, although the backs of her ears and her lower legs were turning a sleek black, her body was haloed in a fuzz of woolly baby fur. This was just the age at which I had seen wild cubs exploring at their mother's side in the vicinity of their earth.

For our first walk I had chosen Hamels on Boar's Hill which became the centre of Niff's activities for the next six years. As an adult she would travel well-trodden fox trails, with pure professionalism ringing in every mincing footfall, in each detour to cut the wind, and in every breathless instant spent in straining anxiously at a jay's alarm call. What a contrast with that first day: she dashed back and forth between the towering stalks of corn, frightening herself, and rushing back to shelter between my boots. Far from the grace of her adulthood, her movements had the frantic air of an upturned bluebottle,

buzzing haphazardly about on the floor. Our excursion took us no more than 50 metres from the car, in which she was now completely at home. As we walked, I repeatedly whistled a curlew's call, and this whistle was to be our long-distance call-sign for the rest of her life.

Twice every day Niff walked me through the fields and woodland of her home range. Those walks gradually increased in length and came to encompass an area of ten hectares—roughly the size of the smallest territories of wild foxes in that habitat. Aside from occasional restrictions imposed by my unwillingness to be led through the densest bramble bush, Niff had complete control over our route and pace. She did not, however, choose the time and sometimes not the duration (often about two hours) of her excursions, and so this remained a restriction on her behaviour. My idea was that her frequent walks would allow Niff to become as familiar with her home range as a wild fox would be. In this way her behaviour, and my field experiments, could be set in a natural context. Her behaviour seemed so like that which I had seen in the wild that the risk that

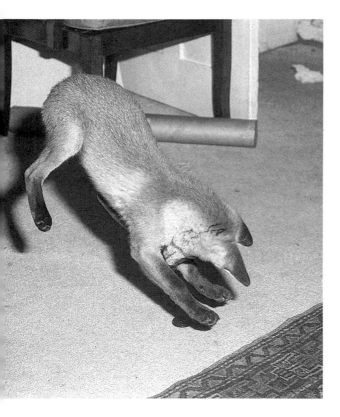

her captive upbringing might result in an unnatural personality seemed to recede.

For my part, I was rapturously immersed under Niff's tutelage. She taught me to pause as we rounded a bend or topped a rise, to see before being seen; to cross slack ground below the icy wind; to circle downwind of anything unfamiliar. Soon I knew that of the infinite number of ways one might cross a field, there were only one or two that were acceptable: I learned that freshly dug molehills have to be pounced and pawed at, that embers of a fire have a mysterious appeal, and that it is unthinkable to pass a tree stump or other good vantage point without jumping up to scan ahead. My expertise as a tracker blossomed as Niff showed me each trick of her trade. And my trip through the looking glass was all the more exciting as her wonderland was so secret.

Something very odd had happened when Niff was ten weeks old: her general friendliness to everybody had suddenly fallen away, and thereafter she trusted only people with whom she had been brought up. Now, if a stranger came to visit us at Swinford Farm, Niff became hysterical with

fear—a wild fox trapped in a room with a human. She would hurtle around the room and scrabble up the chimney, where she hid until the dumbfounded visitor had gone. In the same way, as we travelled the hedgerows and woodland, Niff behaved as any wild creature. At the sight of a distant human she wheeled about, dropped into the dead ground of a ditch and made her escape. Worse still, the sound of a dog's bark would cut through anything she was doing: Niff's ears would flick, she would hold her nose high and little shudders would ripple through her skin. Our walks would often be apprehensive. I think much of a fox's life is spent on a knife-edge, deluged by the acuteness of its senses. In the fox, evolution has fashioned a creature for which every input is tuned to maximum sensitivity: for the fox there is the jolting image of a rabbit's blinking eyelid, the clamorous squeak of a mouse 20 metres off, the dreadful reek of a dog's day-old pawprint. The tension can be put aside, though, and we enjoyed many moments of calm and fun too. What could be more tranquil than lying in a pool of woodland sunshine, a fox curled up and

dozing on your chest? What could be more exhilarating than a game of tag, with a fox wheeling and dodging around the saplings?

Niff became accustomed to our country walks so quickly that, on the 18th May 1974, when she was only ten weeks old, I began a series of trials that would continue for six months. The idea was to test her ability to relocate the hoards of food that she hid so diligently. So, on the first day of each trial, and while Niff was confined to barracks, I criss-crossed her home range, my pockets bulging with dead mice—one of her favourite delicacies. Here and there, at irregular intervals, and on paths which I knew Niff favoured, I dropped a mouse. It lay there, uncovered and awaiting her detection until that evening when I returned to the area accompanied by Niff. Of course, I could not be certain that she would choose to travel the paths on which the mice were waiting, but there was a good chance that she would: foxes almost always circle ploughed fields along paths that hug the perimeter, seldom straying into the field

itself, unless lured in by an attractive smell. Therefore it was on these field-edge paths that I positioned most of the mice.

On the very first day I had no idea how Niff would respond but, in the event, everything went like clockwork. Hurrying along the path that ran between the edge of Aubrey's Field and Bagley Wood, Niff came across the first mouse and swiftly gulped it down. By the time we had reached the far side of the field, and she had eaten several more mice, there was a noticeable bulge in her flanks and less urgency in her stride. Then we came upon the next mouse. Niff picked it up and hurriedly trotted back the way we had come, before swinging off the path into the undergrowth. She pushed through the long grass for about four metres and then, still clasping the mouse in her mouth, began to dig. Soon she had excavated a shallow grave, just deep enough to contain the prize which she gently dropped into the hole, and then poked down with firm nudges of her nose. Taking a pace back, Niff made long strokes with her nose to sweep the soil back over the cache. When no sign of the mouse remained, she pushed her muzzle amongst the displaced grass stalks, weaving them back over the bared earth. The end result was perfect: not a sign remained to disclose the larder's whereabouts.

As we continued our walk, more mice were carefully hidden. My notes were in disarray— Niff had selected such unmemorable sites, and disguised the caches so thoroughly, that I feared I would never be able to find the spots again. However, whether I could find them again was immaterial. The question was could she do so? The following evening, Niff and I returned to the same area. In the meantime, she had not fed and was certainly hungry. I struggled to keep up as she led me swiftly around Aubrey's Field. Before I had recognized the spot, she was busily eating the contents of her first cache. On down the field to the next, and the next, until all the mice had been found and eaten. I need not have worried about keeping notes of the caches' locations: Niff knew precisely where they were.

After six months we had played similar games of hide and seek with 50 mice by night and by day. Of these caches, Niff had subsequently rediscovered and eaten 48. Reduced to a cold statistic, this achievement is impressive enough, but watching the slight frame of the vixen as she wove her course between a hundred thousand identical clods of soil in a 15-hectare ploughed field, one could only be awed by her memory as she navigated, unwaveringly, to an unmarked grave dug more than two weeks earlier.

The next question was whether Niff found the caches by memorizing the exact location, or by sniffing around in roughly the right area. To answer this I ran two sets of trials. In the first experiment, I hid a second mouse within three metres of each of her caches. Niff found almost 90 per cent of her own caches and only 22 per cent of mine. In the second, I actually dug up her caches and reburied them within one metre of their original hiding place. In this experiment she found only a quarter of the transplanted caches. Both results indicated that she was homing in very precisely on the hidden hoard. What was more, during another series of experiments I noticed that she would almost never return to a cache site that she had emptied successfully (although she often scent-marked them after emptying them). However, as many as eight

days later she might try again and again to find a cache that had been 'mislaid' (often due to my interference). It was as if these caches had not been ticked off her list, and she was reluctant to concede that she had lost them.

There were times when Niff grew careless with her larders. Once, after a long period when the misfortunes of the local poultrymen had been our gain, Niff fed well every day and became noticeably sloppy with her caches. One morning she made three caches of mice in such a slovenly way that their tails protruded through the soil. Worse still, she left some other mice uncached. That day I did not feed her, so when we took another walk in the evening Niff led me hungrily to the rather carelessly made caches. Each one had been poached by magpies. Niff ran to the spot where she had discarded other mice on the path and, of course, the magpies had taken them too. I did not feed Niff until later the following day, by which time her appetite was greatly sharpened. Later that evening, before her walk, I again scattered dead mice on her paths. Her lackadaisical behaviour was transformed: every mouse was meticulously hidden.

Despite the success of these experiments, an ominous cloud gathered over our daily walks, in the form of Cindy. Cindy was a large mongrel dog whose perambulations occasionally led her into some of the fields that Niff travelled. At first she was merely an irritation—a distant bark would cause Niff to change route and thereby wreck another experiment. But then came the evening when she was nosing about in a hedgerow at the moment when Cindy and her master appeared through a gate not 100 metres away. The dog barked and dashed for Niff, but mercifully both were on leads. The master shouted at the dog and waved his stick: Niff erupted in panic. In her frenzy, she ran this way and that, flinging herself to the furthest extent of the leash and wrapping it around my legs. Then, as fast as my mud-clogged boots would permit, she hauled me up the field. On into Bagley Wood we rushed, and on and on. Behind us there was no sign of Cindy, she and her master having turned back as soon as he had seen us, oblivious of our panic-stricken flight.

Perhaps the sight of the fleeing fox lodged in the dog's brain because the vendetta was on. Cindy would course the fields, alone or far ahead

Choosing a secluded spot in which to cache the prey.

of the faint sounds of her master's whistle. We changed our routes, but she sniffed us out: we altered our routine, but to no avail. Niff's nerves got so frayed that she pulled and choked on the lead, spooked at the slightest sound, whether or not Cindy was on the rampage. Then, one day, Jenny was walking Niff in a secluded spot when the sound of distant baying told that Cindy had picked up Niff's scent. By now Jenny always carried a heavy stick, purely to ward off Cindy's attentions. The baying drew rapidly closer. Abandoning the walk and experiment, Jenny cut back towards the road where the car was parked. Before she could get there, Cindy was in view and racing towards them. Niff was frantic. Jenny clasped her under one arm and wielded the stick with the other, as the barking dog danced and snapped around her. A pile of brush provided some protection as Jenny ran around it trying to keep it between her and the dog. At last Jenny managed to dash into the near-by lane; Niff perched on her shoulder, half-throttled by her leash and clawing at Jenny's neck. Onto this scene came a startled motorist, whose passage was blocked by the circus. Drawing to a halt, the occupants were even more startled when Jenny

and Niff circled the car, warding off Cindy until her owner arrived.

There was always the nagging thought that to clinch the caching experiments I needed to test Niff's ability to find caches made by other foxes, and vice versa. With this in mind, I set about rearing more cubs. The first newcomers were two hand-reared dog foxes of Niff's age. One was called Oxo, the other Husband, in anticipation of the role he was to play in Niff's life. The arrival of these foxes required accommodation for them. I had been working hard to rebuild, in fox-proof form, a large wooden shed in Dixieland Wood, the heart of Niff's home range on Boar's Hill. The idea was that this would become home to Niff and her future mate, thereby defusing some of the domestic tensions arising from her more destructive extravagances in the house. Niff's Dixieland retreat was not, however, finished by the time Oxo and Husband arrived.

By now, Jenny and I had begun our married life in a greenkeeper's cottage on the edge of Frilford Heath Golf Club. We had modified a brick outbuilding, adding a strong double door system, in which Niff could be contained on occasions when her presence in the house was

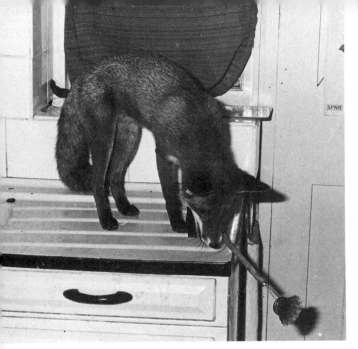
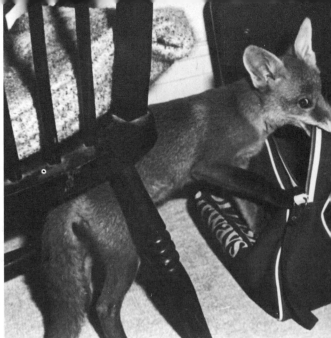

inconvenient. So we decided that one visiting fox could be housed in this outbuilding and the other could live in the kitchen, where no further damage could be done, since Niff had already chewed everything that was chewable. Niff, herself, could spend the few days before her marriage in our bedroom. Plans were laid, accommodation organized, and the newcomers familiarized with the routine of leash walks in the study area, and finally the experiment was begun. I had already tested both dog foxes to establish that they were proficient at finding their own caches. The idea was to see whether they could find the caches that Niff made.

On the first evening, Niff made eight caches along the length of a 200-metre stretch of path running through deciduous woodland. With the first phase of this game of vulpine hide-and-seek under way I returned Niff to Jenny, and set out for a night of radio-tracking. It was shortly after sunrise that I returned, chilled and weary, to find that the night had not passed smoothly. As I entered the kitchen I found Jenny shivering in a sleeping bag on the stone floor, amidst a scene of disarray. It seemed that problems had begun soon after she had gone to bed. Oxo, confined to the outhouse, had discovered that by rasping at the taut mesh of the door with his claws he could generate an extremely loud and resonant twanging noise. Since our cottage was semi-detached, at least half of the pleasures of this incessant

drumming were conveyed to our neighbours' bedroom. They were, in fact, extremely tolerant people, but an hour or so of Oxo's percussion playing was sufficient to bring them to the bedroom window in order to yell a few suggestions to the fox below. Perhaps it was the noise of Oxo's antics, or perhaps the scent of his future bride out of reach upstairs, but something unnerved Niff's husband-to-be residing in the kitchen, and he began to shriek. The only thing that would comfort him was play: he found solace in pouncing games with a pink plastic mouse tied on a long cord which Jenny had to wriggle around the kitchen furniture. Cloaked in her sleeping bag, Jenny had spent the night tiptoeing between the outhouse and the kitchen, trying to cajole each fox into silence. Meanwhile, Niff slept contentedly, snuggled in Jenny's vacated bed. There was no room for debate; within five minutes of my arrival at dawn I had my marching orders and was *en route* back to Boar's Hill with instructions that I would not be allowed back into the house until Niff's Dixieland shed was complete.

So it was, that later that day, and with little ceremony, Niff was introduced to her mate, and they moved into the cosy straw-filled shed, hidden deep in the seclusion of the undisturbed woodland. It was getting towards the end of a fairly bleak 24 hours when I remembered the unfinished experiment.

Collecting Niff's husband from their honeymoon home, I set out to walk through the woodland where Niff had made her caches. We passed within a metre of several. For a moment it seemed that Husband was on the verge of discovering one as, pausing, he sniffed the ground near by and raised his muzzle to scent the air. However, he finished the walk without unearthing a single one. Next, Oxo made the same trip and he too found nothing. There is no doubt that both of them were hungry, so I have no reason to suspect that they were not trying, or turned a blind or disinterested eye to the caches. Later, Niff and I walked through the wood. She went straight to the first cache and ate the mouse. She was listless and none too interested in the walk but she clearly remembered where the next cache was. When I walked close to it, she ran over and nipped me, doubtless thinking I was about to pilfer the hoard. She dug up the mouse and ate it before turning around and returning to her shed. Shortly after midnight we returned and repeated the walk. Niff had recovered her appetite and she dug up and ate a further four mice. She saved the final two until the following afternoon. The outcome of this first rather frantic and sleepless experiment was that the only fox to benefit from the caches was the individual who had made them.

Over the years, and with many different foxes, I have repeated this experiment regularly, if often inadvertently. For example, there was the time when a young leash-walking vixen hid an apple core in a clump of grass. On each of six successive days she returned to the clump, pulled out the core and chewed it, and then hid it there again. Each day up to four of her sisters passed the same spot, jumping nimbly over the tussock and thereby failing to discover the hidden prize.

These results should not be misinterpreted: I do not for one moment believe that foxes cannot discover each other's caches. With their keen senses of smell they clearly can and sometimes do. In fact, generations of fox trappers have exploited the fox's habit of investigating scraps of loose soil—a habit which may have its origins in checking on likely cache sites. Indeed, in the mountains of Italy I have followed fox tracks in the snow, which in turn followed wolf tracks. The tracks showed that the fox had been on its trail in order to loot the wolf's cache. I have also seen plenty of cases where one fox raids another's cache. Also, by burying bio-marked baits, and subsequently recovering the markers in foxes shot in the area, biologist Gwyn Lloyd has proved that 85 per cent of foxes in an area can find man-made caches. Nonetheless, it seems from my experiments that it is very much easier for a red fox to find its own caches than it is for another fox to find them. To this extent they represent a private insurance policy against an unpredictable future.

Having ascertained that foxes do remember where they hide food, another question invited attention. Are different types of food equally likely to be cached? As it happened, field voles were rare on Boar's Hill, whereas bank voles and the racily built wood mice were comparatively numerous. However, their undigested remains occurred in quite different proportions in the fox droppings I examined: field voles were disproportionately common in the foxes' diet. Were field voles particularly easy to catch, or did the foxes prefer them?

With these questions in mind, I altered the field trials. Each trial involved four dead prey—two individuals from each of the two species under test that day. These four corpses were arranged on the ground in a square, about 30cm apart and positioned such that the two specimens of each species were arranged at diagonal corners. All the rodent species looked equally appetizing to me, but Niff had a clear-cut favourite: she trotted up to a bank vole, sniffed it and then took a pace forward. At this point the two specimens nearest to her were field voles, and she sniffed and picked up both of them. Walking past the second bank vole she gave it a cursory sniff but left it. She took the field voles to some nearby grass and put one down while she buried the other. That first cache complete, she picked up the remaining field vole and buried it a couple of metres away. Niff then returned to both the bank voles, sniffed them, and trotted away leaving them uneaten. In the following weeks the procedure was repeated again and again, and irrespective of which species she sniffed first, the results were remarkably consistent. Whenever a field vole was involved in the choice, it was invariably chosen first. Bank voles and wood mice were definitely less favoured (of the two, wood mice seemed to be bottom of the menu).

It was soon clear that not only did Niff prefer to eat field voles, she also preferred to cache them. With time, the fields were dotted with caches, the majority containing field voles, and a minority housing the two other species. This promoted the question of whether the fox remembered which species she had left in each cache. In the following trials I noted the numbers of caches containing each species, and the numbers of each of which she consumed which Niff revisited. The results showed that she returned to and exhumed a greater proportion of caches containing field voles than of those containing other species. In this way Niff demonstrated that she recalled not only where she had made each cache, but also the type of food hoarded therein.

Experiments like these continued over more than 18 months throughout which Niff's liking for field voles was undiminished. However, her tendency to cache less-preferred prey varied. For example, ten days before the birth of her first litter she methodically began to cache food of types that she would previously have discarded. Later, when a group of other adults had grown up around her, and feeding time was characterized by repeated squabbles, she persisted in taking the trouble to hide everything, even less-preferred prey. Both these periods were ones when a full larder could be at a premium. If caching is an insurance policy, it would seem to be a flexible one in which investment can be varied according to risk.

5 | SAMSON'S FOXES

SOME 2,000 YEARS ago, Samson was having marital problems with his Philistine wife and, as reported in the *Book of Judges*, he swiftly caught up 300 foxes, tied firebrands to their tails, and sent them running amok to torch the corn and vineyards of his in-laws' tribe. Putting aside any doubts as to the morals of a chap who ties firebrands to foxes' tails, anybody who can catch 300 foxes in the twinkling of a Nazarite eye was either one heck of a trapper, or Judaean foxes were more easily outsmarted than any I had met. Hoping that the latter was the case, and with the support of a Winston Churchill Fellowship, I flew to Israel in October 1975. If these red foxes were indeed easier to observe than their British counterparts (they are the same species), they would not only allow me to watch foxes in a very different habitat, but also might help me to answer the question which was proving most intractable on Boar's Hill: how do members of neighbouring groups behave towards each other?

One reason for selecting a study site in Israel was that foxes there are protected. I hoped that their protected status would make these foxes easy to watch. Furthermore, the Israeli Nature Reserves Authority had established feeding sites where carnivores are accustomed to eating under the rapt gaze of busloads of schoolchildren. It was to one such site that I was heading.

My base was to be Ein Gedi, on the coastal plain of the Dead Sea. The plain was only a few hundred metres wide, running between the walls of the Syrian–African rift valley and, thereafter, the hills of the Judaean desert. In this arid red landscape less than ten centimetres of rain fell annually. Only sparse vegetation survived amongst the boulders of dolomite and other sediments. Yet two springs sustained incongru-

ous flushes of vegetation. Water from Nachal 'Arugot sustained the date palms and the vineyards which, according to *Song of Songs* (1,14), have provided the little foxes of Ein Gedi with fruity delicacies since prehistoric times. A second wadi, cut between dramatic cliffs, was fed by the other spring, Nachal Dawid, and nurtured a lush flora that was a blinding, almost vulgar, green in this dusty landscape. These plants, known as the Sudanese Vegetation Enclave, were characteristic of an ancient flora somehow trapped for posterity in the rift valley. The feeding site stood in a deserted spot on the rock-strewn plain, some 600 metres from the shore of the Dead Sea. It was under the control of Avi Shaka, the local nature warden, and it was Avi who took me under his wing.

On the night after my arrival at Ein Gedi we drove to the feeding site where the abattoir truck had just paid its weekly visit depositing a dead donkey together with several dozen turkeys and a mass of chickens' legs. The jeep bucked up a sandy ridge and we drew to a halt on a promontory overlooking the unsavoury hillock of corpses 50 metres away. The blazing sun had charged the offal with a foetid aroma that now hung limp in the night air. I slunk from the car, fingers held over the latch and leaving the door ajar to forestall tell-tale metallic clicks. To my horror, Avi bounded out, slammed the door shut and flashed a powerful torch about. Schooled in the belief that the noise of a leaf crumpling underfoot was sufficient to spook every fox in the vicinity, I was sure that Avi's behaviour had sabotaged our chances.

Not a little aggrieved, I began to whisper a diplomatic, but unmistakably stern, caution when he gleefully announced that we had visitors, and flashed his torch full onto a fox trotting

past us, no more than 30 metres away. The fox paused, cast a disinterested glance in our direction, and continued unabashed to the mass of offal. Although a red fox by name, this was a sandy fox by colour. It was small, fine featured and slightly built. Its buff fur was only lightly tinged with red and its ears were huge, the legs were evening-gloved in black, and the brush was tipped white. As Avi's torch flashed back and forth around the site, other foxes appeared, trotting busily about, barely taking time to eat, but caching food as fast as they could.

Over the ensuing evenings I came to recognize ten different foxes, and it was soon clear that they were divided into two social groups, one approaching from the north of the feeding site towards Ein Gedi, the other from the south in the general direction of Masada. I named the groups after these two settlements, and began to unravel their relationship. To the south there were three vixens, distinguished by the size of the white tags that tipped their inordinately fluffy brushes. Small Tag, Big Tag and Enormous Tag shared their range with Sidestripe Dog. To the north

My confidence in such generalizations was soon battered, however, by such sociological conundrums as the extraordinary dance between Star Dog—from the Ein Gedi group—and Enormous Tag Vixen—from the Masada group.

This episode began not long after midnight on the eve of the New Year of 1976, when I was perched on my favourite sand-dune, overlooking the feeding site. It was a warm, peaceful night, and the lights of Jordan twinkled across the Dead Sea. A leopard grunted, a nervous ibex sent a cascade of stones rattling down the cliff, and Enormous Tag lay curled up, apparently asleep, just south of a track which ran beside the feeding site and partitioned the two ranges. In the greenish light of my infra-red binoculars, she blended so perfectly with the rocks that I could only be sure that she was there when she opened one emerald-reflecting eye to peer through the whiskers of her brush, draped like a stole across her snout. I spotted Star Dog as he flitted between the shrubs in a small gully within Ein Gedi territory. He paused to excavate a cache and to play a tossing, head-shaking game with the foetid contents before discarding them.

Moving on, Star Dog barely paused as he trotted brazenly across the track which delineated the border between the two groups. A few paces further into Masada territory and he came to an abrupt halt, lifting his muzzle high as he felt the air for a whiff of Enormous Tag's scent. Slowly, at a radius of about ten metres, he circled her. A reflecting glimmer in the hot-eye's viewfinder betrayed Enormous Tag's wakefulness. Star Dog veered towards Enormous Tag and she, unable to feign sleep any longer, squirmed onto her side in submission. Her lashing tail thumped the ground, sending up a dust cloud as she writhed at Star Dog's feet. She seemed paralysed by him, her legs flailed aimlessly and, unable to get up and run, she wriggled away from him along the ground.

Star Dog leant over Enormous Tag, scrutinizing her with audibly gusty sniffs. At last the frantic vixen sprang to her feet as if to make her escape, but before she could move, Star Dog reared on his hind legs and began to pirouette. Enormous Tag cowered while Star Dog reared high, balancing with extravagant flicks of his tail, his front legs folded and held close to his chest. With his big ears and pert looks, he lacked only a

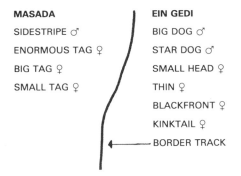

MASADA	EIN GEDI
SIDESTRIPE ♂	BIG DOG ♂
ENORMOUS TAG ♀	STAR DOG ♂
BIG TAG ♀	SMALL HEAD ♀
SMALL TAG ♀	THIN ♀
	BLACKFRONT ♀
	KINKTAIL ♀
	BORDER TRACK

Members of the two groups.

there were four vixens: Thin, Small Head, Kinktail and Blackfront, along with Big Dog. These five foxes in the Ein Gedi group were unorthodox in sharing their range with a second male, known as Star Dog. His name derived from the pure white star emblazoned on his blackish chest, and he was affiliated with the northern group, but apparently only as a 'hanger-on'. Except for this odd phenomenon of two males in the Ein Gedi group, the social system of these foxes seemed straightforward: there were friendly relationships within groups, and hostile ones between them.

frilled collar to be transformed into a circus Chihuahua, rather than the focus of a natural drama in the wilds of Judaea. Enormous Tag was again on her side, shrieking and writhing with submission, every element of her face pulled taut. As Star Dog waltzed before her, Enormous Tag tried more than once to make a dash for it; each time he tip-toed around to block her escape. From her prone position she stabbed up at his chest with her forepaws and knocked him off balance, but in a second he was up again dancing around her. Enormous Tag scrambled up, still wailing, and for a brief moment the foxes boxed, pressing forwards against each other's shoulders. But the force of Star Dog's onslaught knocked Enormous Tag off her feet, and he followed up his advantage with such a succession of flank-slamming barges that the two foxes were engulfed in the dust thrown up by their brawl.

As the dust settled around them, Star Dog was again on his hind legs, pirouetting around the vixen. Again, Enormous Tag reared to her feet and, for a minute more, she lunged with her forepaws at the dog-fox's chest. His back curved proudly upright, taut as an archer's bow, while she hunched with uncertainty. Her squeals were so piercing that it seemed her vocal chords must snap. At last, Enormous Tag broke free and fled shrieking to the south. Star Dog pursued her, again bowled her over, and continued to jig around her, until she once more reared up pawing and stabbing at him. Another minute and a half of bedlam tore the desert calm with the foxes locked in their violent jig, before Enormous Tag broke free and bounded down the bed of a dried wadi, noisily scattering stones as she went. Star Dog dropped to all fours, shook himself and trotted back in the direction from

which he had come, without a glance over his shoulder.

I really do not know what lay beneath this remarkable interaction, but if I were to hazard a guess it would be that the two foxes were disabled by the conflicting forces of territoriality and sex-linked status. The episode took place on the border and the two foxes belonged to neighbouring groups. Much of Star Dog's behaviour was reminiscent of a high intensity attack, or rather half of such an attack since he did not follow it through and Enormous Tag did not retaliate. Perhaps the fact that her adversary was a male prevented Enormous Tag from defending herself, while the fact that he was attacking a female may have inhibited Star Dog. If so, then the result of these social inhibitions was to redirect Star Dog's fierce attack into a bout of shadow boxing as long as Enormous Tag remained in prone submission. Clutching at this straw of an interpretation it became especially interesting to know what variations on intergroup aggression occurred within and/or between the sexes.

By night, foxes were not the only visitors to the feeding site. One night not long before dawn I was sitting on the ground, drowsily propped up against the front wheel of the jeep. More than an hour had passed since I had seen a fox and my eyelids were heavy. Below me, a stone clacked and I forced just sufficient sleep from my arms to raise the infra-red binoculars to my eyes. A cumbersome striped creature was lumbering towards me, a heavy mane of bristles running from its massive shoulders down to its incongruously slim backside. At only ten metres' range I was meeting my first striped hyaena. With shambling steps and a lolling head, the hyaena walked straight towards me. Its broad silver head soon filled my field of view.

My first impression of this disarmingly cuddly creature was tainted by a pang of unease when it sniffed loudly and sneezed, sending a warm gust of wet wind into my face. Dropping the binoculars from my eyes I saw in the moonlight that it was no more than five paces from me. It was not my imagination—I really could hear it breathing. My abiding memory is the view of the hyaena's front paws: they were placed side by side with surprising neatness, and I could clearly see that between each of the claws there protruded a tousle of fur. With a final sniff the hyaena dismissed me and turned back to the feeding site. Striped hyaenas were to become

frequent actors in the nightly theatre at the feeding site, where they had magnetic appeal for foxes. To judge by my observations at Ein Gedi, foxes would seem to be prey to an irresistible and rather churlish desire to make these amiable goofs the butts of their quick wit.

A typical observation began on the evening when a hyaena ambled over the ridge from Nachal 'Arugot with Big Tag Vixen of the Masada foxes trotting at its heels. The fox followed the hyaena's every move and seldom were they separated by more than three metres. Arriving at the feeding site, the fox circled the hyaena as it brought its massive jaws to bear on a dead calf. Up until then, and despite the occasional violent tug at its flesh, the foxes had been unable to break through the calf's hide. Now the hyaena ripped into the flesh and as it dropped a scrap Big Tag rushed forward and snatched it from beneath the hyaena's jaws. Immediately, the vixen cantered off to the south to cache her prize. While Big Tag was away, Small Head Vixen, her neighbour from the Ein Gedi group arrived, and positioned herself beside the hyaena. The hyaena sauntered off to prescribe (as they often did) a circle of some 30 metres radius around the carcass. Small Head Vixen rushed in to the calf and, snatching up all the loose slices of meat which her host had carved, she, too, ran off to cache them in a near-by gully. The hyaena arrived back from its circular tour just as Small Head returned to the calf. The hyaena appeared to grow resentful of the vixen's proximity swinging its head towards her, and shrugging its powerful shoulders. At each nod of the hyaena's head, Small Head jumped back, but in a trice she was at its side again. The hyaena moved a couple of paces towards her and, glowering, its head sank closer and closer to the ground until its nose almost touched its toes. For almost half a minute the hyaena scrutinized its paws, and during these moments the vixen edged closer. The spell snapped when Small Head was within a metre of the hyaena: suddenly disengaging its attention from its toes it charged her. The fox danced in front of the hyaena for over 20 metres. The hyaena stopped. Small Head circled it and trotted back to the calf and began to pull loosened flesh from the carcass. Once more the hyaena took up the appearance of studied contemplation of its forepaws, and once again Small Head's curiosity lured her closer and closer until the hyaena charged her.

This time, however, Small Head stood her

ground, legs squarely asplay and a strip of calf skin hanging from her lips. The hyaena was within a hair's breadth of her when she skipped to one side, before prancing around it. With an air of resignation, the hyaena resumed feeding while Small Head sat down barely two metres away. If I might be forgiven another anthropomorphic thought, I would say that if a fox can wear an impudent expression, then this was it! It took the hyaena half an hour to finish its meal by which time Small Head's attention had drifted and she was investigating a shrub in the wadi below the feeding site. The hyaena wandered off towards the Dead Sea shore whereupon Small Head looked up, ran to the calf and pulled off one last morsel which she hastily cached 40 metres to the north, before cantering after the disappearing hyaena. When she caught up, she fell in at its heels, and the two disappeared from sight.

Every time I saw a hyaena near the feeding site there was a fox in close attendance; if more than one hyaena was in view, each might be trailed by a different fox. Similarly, one hyaena might be followed by two, even three, foxes. However, further afield the hyaenas travelled alone, so perhaps the foxes abandoned them at

their territory borders. Even when they were not vying over food, the foxes sometimes gave the impression of tormenting the hyaenas. For instance, on the 23rd December 1975, Big Tag was circling around a hyaena, her ears perked forward as she craned towards it. Her brush was curled slightly to the side, poised for action. As often as the hyaena turned away from the fox she circled in front of it, only to gambol off and then prance back to within a metre of it. The vixen seemed intent on drawing the hyaena after her. At last, it charged; Big Tag sprinted away, then paused until the hyaena caught up. The fox persisted in capering about, while the hyaena's head hung almost to the ground; it snorted and a little cloud of dust blew up in front of its snout. The hyaena shuffled sideways towards the fox. Big Tag's body tensed to jump, as the hyaena edged closer. At less than a metre, the hyaena gave a shambling lurch, but was left gazing mournfully at the spot where the fox had been standing. At once, Big Tag Vixen was back, and the entire sequence of events was repeated until Big Tag seemed to lose interest in, what I am tempted to call, the game. If this behaviour was a game then it was one spiced with danger. Recently I have heard of two episodes where a

It was soon obvious that a hierarchy operated within each group, in the same way that there was a pecking order between foxes in each Boar's Hill group. In total I documented 100 interactions within the two groups and from these it was clear that Enormous Tag was the dominant vixen of the Masada group, whereas Small Head was matriarch of the Ein Gedi foxes. The next question was whether these differences in status within the group had any bearing on the role each fox took when it encountered members of the neighbouring group. Sometimes the clashes between the groups were violent, others were protracted staring matches. At 10.00pm on 18th December, a scuffling of stones drew my attention to a small lean fox as it topped the rise and trotted towards me. It was an especially memorable night, the moon so bright that I could see the fox's shadow. I recognized Thin Vixen from the Ein Gedi group. She made straight for the feeding site and began to busy herself trotting about as she cached chicks singly here and there. Meanwhile, all three vixens from the Masada group had gathered on the south side of the track, where they sat abreast, watching Thin. Gathering up another chick, Thin Vixen turned to leave and then, seemingly for the first time, noticed her audience. At once her behaviour changed: she turned back and picked up as many chicks as she could squeeze between her bulging jaws. Now she ran off, pausing frequently to glower at the Masada foxes. Thin carried her booty towards Nachal 'Arugot. At the instant when Thin topped the rise and disappeared from sight, Enormous Tag Vixen stood up and moved slowly across the track towards the feeding site, casting frequent glances around her. Then as if a starting pistol had been fired, Enormous Tag sprinted to the feeding site, grabbed a chick and raced back. As she crossed back to the south of the track her group mates, Big Tag and Small Tag, dashed forward to steal her booty. Sprinting southwards, Enormous Tag dodged between the other vixens. Big Tag and Small Tag gave half-hearted chase. Even as they ran, Enormous Tag whined aggressively, and, paradoxically, her pursuing group mates lashed their tails in submission. It seemed as if their lower status inhibited their attempted piracy.

Enormous Tag cached her chick some 100 metres into the Masada territory, and cantered

fox taunting a hyaena mis-timed its ruse and ended up crushed in the hyaena's jaws. At least one of these foxes was then eaten.

The foxes generally abandoned a hyaena that crossed the path dividing their two groups. Indeed, I even saw a hyaena swop foxes as it crossed the border track. I soon came to realize that the lay of this track, within just a stone's throw of the feeding site, provided an extraordinary opportunity to study territorial behaviour. During that winter in Israel, I documented 49 border clashes between the two groups—far more information than I have gleaned in years of watching shy foxes in the dense vegetation of Oxfordshire. The flow of aggression between the two groups was very one-sided. More than nine out of ten attacks were launched by the Ein Gedi group. From the Ein Gedi perspective, almost one-quarter of these were provoked, in so far as they were reprisals launched by Ein Gedi foxes when Masada foxes were caught pilfering food north of the border. The feeding site seemed to lie squarely in the Ein Gedi territory, albeit only 20 metres from the border. However, foxes from both groups relied heavily on it. The Masada foxes were therefore shackled to the lifestyle of sneak-thieves.

back to the feeding site. Grabbing two more chicks, she placed them neatly together on the ground. Running hither and thither she gathered three more and added them to her growing pile. Big Tag Vixen slunk towards this pile and Enormous Tag wheeled to attack her. Dust flew up as the two vixens scuffled. Lurching sideways they locked into a crab-like cufuffle of sideways barging, from which Big Tag broke free with her ears pasted flat back against her head, whining as her brush beat the ground. Enormous Tag tried to pick up her pile of five chicks but could not hold them all at once and, in a frenzy of frustration, she repeatedly dropped one and then another in attempting to retrieve the first. Finally, she gave up, dropped all five chicks and ran to gather up a further three, pausing once to rush at Big Tag who was again venturing close. Enormous Tag returned to her pile, picked up four of the original chicks before cantering off 150 metres south-west where she cached all seven in a communal grave.

Enormous Tag was hurrying back to the feeding site for a third time when Thin Vixen returned from the wadi. Enormous Tag stumbled to a halt just on her side of the track, as Thin walked slowly around the feeding site, sniffing carefully at the remains of Enormous Tag's depot of chicks. Enormous Tag hunkered slowly forwards, to the middle of the track. Thin sat down abruptly and stared at Enormous Tag, a chick's leg dangling indolently from each side of her mouth. The two vixens were separated by no more than 15 metres. Facing her trespassing neighbour, Thin chewed loudly on the chick, while Enormous Tag's ears flicked back and forth at every crunch. Thin stood up and, casting fierce glances at Enormous Tag, tried again and again to cram more chickens into her mouth, but each time she paid the price of dropping another. Three long minutes passed on this fruitless task before Thin trotted off up the path north-eastwards. Again, Enormous Tag Vixen rushed forward, grabbed a mouthful and sped south to cache them. As fast as she could, Enormous Tag was back at the feeding site, then away again to a different hiding place. While Enormous Tag was away, Thin returned and the whole cycle began once again.

Meanwhile, Big Tag and Small Tag Vixens were foraging in a nearby gully. Within the Masada group they were clearly subordinate to Enormous Tag, and perhaps their lower status was reflected in their greater reluctance to trespass in Ein Gedi territory when Thin Vixen was in the vicinity.

Observations like these eventually allowed me to draw some general conclusions about intergroup relationships. Most episodes of territorial aggression were between vixens but there were a dozen occasions when the male of one territory attacked a female from the neighbouring group, and one occasion when neighbouring males fought. However, there were some occasions when dog foxes were very tolerant of neighbouring vixens, so I think there is considerable ambivalence in territorial behaviour between the sexes (whereas relations between neighbours of the same sex invariably seem to be hostile). The only combination which I never saw was a vixen attacking a neighbouring dog fox. Taking into account the fact that there were more vixens in the groups, on average, males and females were involved in the same numbers of territorial disputes. However, that average hid a great disparity in the involvement of different females. In fact, the two dominant females, Small Head and Enormous Tag were the initiators of the bulk of serious aggression against their respective neighbours. Among the Ein Gedi vixens, Thin also maintained a high profile in border clashes, and seemed to have an especially close relationship with Small Head.

On Hogmanay, Thin and Small Head of the Ein Gedi group were suffused with anything but goodwill towards their neighbours. As it happened, they were both elsewhere when Enormous Tag Vixen appeared on the scene, but she was caught red-handed at the feeding site when Small Head Vixen arrived back. Too late, Enormous Tag saw Small Head. While Enormous Tag tried to sink into the sand, Small Head stalked purposely forward, picked up some offal, and carried it 15 metres off. There, she stopped and stared at the cowering Enormous Tag for almost 40 seconds. Very slowly, Enormous Tag stood up and, pace by pace, retreated across the border track. Small Head opened her mouth, letting the food drop. The two dominant females stared at each other, motionless. I do not know which vixen broke the spell, but in an instant they were sprinting south. Small Head quickly overtook

Enormous Tag who tripped herself in the attempt to run and submit simultaneously. Small Head fell upon Enormous Tag in the rising dust. The final chase spanned 100 metres of stumbling, rolling, onslaught. Although far over the border into Masada territory, Small Head was deaf to her victim's submissive shrieks. When Small Head had vented her spleen, Enormous Tag was left to hobble away, badly lamed.

Meanwhile, through the infra-red binoculars, two glinting beads shone on the ridge above the battling vixens. Now these eyes moved, disclosing that Small Tag Vixen had been crouching nervously beside the combatants, without coming to her group-mate's aid. As Small Head returned to her home ground she bounced with the victor's prancing stride. Later, as Thin and Small Head fed at the site, Enormous Tag limped hesitantly up to the border track, where she curled up and peered at the two feeding vixens through the veil of her brush draped across her face.

All four vixens in the Ein Gedi group varied in the frequency with which I saw them in border skirmishes (Thin most and Kinktail least). Gradually, it became clear that there was another difference between them, most markedly between Thin and Small Head, and it involved food. Small Head attacked on sight any Masada interloper that strayed over the border, and when she attacked it was generally in earnest. In contrast, the majority of Thin's attacks (and almost all the serious ones) were directed at intruders caught red-handed while pilfering food. As a generalization, it seemed that Small Head was most concerned with defence of the territory. She was involved in by far the greatest number of spontaneous, serious attacks on neighbours. In contrast, Thin was most concerned with the defence of the feeding site.

If dominant vixens within a group tend to be those most involved in territorial defence, what effect does social status within a group have on the outcome of encounters between groups? What happens, for instance, if a subordinate vixen from one group encounters a trespassing dominant neighbour? This is exactly what happened on 26th December 1975, at 8.00pm when several Ein Gedi foxes were in sight. Blackfront Vixen trotted past her group-mate Thin and, a few minutes later, I noticed that she was peering into the darkness with her tail curled. My first thought was that this apparent apprehension was in response to Thin, since Blackfront was subordinate to her within the group. Then I spotted Enormous Tag, matriarch of the Masada group. Enormous Tag put down the chick she had just pilfered from the feeding site and ran fast at Blackfront. Blackfront immediately gave way, flicking her ears back and whining as she ran off. This defeat took place despite the fact that Blackfront Vixen was on her home ground.

Thin Vixen, ranked as Number Two in the Ein Gedi group, had paused to watch this interaction. As Blackfront retreated, so Thin moved towards the victorious Enormous Tag. Enormous Tag saw her coming, wheeled round to snatch up her chick and broke into a canter. Thin sprinted into the attack and caught her just on the border where Enormous Tag submitted, while Thin pranced in circles around her. Enormous Tag dropped the chick and at once Thin let her run off. Thin picked up her loot, carried it back into Ein Gedi territory and buried it. After this episode Thin cocked her leg three times in the space of a few moments. Observations such as this led me to conclude that a vixen's social status within her group affected the likely outcome of her encounters with neighbours. This may underlie the sometimes surprisingly tolerant meetings I have seen between some neighbours, not only in Israel but also in British study areas.

In addition to the sexes and statuses of the participants, another factor which might affect the outcome of a meeting is the place where it occurred. With this in mind I began to shift the feeding site at Ein Gedi back and forth across the border track. It was revealing to see the tables turned as Thin sat dejectedly on 'her side' of the track while Enormous Tag fed some 30 metres to the south. On a later occasion, however, Thin ventured south to eat in the neighbouring territory (albeit cautiously) when the only Masada fox at the transplanted feeding station was the most subordinate Masada vixen, Small Tag. That raised another question. If lower status members were less militant towards interlopers, did they constitute little more than dead wood when it comes to territorial defence? The answer is probably that they are useful reserve forces. After all, the Ein Gedi group was the larger of the two (six versus four), and it was they that monopolized

the feeding site (although this might be either cause or effect). Furthermore, although the lower-ranking vixens maintained a subdued profile in inter-group conflict, they were involved in some clashes. Also, several group members sometimes combined forces to pursue an intruder. The most dramatic of such communal chases were the two occasions on which I saw four Ein Gedi foxes racing in pursuit of a single intruder as it sped back to the safety of Masada territory.

Foxes were not the only sociable members of the dog family in Israel. Svi Horesh, the nature warden who drove the abattoir truck on its weekly visits, told me of another site at Ein Feshka, midway between Ein Gedi and Jericho. There were not only foxes but also jackals, the only survivors of an over-zealous anti-rabies campaign which in 1964 had eliminated jackals from the Negev. At that time, Ein Feshka had been in Jordan, but when it changed hands in the Six Day War in 1967, the Israeli Nature Reserves Authority immediately declared it a nature reserve. Keen to see how foxes and jackals interacted, I arrived at Ein Feshka late one afternoon and found a green oasis fed by three freshwater streams. This lush enclave was bounded by an arid plain littered with boulders of dolomite. Warm spring water supported stands of reeds and, to the east, a forest of salt-tolerant tamarisk. Along the bleak shoreline, the waves of the Dead Sea lapped quietly on the raised beach, littered with the skeletal remains of drowned tamarisk forests, mineralized fingers of ancient vegetation encased in stone.

As dusk fell I sat on the roof of the jeep. Just as the last trace of green faded to twilight grey, a jackal called: a single wailing cry threading through the night air to the north. From the shoreline, much closer, came an answering voice. To my ears they were lingering, woeful laments, flung skywards with an explosive whoosh and then, like a firework, drifting back to earth in a cascade of pure tones. In the distance, the jackals' calls were haunting and eerie; another cry buffeted the air, bursting from a bush not 20 paces from me. All around me the cries went up, until a cacophony of 60 or more imploring voices rent the darkness. A party of five jackals slipped from the twilight to appear before me, almost within arm's reach. Together they threw their heads

13. DO WOLVES KILL FOXES?

In fables the wolf and fox are often cast as deadly enemies (*see* Box 8, p.32). What is the reality of their relationship? Although they rarely eat foxes and generally do not hunt them, there is evidence that wolves kill foxes whenever the opportunity arises. Furthermore, when I radio-tracked foxes in a part of Italy where there were wolves, the foxes were often at pains to give the wolves a wide berth (although foxes can also benefit greatly from scavenging at wolf kills).

This enmity appears to be characteristic of interactions between red foxes and other members of the dog family (*see* Box 1, p.10). It may arise because, apart from differences in their size, members of the dog family are very similar. It is a basic principle of ecology that competition will prevent two species from occupying the same niche. So, for example, foxes and badgers can live side by side because, despite many similarities in their diets, there are sufficient differences to reduce competition. One might expect, therefore, the worst antagonism between the most similar members of the dog family, and there is increasing evidence that this is the case. The sizes of North American canids descend through wolves (20–80kg), coyotes (11–15kg), red foxes (5–6kg), grey foxes (2.5–6kg), Arctic foxes (3–4kg), to the small swift and kit foxes (1.8–3kg). Coyotes have spread following the annihilation of the wolf. Similarly, red fox numbers are greater where coyotes are absent. In Canada, Dennis Voigt radio-tracked red foxes and coyotes where they co-existed, and discovered that fox territories abutted, but did not overlap, the larger territories of coyotes. The foxes conspicuously avoided rearing cubs where coyotes were active.

In the 17th century, in the USA large tracts of East Coast forest were felled and the landscape opened for agriculture. The new habitat favoured the red fox which had originally been confined to open areas north of 40° latitude, and red foxes spread south from Canada at the expense of the local grey or tree fox. Red foxes now inhabit the prairie states of the USA where Swift foxes once predominated. In the Californian cotton belt there is a relict population of the endangered San Joaquin kit fox (2kg); the conservation of these little foxes is hampered because they are killed, but not eaten, by coyotes.

The idea that canid species are so similar as to compete directly led Pall Hersteinsson and me to formulate a hypothesis about why the Arctic fox lives further north than the red fox. Previous explanations for this were that Arctic foxes could withstand more extreme cold, or that the red fox was not camouflaged in the snow. However, red foxes can and do thrive in very cold, snowy conditions, and our analyses suggested that the factor limiting the northern extreme of their distribution was cool summer temperatures (not perishing winter ones). Summer temperatures limit plant growth and the primary productivity of the far north; with less plant growth there will be fewer herbivorous voles and lemmings. In short, cold summers ultimately limit the food available for foxes.

---

back, their muzzles silhouetted against the red shores of Jordan and in unison they howled. Slowly, the volume subsided, a few new voices chimed in from the south, the chorus fragmented into stray splinters of sound, and then it stopped. Darkness had fallen, the jackals beside me slipped away, and there was a silence more pure than any I had ever known.

While I waited to watch an encounter between fox and jackal I had plenty of opportunity to observe jackal society. Even around the feeding site these jackals were remarkably amicable. They were much less proprietorial about food than foxes. The only serious bickering that I ever saw among group members was in late December when one jackal, busily chewing on a tasty morsel, was approached by another, seemingly intent on stealing the food. The feeding jackal arched its back and lowered its head with its tail thrust between its legs and its ears flapped back, and this posture was mirrored by the antagonist. Both snarled, their lips deeply retracted, teeth exposed and noses wrinkling—a contrast with foxes which do not snarl (except in taxidermists' displays!). Almost at once, three more jackals stopped feeding and advanced to stand beside the jackal who had originally been feeding. Then, in unison, the four sprang at the pilferer, and for an instant they fought furiously. The defeated jackal disentangled himself and sped away; but after a few strides both victors and vanquished stopped. The tension was discharged and the group's cohesion intact. Seven jackals remained in front of me playing. Three of them found a large piece of cardboard discarded at the garbage tip, and began a three-cornered tug-o'-war. Two

The fact that red foxes are bigger than Arctic foxes means that they require more food, and conversely the Arctic fox can live in conditions too barren to sustain red foxes. Red fox home ranges in the Arctic are enormous—over 3,000 hectares. However, in every respect save size the two species are so similar that where they might otherwise co-exist they are likely to compete. We concluded that the northern limit of the red fox is limited directly by shortage of food (and only indirectly by climate) while the southern limit of the Arctic fox is limited by the red fox. In effect, the two are so similar (they can even mate and produce infertile hybrids) that red foxes probably treat Arctic foxes as poor quality red foxes.

Competition between red and Arctic foxes became obvious as a consequence of fox fur ranching. In the 1830s, the Russian–American Company began releasing foxes onto previously fox-free see-bird islands off Alaska. During the 1920s and 1930s, when fox furs were at their most valuable, red or Arctic foxes were released on almost every island from the Aleutian Islands to the Alexander Archipelago. For the most part, they were left to look after themselves, and harvested annually. In 1936, 26,000 fox pelts were harvested from the Aleutian Island 'farms'. However, it was soon obvious that the two species of fox could not be kept on the same island: red foxes invariably usurped Arctic foxes. One report in 1886 records how, on one small island, a single male, red fox killed all the resident Arctic foxes.

In fact, the decendants of these fur island foxes have imperilled the sea bird colonies (and driven the Aleutian Island Goose to the verge of extinction). Despite 30 years of effort, it has generally proved impossible to eradicate the foxes (see Box 31, p.207), so one idea is to introduce sterile red foxes or coyotes to islands with Arctic or red foxes, respectively, to let the larger canid eliminate the smaller one.

Against this background of aggression between species of fox, how could it happen that in November 1981 a new species of fox was discovered at Ein Gedi in Israel? The new fox lives within a stone's throw of the numerous red foxes visiting the Ein Gedi feeding site. It is probably a species called Blanford's fox (*Vulpes cana*), otherwise known from south-west Pakistan, Afghanistan and south-west Russia (and had not previously been seen within 2,000km of Israel). Apart from some differences in colouration (e.g. a black tail tip and buff legs) Blanford's foxes look like miniature red foxes—just 40cm in body length, with the tail adding a further 30cm. How can the two species co-exist? The answer seems to be that the little Blanford's foxes restrict their movements to the rocky cliffs, a habitat where their small size probably puts them at an advantage over the red foxes. They rarely venture to the plains below, where confrontation with their larger cousins would seem inevitable.

others began a mock fight throughout which their tails wagged vigorously.

While the jackals were immersed in their play I spotted a fox flitting between the scrub 50 metres away. It was soon obvious that the fox was intent upon reaching the feeding site, but was fearful of the company. Moving nervously and using cover it slid to within 30 metres of the jackals, and peered at them from behind a shrub. The fox shied away as the jackals' play reached a boisterous crescendo. Five minutes later I spotted it again, once more peering cautiously from a distance. At that point, three jackals began to stroll in the fox's direction. As far as I could tell their approach was coincidental; they appeared oblivious to the fox. The fox wheeled and fled.

Although a family of foxes lived at Ein Feshka, they were very wary of their larger cousins (see Box 13). There may have been good reasons for this: I found one adult fox at Ein Feshka, dead and badly mauled. All the signs were that it had been killed by the jackals. The only occasion when I saw an Israeli fox look more scared than they were of jackals was when a lone wolf arrived at Ein Gedi. Small Tag caught its scent when it was more than 60 metres off; she was fleeing at breakneck speed even before the wolf came into view. Clearly foxes are in no doubt about the identity of their larger cousins. Others were apparently not so discerning. There was some zoological uncertainty amongst the early Talmudic scholars, with the result that foxes and jackals were often confused in translation. The *Book of Judges* should have related how Samson caught 300 jackals, not 300 foxes—perhaps a more practical proposition!

6 | THE NIGHT OF THE FOX

IT WAS TOOTHYPEG VIXEN who gave me the idea that foxes practise family planning. I first met her in the winter of 1973, at that point in the night when frozen winds begin to coat waterlogged fields with a crackly white veneer. My nocturnal vigils were becoming trials of endurance. Slipping and slithering across the fields, winter's spiky beauty was a lesser preoccupation than the pulsings of a clutch of chilblains. I was launched upon a major, if unsuccessful, drive to catch foxes for radio-tagging, and that night I was already on my third weary circuit of the traps. A heavy stippling of pawprints chiselled a rut around the headland furrows bordering Ducklings Field, and I was anxious not to cross this well-used path for fear of drawing vulpine attention to the scent of my prowlings. So, I cut a wide detour across the plough and doggedly fought off the cowardly hope that for the sake of my numbed fingers the trap would be empty. A heavy cloud drifted across the moon and, with gratuitous malice, spat at me with a torrent of icy wet pellets. From the hedge I heard a rustle and, in the beam of my torch, two points of light flashed back the message that a fox was caught.

Running back to the road, I drove quickly to the Kruuks' house where I tiptoed up the stairs, and tapped on the bedroom door. In minutes, Hans, I and the fox were eying each other in a torrential downpour. After a brief scuffle, I had the fox in hand and its eyes covered with a calming blanket. Our then new (but now archaic) design of radio-collar was fitted (and switched on) by means of the delicate threading of a bolt and several washers through a tongue of braided cable (which also served as the broadcasting antenna). The longevity of the transmitter hinged critically on keeping the contacts clean and dry.

By the time the fifth washer had slipped to electronic doom in the quagmire, the insulating tape had lost its 'stick' in the rain water, and large clods of mud were working their way into the connecting sockets. Our elation at the capture was immersed in rising panic. Finally, the pernickety connections threaded into place and a satisfying string of bleeps pulsed healthily from the receiver. We set about examining those parts of the fox which protruded through the mud. The discovery that she was almost toothless made something of a mockery of our anxieties for our fingers. The old vixen's mouth housed one broken canine tooth, a few worn molars on one side, and a great expanse of naked gum. With hindsight (having counted the growth rings on her tooth posthumously), I now know that at our first encounter, Toothypeg had already seen eight winters. During the remaining year of her life I saw her almost daily, a wiry, grizzled fox gliding over the mat of brambles that carpeted Dixieland Wood where she lay up. Gradually, she came to tolerate my approach to as close as 40 metres as she lay like a gaunt sphinx at the entrance to her earth. I recaptured Toothypeg so often that latterly she scarcely attempted to bite me, but placidly waited while I replaced her worn radio with a new one.

Later that year I radio-collared a dog fox in Toothypeg's territory. Although his worn teeth were all intact, he, too, had left behind the dense fur and full muscle of his prime. Now his pelt had a time-worn coarseness, and his frame was big-boned and wiry. I estimated that he was at least five years old. His face was heavily scarred and cut with reminders of bygone duels. I named the dog fox Scar Nose, and soon discovered that he and Toothypeg shared almost exactly the same

14. HOW FAR DO FOXES TRAVEL?

There are two types of answer to this question, and both vary between habitats. One answer concerns the movements of resident, territory holding foxes, and is the subject of Box 16, p.117. The second answer concerns those foxes, generally adolescents, who disperse, travelling far and wide. These itinerant foxes have been recorded to cover long distances—the record is a straight-line distance of 500km recorded in Sweden. In the USA the longest point to point dispersal was recorded by a dog fox that covered 394km (in Britain the longest is 52km in Wales).

Each spring, cubs are born to territory-holding foxes. If the youngsters survive, then in autumn there may be more foxes in the parents' territory than it can support. Some of the vixen cubs may stay to join the family group, but the remainder, together with almost all the adolescent dog foxes, will disperse. A small percentage of adult foxes may also disperse. Dispersal is in full swing from September until February, but may begin as early as July (and the departure date varies even between litter-mates). Dispersal takes a variety of forms: some young foxes leave home suddenly, others do so after a succession of excursions, some oscillate between two home ranges before finally shifting their base, some weave an erratic course across the countryside, others travel fast and far in roughly straight lines. These variations are not understood. In the context of rabies dispersing foxes probably explain the sporadic outbreaks of disease 30km or more ahead of the front line.

The distances over which foxes disperse vary greatly between individuals and regions. Various biologists have tagged cubs and then measured the straight line distances to places where they were killed as adults (the fact that such studies have a good recovery rate from hunters emphasizes the importance of people as agents of fox mortality—*see* Box 21, p. 144). To the extent that the function of dispersal is securing a vacant territory one might expect foxes to disperse over shorter distances, all else being equal, where territories are smaller or where mortality is greater. Both expectations appear fulfilled. The ranges of resident foxes in Bristol City, Dutch farmland, Welsh hills and the American cereal belt were, respectively, 45, 119, 644 and 960 hectares while the average bee-line dispersal distances for dog foxes in these areas were 3, 8, 14 and 31km. Of course, the actual distances travelled by these foxes would be much further than, but perhaps proportional to, these bee-line distances. Overall, the average dog fox disperses over a straight line distance roughly equivalent to the widths of four to six territories. In Ontario, where mortality was high due to rabies and fur trapping, the average dispersal distance was only 2.4 territory widths. The clearest demonstration of a relationship between territory size and dispersal distance comes from Erik Lindström's study of foxes in the Swedish taiga: to the north lay relatively barren forest and large fox territories, to the south richer land and smaller territories. Foxes which went north travelled further (average 30km) than those (sometimes their brothers) who went south (average 17km).

Another function of dispersal may be to avoid inbreeding. This may partly explain why the two sexes travel different distances. Most studies have shown that dog foxes travel further afield (they also leave home younger) than vixens. In the Welsh hills Gwyn Lloyd found the mean bee-line dispersal distance of dog foxes was 13.7km and of vixens was 2.3km. On farmland in West Wales the figures were 4.7 and 1.9km. Such samples are complicated by animals that might have dispersed had they survived longer, but even so in both areas it seems likely that many vixens had settled in the range in which they were born. Behaviour involved with dispersal and the process of settling down is one of the least known aspects of fox natural history.

range. The very same range was also used by two other vixens, Four-Ten and Husky—the two Toothypeg look-alikes. I continued to track them without incident until one night, late the following January, the whole world seemed to converge on their territory. At the time I was on the trail of a yearling dog fox named Half-Cut. I had originally caught and radio-collared Half-Cut on 10th January in the heart of the neighbouring White-legged group's territory. He weighed almost 6 kg and had the lean rangy look which, along with an almost pristine comb of serrations on his incisor teeth, convinced me that he was a yearling. Nevertheless, his testes and tail gland were large and he had already acquired a network of fresh scars on his muzzle, and one canine tooth had recently been smashed. Since our first meeting, Half-Cut had woven a seemingly erratic track across Boar's Hill and further afield too, apparently regardless of territorial demarcation. He was leading the typical life of an itinerant fox, doubtless in search of a mate and territory—footloose and fancy free you might say, but more likely an exhausting, harried and perilous struggle against the odds (*see* Box 14, p. 88).

On the night in question, Half-Cut arrived in Toothypeg's territory before midnight. Soon his radio signal converged with Toothypeg's and Scar Nose's. I crept up Bayworth Lane. The barrage of radio signals pounding in my head-phones indicated that the three foxes were just the other side of the hedge. Sounds of scuffling and whimpering told just how close they were. At 11.35pm, the three foxes (a leash) were joined by another radio fox: Scalpie, a 7-kg dog fox who normally operated behind the village of Old Wooton. Moments later, Half-Right, another itinerant radio-male arrived too. Four radio-col-lared dog foxes, and goodness knows how many others, were gathered around Toothypeg and from the furore of gekkering that broke out, they were not too pleased to see each other. I crept over the ditch into Mr Dixie's garden where it adjoined the woodland. A curtain of wet veg-etation reflected the infra-red light from the hot-eye. Now and then I caught a flash of vulpine eyeshine. Twigs snapped, leaf-litter rustled and a vixen's shriek ripped through the tension. Hidden in the vegetation, foxes fought in the darkness and I was probably as close as I have ever been to seeing wild foxes mating.

I doubt that Half-Cut fared well during that hot-headed night, for beside the likes of Scar Nose and Scalpie he was a mere stripling. Half-Cut remained in the vicinity until 2nd February and then he disappeared. However, the lie of the land on Boar's Hill obviously stuck in his mind, because on the night of 12th March I picked up his signal far out on Chilswell Farm. He was moving east and towards Toothypeg's territory. By 2am he had passed through Toothypeg's territory and into Roger's, where he remained until 4.25am when he visited the feeding station in Hans' garden before retiring to spend the day in the same earth in Dixieland that he had frequented during his previous sojourns on Boar's Hill.

By midnight the following night he was four kilometres to the south, returning to Hans' garden the following night before leaving Boar's Hill and heading out across farmland two kilometres north-west. Shortly before 5am he

made his big mistake, and returned to Toothy-peg's territory where his radio signal converged with Toothypeg's. A few moments later Scar Nose's radio signal showed that he had joined them. Almost at once, Half-Cut was moving fast. I spotted him as he broke from the woodland and sped across a field with Scar Nose hard at his heels. He had barely shaken him off and crossed into White-legged territory when Sampson materi-alized, bowled him over and chased him hard to the east. Half-Cut swung in a wide loop and by

5am he was underground in his *pied à terre* in Dixieland. Shortly after midnight the next evening he was travelling fast north across Chilswell Farm in the direction from which he had come three nights earlier. I never found him again.

Old Toothypeg gave birth in March 1974, and a month later a single male cub emerged from the earth. The two younger vixens of the same group, Four-Ten and Husky, showed no signs of whelping, or even of pregnancy. Toothypeg's cub was born in an earth dug deep into a sandy bank, in the wooded grounds of Plater College, secluded from all intrusion save the occasional strollings of the trainee curates resident in the college.

The old vixen had lain up in that same earth almost every day throughout the winter, and occasionally she had shared it with Scar Nose or Four-Ten Vixen. Now, radio-tracking revealed that the other group members visited mother and cub frequently during the nights following the birth of her cub. Situated on the steep bank, Toothypeg's earth was ideally positioned for observation. Several lengths of angle-iron struts

and some planks of wood were quickly fashioned into a high-seat which was, at least in theory, portable. In practice, with its long, lance-like legs, negotiating the woodland led to quixotic jousting matches with an army of obstinate trees. Over the course of a week of familiarization I manœuvred this uncompromising structure progressively closer to the bank until it leant uncertainly against a tree only 15 metres from the earth.

By then the cub was almost two months old and spent most of its time in a trailing mass of brambles at the foot of the bank. Now my vigil began. Each evening, before dusk, I crept through the woodland and climbed into position on the high-seat.

As dusk fell on the 26th May, two and a half hours after I had slunk to my hiding place, I caught sight of a fox moving beneath me. It was a big, lean fox wearing a radio-collar. My radio receiver was clasped firmly between my knees, and the receiving antenna hung from a nearby branch. Using headphones, so that the fox could not hear the signal. I tuned to the frequency

A dominant vixen (out of shot) approaches her group mates, whose postures illustrate their respective social statuses. The dog fox stands relaxed and unconcerned, the second vixen (foreground) adopts a slightly submissive posture, whereas the third vixen crouches in intense submission.

which confirmed that this was Scar Nose. Moments later Toothypeg appeared nearby. Scar Nose stood with his head held low, giving his hackles a peculiarly gaunt appearance, and uttered a throaty warbling greeting. Toothypeg sank to the ground and slithered towards him in cloying submissiveness. Scar Nose took a pace towards the earth, and Toothypeg followed behind him. The old dog fox seemed oblivious of her fawning, and walked, sniffing, to the entrance of the earth. Toothypeg's whimperings rose to a fulsome shriek. Scar Nose turned towards her and, flat to the ground, she crept forwards and licked his muzzle. Toothypeg fell to a rapturous writhing while Scar Nose urinated ostentatiously into the mouth of the earth, before trotting down the bank into the rhododendron bushes below. Toothypeg, her ears still flicking and brush twitching from side to side, sniffed long and hard at the urine-splashed sand.

The whimpers of another greeting erupted from the bushes, and Husky slithered to Scar Nose. However, Husky's paroxysms of submis-

sion soon passed, and she squirmed away from Scar Nose and trotted up the path towards Toothypeg. On reaching her, Husky crouched flat to the ground, tail lashing to the older vixen, who ignored her. Husky continued up the path until out of sight. Soon, Scar Nose and Toothypeg also melted from view. Half an hour later a fourth fox briefly visited the earth: it was Four-Ten Vixen. As the night passed, the adult foxes came and went below me. It seemed that the earth and cub were a focus of attention for many, perhaps all, of the group's members. An adult's arrival generally prompted excited squealing from the cub whichever individual was involved. I was almost sure I could hear chewing noises after one of Four-Ten's visits—was the barren vixen feeding Toothypeg's cub? A curtain of undergrowth prevented me from confirming this.

Exciting though adults' visits were, they were fleeting, and the intervals between them long and boring. Pins and needles spread through my backside, and I was reduced to time-

A vixen writhes in greeting as her mate sniffs her.

consuming distractions such as reciting Edward Lear's nonsense dredged imperfectly from childhood memories. Between verses of *The Owl and the Pussycat* I mused on something I had been told by a gamekeeper friend. On several occasions, having killed a 'milky' vixen, he had thereafter shot a 'dry' vixen seemingly bringing food to the orphans. Indeed, he knew of such barren vixens trying to dig out an earth that had been gassed. These snippets of keeper's lore, along with Four-Ten's and Husky's involvement with the cubs on the bank beneath me, fanned the suspicion that I was getting close to an important secret of fox society. Night work provides plenty of time for such optimistic speculation. Every hour or so, at moments when faint radio signals indicated that the foxes were far off, I allowed myself the luxury of a ration of coffee from the Thermos flask. And so that night, like many others, passed.

During that year, neither Four-Ten nor Husky reared cubs of their own. In many areas, most vixens breed as yearlings, so there could be no question that these two vixens were barren

due to immaturity. Both were in their prime: Four-Ten was five years old, whereas Husky was probably two. Was it merely chance that only one vixen, and she the oldest, reared cubs that year? It would be stretching coincidence to dismiss also the fact that of the four vixens in the White-legged group there had been no sign of two (Equal-White and Up-White) having cubs the previous year. Out of these observations a question arose whose ramifications were to determine the course of my study for almost a decade: was some unexpected restraint limiting the birth rate of foxes, at least on Boar's Hill?

Published studies, and conversations with other biologists, all suggested that across much of continental Europe and North America well over 90 per cent of vixens breed in good years. In Britain, the only hint of an exception was one sample in which Gwyn Lloyd had found only about 80 per cent of vixens had bred. So, there had been little prior reason to think that any healthy vixens would not breed in my study areas.

With mounting excitement, I lived on the

15. HOW MANY CUBS DO FOXES HAVE?

Two factors affect the numbers of cubs born in a fox population—the number of cubs per litter and the proportion of vixens bearing cubs—and both of these vary regionally (about two-fold and six-fold respectively).

Vixens are capable of conceiving at least 14 cubs in one litter, but in many areas the average litter size at birth is between four and five. The known extremes are averages of three in Jämtland, Sweden, and eight in Southern Ontario, Canada. In some regions the average varies not only from place to place, but from year to year (e.g. from three to six in northern Sweden). Larger litters are typical of areas where there is heavy mortality (in Ontario there is a rapid turnover in the fox population because many die of rabies and due to fur trapping). If mortality reduces the breeding population below that which might otherwise be supported by the food supply (i.e. below 'carrying capacity'), then there will be more food available to each of the survivors (see Box 32, p.208). This extra food for breeding vixens may partly explain their larger litters (equally, it might result in greater juvenile survival). The result is that high productivity may compensate for high mortality.

The proportion of vixens bearing cubs also varies regionally. In the American prairies (where fox trapping for fur is intensive) 96 per cent of all vixens examined *post mortem* had been pregnant. In Southern Ontario, with its heavy fox mortality, the average was similarly over 90 per cent, as it was in parts of Switzerland and Germany (areas where hunting and rabies took a heavy toll). In contrast, on Boar's Hill I found that 60 per cent of vixens did not rear cubs. Similarly, in London, Stephen Harris found that 24 per cent were barren. The combined effects of variations in litter size and proportions of vixens breeding can lead to ten-fold regional variation in the average number of cubs produced per average vixen: even in one area of the northern forests of Sweden it varied almost five-fold (between 0.8 and 3.9 per vixen) in successive years.

In general, yearling vixens are less likely to produce cubs than older vixens. In Ontario, 89 per cent of yearlings had been pregnant in contrast to 99 per cent of older vixens. In Wisconsin these figures were 59 and 89 per cent respectively, in London 48 and over 90 per cent respectively. In Stephen Harris' study in London there was evidence that litter size fell (and the proportion of barren vixens rose) among vixens older than five years—in most areas vixens do not live that long (see Box 21, p.144).

These findings could be explained by either or both of two compatible processes. In areas, such as Boar's Hill, where vixens live in stable family groups, most of the barren females may be subordinate group members (and since social status is often linked to age one would expect a greater proportion of non-breeding yearlings). In areas where vixen dispersal was common some might fail to secure territories and for that reason might not breed (and because yearlings are more likely to disperse than older vixens one would again expect a greater proportion of them to be without territories and therefore without cubs).

Which mechanism is more likely in a given area hinges on very complex questions about how the sizes of foxes' territories adjust to the fluctuations in food availability within and between years (see Box 16, p.117). As an indication of this complexity, compare three areas of Sweden. In mixed farmland and forest where there was diverse prey and rather low mortality, two-thirds of yearlings were barren (maximum 81 per cent) in comparison with about one-third of older vixens (and two year olds were more likely to be barren than three year olds). An increase in vole populations led to an increase in litter sizes, but not in the proportion of vixen's breeding. In contrast, in the Boreal forests in the far north, foxes lived largely on voles and there the litter sizes and proportions of vixens breeding were more similar for all age groups, and varied greatly from year to year depending on the abundance of voles (see Box 18, p.122). The foxes in these two areas were studied by Jan Englund, but in a transition zone between them Erik Lindström found that voles were of intermediate importance in the diet. There, he found that litter sizes went up and the proportion of vixens breeding went down as vole numbers reached their peak.

These three outcomes might be explained as follows: (i) Mixed farmland and forest (voles of minor importance): territory sizes stable, group sizes large, and social suppression of reproduction occurs irrespective of vole numbers, (ii) Transition zone (voles of intermediate importance): territory sizes stable, but group sizes increased by addition of non-breeding yearlings as vole numbers increase; non-breeders expelled as vole numbers decline, (iii) Boreal forest (voles of paramount importance): territories shrink or expand or even disintegrate to accommodate massive changes in vole numbers; one vixen per territory and no opportunity for family groups to develop. When voles abound, most vixens secure a territory and most breed; when voles are scarce, most vixens do not secure a territory and do not breed. These interpretations are simplified and partly hypothetical but they illustrate how food supply, territoriality and social behaviour might interact in complex ways.

heels of the vixens on Boar's Hill throughout the cubbing season. By the summer of 1974 I was confident that, of the 15 adult vixens that I knew most thoroughly, only six had reared cubs. What was more, within each of four social groups, what I had seen of social interactions indicated that the vixens which bred were the most socially dominant ones. I began to suspect that I had stumbled upon what, at the time, was an unexpected social mechanism: fox family planning. Of course, I do not imply by this term that birth control is a matter of conscious thought or decision by these vixens, or even that it is voluntary. Rather, I am suggesting that there is a social mechanism which determines whether or not a vixen breeds, and which has the effect of concentrating the available resources for the well-being of a select few offspring.

But why were my results so different from those of studies elsewhere? An important clue lay in the results of a massive post-mortem study published in 1970 by a biologist called Jan Englund. Collecting dead foxes from hunters in different regions of Sweden he had found that the proportion of pregnant vixens varied regionally and that this variation was greatest among yearlings (from 88 per cent down to only 5 per cent pregnant). Most important, his data suggested that, in any given area, a greater proportion of yearlings were barren than older vixens. Although nobody had ever thought of Swedish foxes living as any stable unit larger than a pair, it seemed plausible to speculate that some of these barren yearlings were low-ranking members of family groups similar to those on Boar's Hill (see Box 15, p. 93).

My hypothesis took the following shape. Some vixens live in groups and climb to different heights on a social ladder: those dominant vixens at the top of a roughly linear hierarchy somehow have a monopoly on breeding. Other vixens are not members of such social groups. They live alone with their mates, and these vixens are not subject to social pressures on their reproductive lives, with the result that all of them breed as soon as they are mature. Put this way, the difference between my findings and those of other people's studies could arise as a result of the foxes on Boar's Hill living in stable groups, when those studied elsewhere were not. This question begs another question: why do foxes in

some areas live in groups while elsewhere others live in pairs? I think the answer to this fundamental question has to do with variations in both food supply (its availability and patchiness) and mortality between different areas. I will return to that later, and continue now with the question of whether the breeding of foxes which do live in groups (for whatever reason) really is affected by their social status.

If the reproduction of low-ranking vixens really was inhibited, and only the top-ranking vixens bred, then one consequence of this arrangement would be that the average productivity of cubs per vixen would fall as the number of vixens in a group increased. This could be a case of density-dependent regulation.

Density-dependence is a very important idea for ecologists. In a nutshell, it is that the intensity with which the mechanisms that control the numbers of animals in a population are exerted varies with the size of that population—a sort of negative feedback system. The idea has been widely applied, but in this case it would be that the mechanism whereby the numbers of cubs born were regulated have a disproportionately bigger effect in bigger groups (e.g. in a group of two vixens only half would be barren, but in a group of four, three-quarters would be barren). It was an odd coincidence that at the time I was beginning to develop these ideas I first met one of the oldest vixens on Boar's Hill, Black Agnes, who lived in the Lack's family garden. David Lack was one of Oxford's great biologists and it was he who, in the 1950s, was one of the first to be concerned with factors affecting family size in animals. Black Agnes provided a further instance of an elderly breeding female in a group of less venerable, but barren, vixens.

My finding that the breeding vixens were the socially dominant ones had a logical weakness. Most of my observations on their social behaviour were made after the cubs were born in March or April, and almost all were made after the vixens had become pregnant in January. This was for unavoidable practical reasons, such as the great difficulty in making observations during the long nights of winter darkness. Therefore, I could not be sure whether high social rank was a prerequisite to a vixen becoming a breeder, or whether becoming a breeder bestowed high status on a vixen. To resolve this one would

require knowledge of social relationships throughout the year.

Considering the many uncertainties that beset behavioural inferences drawn from post-mortem studies, and the impracticality of watching adequate numbers of wild foxes, I decided that my best hope for exploring birth control lay with Niff. Along with her mate, she was now living in the Dixieland shed, and continuing her experimental walks around the countryside. My aim was to build a captive group around Niff whose composition mirrored that of wild fox groups on Boar's Hill. I would know all the kinship and social relationships amongst these foxes. It would take at least two years, and probably much longer for the group to develop. In the first year Niff must rear cubs. When that

first generation reached adolescence, I would remove the young males since, in the wild, they almost invariably disperse anyway (see Box 14, p. 88). The young vixens would remain with their mother, just as Four-Ten Vixen and Husky had done; they were probably Toothypeg's daughters. Detailed observations would then allow me to disentangle the pecking order among this family group.

In the second year I could test my first prediction: only the dominant vixen should breed (this would probably be Niff as the eldest female). In this case, I would again retain a few of her second generation of daughters, and so on, year after year, until a group of variously aged relatives had developed. Of course, if my hypothesis was wrong, that is if social pressure was not behind the failure of so many wild vixens to breed, then doubtless vixens of high and low status in the captive group would not differ significantly in their reproductive success. Either way, perhaps I would glean observations to shed light on my hunch that in the wild, non-breeding vixens in the social group were taking food to other females' cubs.

The plan was straightforward, but would Niff and her unborn family cooperate? Furthermore, while her shed was an ideal and secluded base from which Niff could take her daily walks, it would hardly suffice for a family of foxes. I needed an enclosure large enough for conditions to be as natural as possible yet not so large that the inmates could elude detailed study of their private lives. As far as Niff was concerned, the purpose of the enclosure was not really to keep her in—she was so tame that she would run to the curlew-whistle (and even to the individual chugging of my car's engine)—rather it was to protect her from the unwelcome, and sometimes unconscious, attentions of dogs, people and wild foxes. Luckily, I knew a suitable site—the disused tennis court at which the White-legged foxes had reared their cubs in 1973.

One day, while tracking foxes in the grounds of Hamels, I had seen long plumes of smoke spiral above the house. In minutes the plumes gave way to an inferno. The house, converted from a wooden Kentish barn, went up like a tinder box. Having only recently bought Hamels, the owners, Robin and Nitza Spiro, were living elsewhere (actually in Mottle Vixen's territory, and we had become friends after meeting while I was trespassing in their garden). Now, with the burning of Hamels, their misfortune became my salvation. With a generosity and enthusiasm that was to extend for more than seven years, they permitted me to build the first fox enclosure on the site of the old tennis court, and to use the six hectares of Hamels as a centre for the project.

Early spring of 1974 found Niff pregnant and behaving like a wild fox in every way except in her friendship for Jenny and me. Plans for her enclosure were well in hand. The single blemish on our good fortune for the project was that we were broke, and facing an estimated bill of £200 for wire required to fence the enclosure. Also, the high mileage necessitated by radio-tracking was drinking petrol at a rate which my grant could

not sustain. This was the first of far too many occasions when I faced the reality that the project faced financial collapse.

By coincidence, I had worked now and again for BBC television's Natural History Unit, and, of course, I had chatted with friends there about the progress of my fox project. Just when it seemed that lack of funds would surely put the kibosh on Niff's enclosure, Mick Rhodes, then Director of the Unit, authorized a 50-minute documentary film about my work. It was agreed that if I did the labouring, the BBC would pay for the materials needed for the enclosure. In return they would be able to film in the enclosure.

So, with less than a month to go before the expected birth of Niff's cubs, I found myself standing in the ramshackle tennis court. It was a wonderful place, with the Gothic atmosphere of a secret garden. Cloaked in an impenetrable wall of a tall bramble thicket, it offered only one entrance—a passageway beneath the thorns that could be passed only by squirming along on hands and knees. Ancient court markings were still traceable across a pitted and fissured tarmacadam. Mighty nettles had pushed up slabs of the court. Remnants of a blue tit nest spilled from a rusty cavity in the winding mechanism of the net support. The chain link fence was overwhelmed in brambles, and the brittle wire could be kneaded into a rusty powder between finger and thumb. Corner posts that had supported the fences were etched with rust. No normal thinking person would have been deluded into the belief that this derelict wilderness could be transformed by a couple of amateurs into a robust, fox-proof enclosure within a fortnight or so. There is no doubt that in this undertaking, as in so many others, my greatest assets have been my inexhaustible naïvety, and Jenny.

Day after day I flayed with axe and scythe. Each afternoon, when Jenny had finished her day's work as a schoolteacher, she sped to the tennis court to gather up the debris and carry away thorny armfuls. As daylight faded, Jenny walked Niff down from Dixieland, and the increasingly rotund vixen sniffed and probed and dug in and around her future home.

Soon the brush was cut back, but this achievement disclosed unexpected problems: the corner posts, misleadingly robust where they had surfaced above the saplings, had rotted at soil level. We could not afford new iron posts but John Gee rescued me with the loan of an arc-welder. With a hacksaw I felled the existing iron posts, excised the rusted lengths, and transported the usable segments to Denman's Farm. There I welded them together and, with lengths of iron salvaged from John's scrapheap, welded tripod support struts onto the new corner posts.

A daily routine emerged: I cleared vegetation all day, and then worked on the welding after dark. I set about digging holes for the rejuvenated corner struts, and for the four-metre spruce poles we had prepared as intermediate uprights. Then came another set-back: the tennis court was built on almost pure blue Oxford clay beneath which the water table lurked just a few centimetres down. The term digging is a honeyed euphemism for the process of clawing out glutinous lumps of clay which, in the icy February weather, clung to the spade with wearying tenacity. And as the holes went deeper, so they filled up with freezing water. The task was akin to shovelling golden syrup out of a deep fridge.

At last the enclosure was finished. Inside I built an artificial earth, with a cosy nest cavity backed by a glass window, designed for filming. Niff took to it at once. She did not revert to the wild in the relative freedom of the Tennis Court. If anything, she became more trusting—at least with Jenny and me. Anyone who struggled through the curtain of vegetation that shrouded the enclosure saw not so much as a glimpse of the inmates. Unless the wind carried the scent of a friend, Niff and her mate hid at the slightest sound of human approach. I do not know how many thousand visits I made to the tennis court, but each time, on seeing it devoid of foxes, I felt a pang of dread that they had escaped. Then, I'd give the curlew whistle, and the thrill never palled when Niff sprang from hiding and rushed over in an ecstasy of tail-lashing welcome.

On the 19th March 1975 winter threw a Parthian shot at advancing spring, and large watery snowflakes drifted down on the enclosure. Niff emerged from the snug protection of her artificial earth, her swollen belly hung low with the great weight of unborn cubs pulling her skin taught across her narrow hips. She waddled to a large pile of thorny brushwood in the centre of the court and crept below it. That night the snow fell, cold winds lashed the tennis court, and

Niff gave birth below the windswept brush pile. The next morning found me there, fraught with anxiety and indecision. In country slang, cubs whelped above ground are termed 'stump-bred', and huntsmen have it that such cubs are especially robust. I hoped that they were right, for with the freezing wind I feared their chances were very slim indeed.

Outside the enclosure, Hugh Maynard, the cameraman, was hidden on top of a tall observation platform. For our film to make sense, we had to have footage of Niff and her newborn cubs. The plan had been to film the family through the glass window I had built into the artificial earth, but Niff's last-minute shift of den to the brush pile put paid to that scheme. Instead, with my hand-cranked Rolex, I was to creep into Niff's nest and film the family, while Hugh would film me doing so. The problem was that everything depended on the cubs—not only did the film depend on their survival but so too did my research. I had sought advice widely from fox farmers and experts on the captive breeding of wild animals. Their answers had an unnerving unanimity: meddling with the newborn litter would probably distress the mother to the extent of deserting or even killing her offspring. If my interference now, for the sake of a few minutes of film, precipitated disaster, then months of effort would go down the drain, and my doctoral thesis might well follow it. However, weighed against these fears, and based more on sentiment than on logic, was my faith that Niff would tolerate my impertinence.

Hidden on the observation platform Peter Bale, the BBC producer, waited nervously. Standing beside that brushpile I heard, for the first time in my life, the wonderful mewings of suckling fox cubs. Dropping to my hands and knees, and pushing the camera ahead of me, I began slowly to crawl under the brush pile. As I edged forward I whispered softly to Niff. Every few centimetres I paused, waiting anxiously for any sign of alarm or aggression. At last I could peer forward and see Niff looking at me from barely half a metre away. A tremble of greeting rippled through her. A barrage of thorns were gouging a course along the back of my scalp and prevented me from lifting my head high enough to see over Niff's flanks to the cubs mewing at her side. Painfully, I broke off the pliant thorny twigs to create an alcove from which I could view the cubs and get the camera into position. At last I could see them—five mole-like bundles, wriggling at Niff's teats. Through my viewfinder, the family scene more than filled the screen. I faced the last hurdle and pressed the button. The noise of the camera's mechanism exploded like a tractor engine at full throttle. Niff looked straight at the lens, but did not move. With the camera running, and pivoting my weight on my right elbow, I stretched forward with my free arm. Through the viewfinder, I saw my hand come into frame and timorously make its way towards Niff. I saw it stroke her ears and then run on, until my fingers nestled amongst the babies at her teats. Niff turned, nuzzling the cubs and licked my hand. I thought my heart would burst.

Niff was an excellent mother, and the four vixens and one little dog grew apace. Perched aloft the observation platform, Hugh patiently filmed marvellous pictures of Niff's tender motherhood, and the cubs' rumbustious play. Both Jenny and I spent hours in the enclosure recording the family's behaviour. In the early days, while their vision was still cloudy, the cubs tolerated us as long as we pretended to be tree-trunks: we lay motionless on the ground and

they clambered over us. But as their coats turned from brown to red they grew wary and soon they were as shy as any wild cubs.

Summer turned to autumn and, with the approach of Christmas came the critical stage of my experiment. We removed the young male so that at the next breeding season the group would consist of Niff and her mate, and their four yearling daughters. Who would breed? We faced an unexpected difficulty in answering that question. The young vixens had grown up such 'natural' foxes that they hid whenever they sensed us near by. With hindsight it seemed that their mother's trust of us had not been enough. Perhaps the only way to keep them tame would have been to hand-rear them, but that would have compromised the experiment by destroying their relationship with Niff. Furthermore, the prospects of filming such self-conscious stars were zero. We fantasized about a night vision camera that would work along the same principles as the hot-eye, and which could be oper-

ated by remote control—thereby overcoming both the problems of darkness and the foxes' timidity. Not for the first time in this project, our dream became reality.

Two BBC engineering trouble-shooters, Paul Townsend and John Noakes, were brought in and became infected with our dream. They worked all hours to find a solution. Without major funding they built prototypes from scavenged equipment, mostly from bits and pieces found unused in cupboards. Four large infra-red lights were built. One of these 1200-watt monsters was mounted at each corner of the tennis court. Each contained a powerful electric fan to dissipate the tremendous heat generated by the bulbs as they floodlit the enclosure in invisible light—'black light' as the producer called it. An old television camera was weather-proofed and modified to be sensitive to infra-red light. The army was brought in to help design an electronically controlled tripod head, and circuitry was designed so that the camera could be

panned, tilted and focused by remote control. Next, pantechnicon lorries arrived at Hamels laden with coils of heavy-duty cable which were trailed from the enclosure to the BBC outside broadcast caravan 200 metres away. Inside, facing a battery of TV monitors, circuit boxes and tangled leads, we sat with a box of joysticks which controlled the camera, and fed signals to a video tape recorder. Miraculously, it worked. The foxes behaved completely naturally, totally oblivious to our distant surveillance, and by remote control we could see and record every detail of their activities.

On the night of the 22nd January 1976, if the mood in the tennis court was highly charged, that in our caravan was electric. Eight people and twice as many Thermos flasks were crammed around the video monitor. A producer, his assistant, two engineers, a cameraman, a soundman, Jenny and myself, bundled together in a downy matrix of parkas, woollies and wellies. All those people had worked hard for 12 months preparing for these nights of filming in darkness, and now their efforts hung on my guesswork. They had made equipment that people had said could not be made, and to do so they had swum hard against the bureaucratic current. The night

camera was set up and working, but we were manacled by the availability of the video tape recorder, without which we could not record the pictures we saw on the monitor. In the entire BBC there were only two appropriate machines, and both were in constant demand. We could book the VTR for three nights only, and the big question was which three. Days in advance, it fell to me to make the gamble. I knew that vixens are on heat for only three or four days each year, and that they might mate on only one of these. So, from the months of abstinence I had to pluck the days of sexual receptivity. If I guessed wrong there would be a lynching, I chose the 22nd to the 24th January.

On the screen, Niff's mate trotted into view, glowing an eerie green. He was gripped by restlessness. With determined gait he moved across the tennis court, our hidden microphones picking up his footfalls and the dull whirr of the servo unit on the tripod as it panned with him. He stopped, pawed the ground, then decisively turned on his heels and trotted back towards Niff, who was dozing under a tree. Three metres away from her he paused, stared, craned his neck towards her and sniffed audibly, before spinning off again to some urgent business elsewhere in

the enclosure. Again and again, at intervals of never more than three minutes, he returned to monitor Niff's slumbers. As soon as she awoke and began to move, he was beside her, dogging her footsteps wherever she went, and sprinkling urine on every object that he passed. And as he moved there was a remarkable thing about his demeanour—his brush, which was full and bushy and normally draped in a luxurious curve, now stuck out horizontally, ram-rod stiff. Occasionally, he would edge even closer to her and it seemed that at any instant he might mount her, but Niff whirled around, mouth agape, head twisted to one side, and snirked at him. So, bouncing tautly in her wake, he passed the night, and gave not so much as a glance at food.

All day the dog fox lay curled up, as close to Niff as she would permit. By nightfall he was overwrought, matching Niff's every movement, pace by pace. With brush flagged high and snout craning forward, he shadowed her to within a metre. When she paused, he tiptoed forward, raised a paw and placed it on her rump. There was no rebuke. He put more weight on the paw, began to rear up, and Niff wheeled in gekkering antagonism. For another hour he padded at her heels. She curled up to sleep. He stood near by.

Tiring, he scraped a small depression and turned several tight circles before curling up. But the infra-red light reflected in his eyes betrayed his piercing stare that never wavered from Niff. She moved on and paused. He followed, gingerly leant his chin on her rump, and was cuffed for his temerity. All the while, the VTR whirred around, making television history as it recorded, for the first time ever, broadcast quality, infra-red images.

Niff's mate only had eyes for her, but the other vixens were vibrant with excitement too. They seemed keen to attract the dog fox's attention, but were also drawn to Niff. One yearling vixen reared up and mounted her mother, embracing her in a lurching sexual clasp. Niff's ears flicked back and sideways in aggression as she struggled to free herself, but the younger vixen clung on. At last Niff swivelled around and reared up on her hind legs within the vixen's embrace, poking her away with stabs of her forepaws. The Rabelaisian mood spread, the young vixens snirked and gekkered as they made fumbling attempts to mount each other and even the dog fox. Then they turned their attention to a chicken carcass and fell into a three-cornered tug-o'-war.

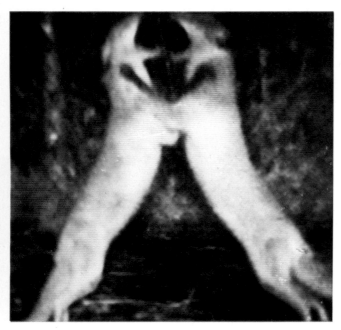

Infra-red picture of Niff's daughters observed by remote control.

Shivering in the darkness of the caravan we watched in rapt silence. This was indeed the night of the fox—the title we would eventually give to the film. The excited vixens had dragged the chicken beneath a sapling. In the greenish light of the infra-red picture the silvery leaves shimmered as the vixens rampaged beneath them, pulling the chicken carcass hither and thither: the harsh cackling sounds of their gekkering becoming a riot of noise in the brittle, frosty air. An owl hooted, and we heard it twice: once immediately outside the caravan, and a second time, more distantly, through the microphones in the tennis court. One vixen struggled in a tug-o'-war with her sister, while a third took advantage of their preoccupation and mounted the first. Tails lashed, jaws gaped, backs arched and flanks slammed into each other in a frenzy of excitement.

Suddenly a racket of wailing and whimpering broke out. Joysticks were pulled from side to side, the zoom button pulled full out, as we scanned for the source of the excitement. Then we saw it: a wild fox on the outside of the enclosure faced one of Niff's daughters through the wire. Niff dashed into view, barging the yearling aside. Niff was the matriarch and this

intruder was her business. A remarkable charade followed. The stranger was big, broad-headed, stocky. With its ears pressed backwards and jaws agape it sat, wailing at Niff. She replied in staccato bursts of clicketting calls, stabbing at it, through the wire with her forepaws. The shrieks reached a crescendo: inside the enclosure, foxes were dashing around Niff, but she barged them aside and maintained her place, face to face with the outsider. Niff's mate took no notice of the outsider, convincing us that it was a vixen. At last, it stood, tail held in an uncertain curve to the side, and slowly turned to melt away into the undergrowth. Again Niff's mate tried to mount her, his fourth serious attempt, and her equally serious rebuff, that night. It was 3.30am.

Two of Niff's daughters began to play, their antics full of sexual innuendo. And then their mood snapped, the play was gone, and the contest was in earnest. The two young vixens whirled and spun, each attempting to land a solid sideways barge on the other's flanks. Suddenly they were locked in stalemate, flanks pressed together, four feet splayed and shoving, heads turned away in perfect symmetry. We zoomed in, praying that the video tape would not run out as this extraordinary battle filled the frame, and the sounds of their gekkering rattled through the caravan. In the caravan, a cameraman was filming us as we taped the foxes, and recorded a cluster of rapt faces around the monitor, our jaws sagging in disbelief at the spectacle on the screen. The two vixens snapped apart and whirled at each other, rearing on their hind legs. Again they locked in stalemate, upright on tiptoe, forepaws resting on each other's shoulders, heads thrown back, mouths open to the sky. Broadside to the camera, they made the perfect picture, their ghostly green images glowing in perfectly matched rivalry.

Long seconds slipped by. The producer was in ecstasy, clasping my shoulder and whispering 'my dear boy', over and over again. The sound man's face was split with a grin from earphone to earphone, the tape engineer was groaning 'it's going to run out, it's going to run out'. Back and forth the vixens waltzed, a pace forward, a pace back, neither would yield. Then, ever so slowly, one vixen's stance dropped lower than her sister's, her head was thrown further back, her tail began to curl to the side, slowly like paper curling

Postures and expressions betray the likely outcome of this rather ritualized and intensively aggressive encounter between two vixens. They are almost equally matched, but at each stage the fox on the left faces away slightly more, gapes wider, crouches fractionally lower, and has her ears rotated further backwards. In the final picture, she is about to be pushed backwards, off balance, before being chased off.

near a flame. It was decided, but not over. She was pushed a pace back, and another and another, then she broke, springing backwards to disentangle and flee. The victor stood, looking a trifle surprised, and our tape ran out. A year later, those book-end boxing vixens were the high point of our film and led, I think, to its nomination for a British Academy of Film and Television Arts award as best documentary film of the year. Five years later the victorious vixen inherited the matriarchy from her mother.

Niff eventually mated around dawn that morning—shortly after the engineers had headed wearily for bed. This discreet timing ensured that the union was not recorded on film. Of the five adult vixens in the group during that winter of 1975–76, only Niff conceived. Indeed, the dog fox paid scant attention to the others. So we settled back for another summer to pass before the next chapter of the birth control story would unfold. However, when Niff's four cubs were born on 14th March 1976 a new story began.

Mother and infants became a focus of interest for at least two of the non-breeding vixens. Soon these barren vixens took to lying in the den with Niff and her nursing family. When the cubs were 14 days old, Niff injured her forepaw seriously while fighting with a wild fox through the fence. Infection set in and soon she was too sick to stand. Increasingly, other vixens lay with her and her cubs as she recovered until, on 7th April one 'babysitter' took over supervision of the cubs while Niff slept peacefully in a den at the far end of the tennis court. In the following days the swelling went out of Niff's paw and the crisis seemed to pass. The older sisters spent long periods with the cubs, grooming and nuzzling them. Niff began to take solid food to the cubs when they were 25 days old.

When the cubs were one month old, she had another fierce battle with a wild enemy. Two toes were ripped from her other forepaw, which was deeply gashed. Weakened by the strains of motherhood and incompletely recovered from the earlier injury, Niff's condition deteriorated fast. The following day she lay motionless and remained unmoving for 24 hours. For several days it seemed certain that she would die. She ceased nursing the cubs and for two weeks the barren vixens took over the care of their infant

siblings. They lay with them, groomed them, carried them, and even split them between two dens, half the cubs with one older sister, half with another. During these days the cubs grew apace and remained in peak condition despite Niff's complete incapacitation. The dog fox was feeding them and I suspected that the babysitters were doing so too. Although we saw them carry food to the den, we never actually saw them give it to the cubs. Nonetheless, by the time Niff had recovered and even begun to suckle the cubs again, we were convinced that the family's survival was due to their adoption by the elder sisters. It seemed to be a remarkable case of cooperation for such a reputedly anti-social creature and I could not ignore nagging doubts that it was an artefact of captivity. This doubt was dispelled five years later when, in Sweden, Torbjorn von Schantz published a fascinating observation of a wild subordinate vixen adopting and successfully rearing the orphaned cubs of the dominant in her group. However, adoption is a response to crisis, and we still lacked direct evidence of whether, under normal circumstances, the non-breeders played a useful role in fox society.

Meanwhile, the simple task of maintaining the enclosure proved most time-consuming. On one side of the fence, the foxes were busily digging escape routes, and this led to an unending search for heavy logs and boulders with which to block up their tunnels. Much worse, it dawned on us that on the other side of the fence attempts were being made to get in. The warning signs came when Jenny arrived one night to feed the foxes and found them dashing around the enclosure in panic. Over the weeks the evidence mounted: Niff was often too jumpy to go out on her experimental walks, so long-term trials were set back. Our carefully preserved barricade of thorns was worn down, and the long grass of the neighbouring meadow was marked with tell-tale depressions of human foot falls. There was no doubt—people were trespassing around the tennis court. So began a blemish on our lives that was to linger with varying severity for the next six years.

One day, in summer, we found a hole torn in the wire that linked the main fence to the inwardly cantilevered envelope of mesh which prevented the foxes scaling the walls. Clearly,

The dog fox trails behind the vixen, and suffers frequent rebuffs, until they mate during the 2–3 days of her receptivity. In common with other members of the dog family, mating foxes remain 'tied' for 30 minutes or more. The couple are firmly locked together (due to the arrangement of blood vessels and a bone, the bacculum, in the male's genitals). This may diminish the risk of another male mating with the vixen before the first one has fertilized her.

someone had climbed into the tennis court and had then been unable to get out without cutting an exit. Miraculously, no foxes had escaped— they had been so terrified by the intruder that they had remained in their hiding places and not investigated the new exit. In the days that followed it was obvious that children were climbing onto the top tension wire and balancing along the in-sloping flap, thereby bending it downwards and greatly weakening the structure. Catapult-sized stones and spent airgun pellets began to appear in the enclosure. Jenny devoted the next weekend to lying in wait.

In the late afternoon, a band of urchins arrived. Most escaped in the ensuing pursuit, but Jenny overtook one straggler, too youthful for the chase and deserted by his elder brother. This poor unfortunate turned out to be a pupil in Jenny's infant class, a situation that put him in a very weak position for negotiation. The immediate problem was cured, but only temporarily.

Aside from successive generations of rascals, we would find insensitive adults standing beside the enclosure, complaining that they could not see any foxes while their dogs barked in frenzy at the terrified inmates. Bank holidays were the worst times, and for many years Jenny would spend them sitting in the enclosure with a book, ready to repel intruders. Furthermore, humans were not the only problem: in the last days of December 1975 two dog foxes scrambled into the enclosure, only to find that they could not escape. Our attempts to evict them developed into something of a farce. Jenny and I strung out a net in the shape of a funnel and tried to drive the intruders into it. The plan was foiled as they fell to furious combat with Niff's mate who flew into the attack each time an intruder passed him. During these fur-flying flurries, however, the interlopers forgot themselves to the extent that we were at last able to corner them.

From Niff's litter of 1976 I kidnapped the

male, named Fox: he was to be hand-reared and become our first really tame dog fox. The experiment was in full swing, and by January 1977 the group contained Niff and her mate, three of their two-year-old daughters and one yearling daughter. On the 25th January 1977 Niff mated once more, and she alone of the five vixens bore cubs. That autumn, as before, I removed the adolescent males, leaving four vixens. In 1978, it was only Niff again who produced a litter. Although she was smaller than most of her daughters and, latterly, her teeth were worn and broken, Niff remained socially dominant to them all. In this respect the perfect parallels between Niff's behaviour in captivity and Toothypeg's behaviour in the wild lent validity to the observations in the enclosure and went some way to vindicating my approach.

Perhaps it was their social dominance that underlay Niff's and Toothypeg's prerogative of breeding. However, there were other possibilities. Was the restraint on breeding actually due to the dog fox or the younger vixens? After all, he was their father and an incest taboo might inhibit matings between them, since inbreeding can be damaging. Were the non-breeding vixens sexually attractive to other dog foxes, even if apparently not to the patriarch of their own group? Each explanation could have several variations, and to test them would be a long and painstaking task. Even then, conclusions based on the history of only one family would hardly constitute a convincing sample. The minimum starting point was two additional family groups, and a great deal of good luck. In terms of scientific productivity, the effort that would be required to establish and maintain these groups would make the venture hopelessly time-consuming. Nonetheless, I took the gamble and, in due course, two further captive groups were established, and manipulations of their memberships shed much light on the question of reproductive restraint. But before describing these other groups, I will finish the story of Niff's part in the experiment.

In 1978 I planned an experiment to remove Niff from the tennis court, after four successive years as breeding matriarch. My idea was to see whether the old dog fox mated with any or all of his daughters following Niff's removal. This should answer the question of whether he and/or

they were constrained to avoid inbreeding, or whether fox family planning was solely the product of the matriarch's dominance over her daughters. Sadly, lack of many facilities, time and forethought ruined the experiment. Niff's new enclosure was not completed until late December, so the breeding season was almost upon us when she was removed from the tennis court. Furthermore, her odour was in the vicinity and on our clothing when we visited the enclosure every day. The fact that no cubs were born that spring is, with hindsight, hard to interpret. In the future I would return to the question of incest taboos, but in the meantime I decided on another approach, hopefully one guaranteed to yield, at least, some results.

In May 1979, Niff's old mate was also removed from the tennis court, and replaced by Basil and Snipey, two young, tame dog foxes, unrelated to each other or to Niff's lineage. It worked like a dream: with Niff gone, only the

eldest, and most dominant of her two remaining daughters, barren for five years under her mother's domination, was seen to mate with only one of the males, Basil. Later, Basil provisioned her cubs while Snipey ignored them. A new family group developed: the breeding female and Basil, their son and daughter, and the unrelated Snipey. With this carefully formulated combination we awaited the spring of 1981. If only the dominant pair bred then the proposal that birth control was imposed through the matriarch's domination of her subordinates would be strengthened. Also, the inbreeding argument would be gravely weakened if Snipey did not at least attempt to mate with the young vixen. As a secondary experiment, either Basil or his younger son, or both, might court the yearling vixen if Snipey did not, exposing any possible difference between father–daughter and brother–sister

incest. Finally, the reactions of the three males, variously related as they would be, to any forthcoming offspring would shed light on aspects of paternal behaviour. Then, just as the breeding season approached, Snipey contracted a bacterial infection and died. Nonetheless, the survivors' courtship answered several questions. Only Basil and his dominant mate bred. Neither Basil nor his son showed any interest in the yearling vixen.

By late 1981, after an experiment that had taken almost eight years to run, Niff and her offspring have allowed us more than a glimpse of the genealogy of power within a fox family. Now, as heiress to the matriarchy, her eldest daughter held sway just as Niff had before. Explanation of the mechanism and consequences of this Machiavellian system would have to await developments in our studies.

7 | ON THE FOX'S SCENT

WAKING WITH A guilty start, I found myself slumped across a table in the Kruuks' sitting room, a stale cup of coffee mouldering beside me. I had crept in for a break at 3.30am, and unintentionally dozed off. Now, as if the pins and needles in my limbs were not retribution enough, I realized that I had wrecked the night's radio-tracking data, and missed the opportunity to be hidden at my observation post before the sun was up. Bleary eyed, I hurried towards Back Field, my irritation heightened as my trousers sucked cold dew from the barley heads like blotting paper. The sun was well up and Mottle Vixen and her crew had gone. Dejectedly, I jumped the ditch into High Gate Field and, wringing wet, stumped homeward.

I was within 40 metres of the dog fox when I spotted him. Luckily, he had his back to me. I slowly dropped to the ground, and began to crawl through the long grass to the cover of a patch of thistles. I could hear the snap and clatter of his teeth on the splintering wing cases of beetles. Not long after, the fox began to scratch at the ground, and wedging his nose into the resulting hole, snorted loudly. He seemed to be eating the soil. This odd meal swallowed, he wandered towards the High Gate, repeated the whole performance, and then trotted out of sight. I carefully marked the last spot where he had been digging. There, amidst a parting torn in the grass, a small divot had been raked up. Pressing my nose to the ground, the earth smelt foetid. In one small spot the soil was slimy. Probing with the blade of my penknife, I exhumed the decaying corpse of a long-dead earthworm. At once I thought of the fox droppings I had been collecting, and of my careless assumption that the soil which they often contained had been swallowed accidentally while digging up rodent burrows. I wondered if the soil could actually have been the remains of a meal of worms. Back in the laboratory, I selected a particularly earthy fox dropping from my oven-dried collection. Crumbling off a pinch of soil, I hurried to the microscope. Sure enough, shimmering through the lens were hundreds of miniature billhooks—the so-called chaetae with which earthworms gain traction on their burrows.

The foxes of Boar's Hill lived in larger groups, smaller territories, and therefore at greater population densities than those which other biologists had studied. This state of affairs, of course, prompted a whole string of questions, but a logical starting point was to ask why so many foxes lived there. Now, through one chance observation, I was sure that I had found the answer. Literally millions of worms must die annually in the topsoil of each fox's territory. With their sharp noses, the foxes could simply 'hoover' along, sniffing out a decaying bonanza of free food. Surely this was how Boar's Hill could support so many foxes. As it happens, I was right that worms were important in their diet, but wrong to conclude that they were taken as carrion. In the ensuing 12 years I have never seen another fox dig up a decayed earthworm, but I remain grateful to that one oddball fox for pointing me in the right direction. How, then, do foxes catch earthworms?

Earthworms, as every fisherman knows, crawl to the surface when the weather is right. On still, warm nights, in their quest for delights of the flesh and the occasional mouldy leaf, some slither unprotected through the jungle of grass; others, perhaps of lesser mettle or greater prudence, retain a toehold in the soil, with tails

Poised to catch an earthworm.

anchored and chaetae well dug in. On nights when the worms are up, foxes meander slowly but purposefully across the fields. They especially seek the dung-rich pastures where horses graze and worms abound. There, close-cropped grass affords easy access to succulent, crawling fare.

There is great precision in a fox's pursuit of worms. Each fur-padded footfall follows a measured pace. Long pauses punctuate the quest, while the fox, with head cocked and ears perked, struggles to listen over the din of rustling leaves. Suddenly, the fox freezes, brush poker-stiff, its ears flicking. Below its snout an amorous pair of worms have incautiously rasped their chaetae on the grass in a moment of hermaphrodite rapture. The fox's snout points like a laser at the noisy indiscretion, and plunges down into the grass.

Too late the unfortunate couple disentangle from their mucilaginous embrace, and one finds its head neatly clamped between the fox's incisors, its tail wedged 'safe' in the burrow. Skilfully, the fox avoids snapping its victim. Rather, it pauses, holding the worm momentarily taut before raising its muzzle in an arc, slowly at first but accelerating as the prey is drawn smoothly and intact from its sanctuary. Flinging itself into contortions, the earthworm winds around the fox's muzzle, but the captor, its jaws manoeuvring with the dexterity of an Italian's fork, deftly slips this animated spaghetti down the chute.

As many as eight earthworms per square metre may surface when conditions are ideal. With a daily requirement of about 600 calories, and with a worm being worth only 2.5 calories, a fox would need to eat 240 worms nightly to satisfy its energy requirements. But how many worms can a fox catch? I found the answer to vary widely from night to night, with a maximum of four worms per minute. Under ideal circumstances a fox might make its living in an hour of leisurely strolling. Having now analysed 2,799 fox droppings from Boar's Hill, it seems that some foxes do just that thing! Some droppings were solid soil, and most contained some traces of a meal of earthworm. On average, half the volume of each dropping was soil—soil from the guts of earthworms which had been alive, well, and busily digesting detritus when plucked from the surface by foxes. The consumption of earthworms not only varied seasonally (most in February, least in July) but also from territory to territory. In late winter, the average fox in Scar Nose's territory was eating about 150 worms each night, while neighbours in Sampson's territory ate only 25 or so (and made up the difference with more household scraps).

Many people are surprised that foxes eat earthworms, and ask if it is a dietary quirk of those on Boar's Hill. In fact, subsequent studies have shown that foxes eat common earthworms in other areas too. However, I once saw something which made me wonder if they have to learn the technique. One dark, moonless night I stalked across a favoured worming pasture with the hot-eye. After many minutes of silent footsteps, I reached a ridge, raised the binoculars to my eyes, and peered over. There I saw Toothypeg, standing not 30 metres from me, accompanied by her leggy cub.

It was the first night on which I had seen that cub away from its den. It had rained heavily that afternoon and the grass was still moist. The air was so still that even I could hear the rasping of worms on the move. The old vixen paced silently to and fro. Repeatedly, she quartered the same patch, pausing, pinpointing the grating of worm-bristles on grass, stabbing her nose into the sward. Thrashing wildly, worm after worm wrapped itself around her snout. Once, when she caught a worm, the cub ran to investigate her prize. In his gangling youthfulness he too had been trying to catch worms, leaping high into the air and thudding down on them with out-stretched forepaws. Pouncing with this characteristic 'mouse leap' may be ideal for pulverizing wood mice, but applying the method to these slippery delicacies left the cub biting fruitlessly at his feet as the worm slithered, unharmed under his toes.

The cub turned his attention to Toothypeg and within seconds she had caught another worm. This one had its tail firmly anchored. Instead of drawing her prize clear from its burrow, the old vixen held it taut until her frolicking offspring summoned the temerity to take hold of it gingerly. With an incompetent tug, he snapped the worm in two, and clacked his teeth noisily on the gritty morsel. Methodically, the vixen caught another, again held it taut, and let the cub take it, but once more he fumbled. But now she had his full attention. As she searched, he was at her side, his nose tracing the same course as hers. The next worm that she caught was so well lodged in its burrow that Toothypeg could barely grip it. Normally, she might have cut her losses, rewarding such annelid obstinacy with a body-snapping flick, but now she paused, holding the tip of the worm in her front teeth, while the cub excitedly sniffed her muzzle. Astonishingly, Toothypeg began to tap her captive gently with her forepaw. The worm heaved valiantly in this mortal tug-o'-war, pinioned and pulled by an adversary some 1,000-fold its weight. At first, only a paw's width of worm was free from the soil and it seemed that its injuries might be limited to the amputation of a few replaceable segments. But Toothypeg's hypnotic massage was irresistible; again and again, she gently brought her paw up to stroke at the straining sliver of life. Ten long seconds edged by. Caressed like a guitar string, the worm's crampon-hold on its burrow began to weaken. Bit by bit the vixen patted it free, until, vanquished, it was two-thirds drawn from the ground. She held it for the cub to snatch greedily. His appetite whetted, the cub redoubled his efforts to capture a worm of his own. But he was transformed: gone was the infantile bungling of the mouse leap. True, he still caught nothing, but in a few short minutes he had learnt the principle: inept maybe, but now he foraged with the adult technique.

Several days later, I saw Toothypeg and her cub again. Experience still weighed in the old vixen's favour; she caught four worms each minute, to her cub's one. But by the time our paths crossed again, a month later, he had

graduated with distinction, and was catching as proficiently as his mother.

The great abundance of worms (and lots of other food too—*see* Diet box 17, p. 118) was the obvious answer to why foxes were numerous on Boar's Hill (another part of the answer was their freedom there from persecution by man—*see* chapter 11). The profusion of food also seemed to explain why Boar's Hill foxes' territories were smaller than those reported elsewhere (*see* Box 16, p. 117). On further thought, though, this question became more interesting when rephrased: why were the territories not smaller still? There were two separate reasons for asking this question. First, even the smallest territory housed a huge population of worms (I estimated 350,000 worms in just one pasture in Roger's territory) of which the occupants probably ate

less than six per cent. The second puzzle was that up to six adult foxes were sharing each territory, and apparently the result of this cohabitation was that the majority of vixens were not breeding. Why not split into breeding pairs, each in proportionately smaller and conveniently compact territories? After all, the smaller the territory, the easier its defence, and all the better to know its nooks and crannies. With these thoughts, the question of what determines territory size became inseparably linked to the question of why do some foxes live in groups? In order to tackle this I determined to discover more about the foxes' food supply, using the earthworm as a case study.

After 20 months of trying to watch foxes hunting for worms, I ended up with 121 good observations, gathered on 92 separate nights. Three-quarters of these observations were in only

two of the ten fields in which I regularly took a census. Why were the foxes concentrating their efforts in this way? To tackle this question the first step was to assess the abundance of earthworms. It so happens that pouring water laced with formalin on the ground irritates the earthworms below and they crawl to the surface to be counted. Lugging six-gallon drums of this solution back and forth to all ten fields, I sampled the numbers of earthworms.

The variation between fields was immense. Each square metre of cereal field yielded as few as one worm, whereas 15 or more large succulent worms might crawl to the surface in the same area of permanent pasture. So, these prey were patchily distributed, and not surprisingly this patchiness was reflected in the foxes' movements. Furthermore, there was a patchwork of worm distribution even within fields. For example, within the most bountiful pasture, worm counts varied twofold from place to place. To test the hunch that this had something to do with the horses that grazed there, we set about mapping the location of each heap of horse dung. This tedious task took several days—time enough for our antics to be widely observed and generate considerable ridicule. But they paid off—the horses dunged only in certain areas of the field, and never grazed in those areas. Presumably the greater fertility of these latrines enriched the soil and explained the fact that these were the areas where worm numbers peaked. When we repeated this exercise with cattle it transpired that they, in contrast, ate and dunged throughout the field. So I found that the distribution of worms within a field, and therefore the behaviour of foxes hunting them, depended on whether a field was stocked with horses or cattle.

A huge population of worms underground would be small consolation to a fox above with an empty stomach. What matters to the fox is the number of worms that can be got at on the surface—and sometimes this was nil. This distinction is part of the answer to why territories were not smaller—the foxes could not rely solely on worms. Nonetheless, there were many nights when the ground seethed with them. How could a fox predict where and when to look? Hans Kruuk was battling with the same question since his study of badgers had shown that worms were their staple diet, too.

To answer this question Jenny, Hans and I tried our hands at worm-catching. Arming ourselves with torches swathed in red cellophane (red light being invisible to worms but, unfortunately, not to householders) we wandered the fields and gardens counting worms on the surface. These activities did not go entirely unnoticed. Not long after midnight, and having checked for fox and worm activity, I had just made my way over the wall of a theological college when I was blinded by the beams of headlights as cars screeched to a halt from both directions. Policemen jumped out: a telephone caller had alerted them to a malevolent intruder sneaking into the college, carrying a sawn-off shotgun and wearing an Irish Republican Army uniform (of which there is no such thing)! It was not long before I knew the squad car drivers well; they took the fox project to heart, and often brought me a thermos of coffee. I forget the exact tally, but I think it tops two dozen occasions that they have been called to investigate my suspicious behaviour.

Our worm counts soon confirmed that the greatest numbers surfaced on mild, still nights with high humidity. At the same time I noted the capture rates of foxes hunting for worms and found that it increased when rain had recently fallen, when the humidity was high, and when it was mild. Furthermore, the length of grass affected the humidity of air at worm-level, so in the long grass of those horse-dunging areas many more worms surfaced than on the neighbouring grazed patches. On the other hand, capture rates plummeted when there was a cold wind. I remember an exception which proved this rule: late in the summer there had been no rain, and the ground was so parched that most worms were inactive, deep in their burrows and so I was surprised to see foxes catching worms at a good rate in certain gardens. The paradox was resolved when I quizzed the householders: the foxes had sought out those lawns on which sprinklers had been showering water all the previous day!

The importance of these intricacies in the fox's behaviour as a predator upon earthworms is that they illustrate a general point: namely, the fox's prey is often patchy and unpredictable in availability. This applies to almost all the food which the Boar's Hill foxes ate: worms, beetles, mice, rabbits, birds, blackberries, apples and scraps from bird-tables and compost heaps (*see*

16. HOW BIG ARE FOXES' TERRITORIES?

(1 hectare (ha) = 2.4 acres; 100ha = 1sq km; 259ha = 1sq mile).

Some foxes become resident in a particular area and establish a stable home range there, others are itinerant and of no fixed abode. The sizes of these residential home ranges vary between neighbours and areas. For example, on Boar's Hill, in a mixture of large gardens and farmland, home ranges average about 40ha , but vary between 10 and 70ha. On nearby mixed farmland most are between 100 and 250ha, while in Wytham Woods they average 60ha, but vary between 20 and 100. Between these three habitats lies Oxford City, where the situation is rather different because foxes' home ranges are less stable there. Over many months I found them to average at about 90ha, but during any given month they used only 40ha.

All these range sizes are rather small—a Boar's Hill fox could probably run the width of its home range in less than a minute, and yet might spend several years within its confines. The situation is markedly different in the fells of Cumbria, where home ranges average more than 1,000ha. Recently, Ian Lindsay and I analysed the movements of a single dog fox which occupied a fairly stable range in the deserts of Oman—its range spanned 5,000ha. So, the short answer to the question of how big are foxes' home ranges is that they vary greatly.

Over the last two decades, several biologists around the world have measured fox home ranges, and their findings give an interesting picture of variation. In the rich farmland of West Wales, Gwyn Lloyd has found ranges averaging 30 to 50ha, whereas in the uplands of mid-Wales they average 400ha. In farmland in southern England, Jonathan Reynolds tracked foxes occupying 270 to 310ha, while in a more wooded area in the Netherlands, Freik Niewold described range sizes of 150 to 250ha (in Dutch heathland they averaged 880ha). In southern Sweden, Torbjorn von Schantz has found foxes travelling 400ha ranges, while in the Swedish Taiga, Erik Lindström measured ranges which averaged about 650ha (250–1150ha). In France, in the lowland farmland around Nancy, Marc Artois found ranges averaging 350ha, whereas in the mountain meadows of Italy, Paolo Barrasso and I found ranges between 400 and 1300ha. Urban fox ranges tend to be small: in

Bristol, Stephen Harris found that in semi-detached housing they measured 25 to 40ha (in council housing and industrial estates this increased to about 90ha).

The home ranges studied in North America tend to be larger than most recorded in Europe. In Iowa, Gerry Storm has found ranges of nearly 700ha and, subsequently, in Minnesota, ranges averaging 960ha. In Ontario, Dennis Voigt's foxes covered an average of 900ha, with individuals varying between 500 and 2,000ha. In the barren cereal plains of North Dakota, Alan Sargeant found foxes travelling 2,000ha, and in the Arctic they can reach 3,400ha.

Are fox home ranges territories? A territory is a special kind of home range, the simplest of several definitions being that they are defended as 'private property' from neighbours and intruders. Territoriality is a system whereby animals are spaced out. For the occupants, the advantage of owning a territory is that it secures their access to sufficient resources (generally food) that are in short supply. However, territories bring costs as well as benefits—they have to be defended. It seems that the home ranges of resident foxes are almost invariably territories, in that the movements of neighbours overlap less than might have been expected by chance. Indeed, they generally abut almost perfectly, with minimal overlap. Two or more foxes may share a territory, their movements overlapping to a greater or lesser extent with each other, but overlapping much less with those of neighbouring groups.

What determines the size of fox territories? Fundamentally, there are probably two crucial factors: first, the availability of food, and second, the costs of defence. Territory size will depend on the balance between these benefits and costs, and this balance will obviously vary with circumstances. Territories are expected to be of the minimum size necessary to satisfy the requirements of the occupants, because further enlargement would bring extra costs of defence without net benefits. So, all else being equal, territories can be smaller where food availability is greater. Also, all else being equal, defence costs are likely to increase with territory size and to be greater where foxes are abundant, because the territory-holder will be bombarded by more intruders. Therefore, where fox mortality is high, foxes may be able to afford to expand their territories, up to a size beyond which there is no further net advantage in doing so.

17. WHAT DO FOXES EAT?

Foxes are such opportunistic hunters and scavengers, and have such catholic tastes, that they will eat almost anything. The result is that their diet can vary greatly from one area to the next, and even between neighbouring territories.

There are several ways to discover what foxes eat. The obvious one is to watch them, but this is often insuperably difficult. A seemingly straightforward method is to look at uneaten prey remains around breeding earths. However, this approach is prone to many sources of bias. For example, small, perishable items are less likely to be found than large indigestible ones, and the remains of uneaten food are likely to give a distorted picture of what was eaten. Furthermore, it is likely that bigger prey are more likely to be carried back to the den.

A much more reliable method is to examine the stomach contents of foxes. However, this has the disadvantage that it necessitates the subject's death. A reasonably satisfactory alternative is to tease apart the undigested food remains found in fox droppings. This method also has its drawbacks (principally the difficulty of allowing for differential digestibility—a large lump of meat may leave no identifiable trace, whereas the indigestible carapace of even a small beetle is conspicuous). Nonetheless, faecal analysis can reveal a lot about fox diet. Viewed under a microscope, the patterns of scales on a single hair are sufficient to distinguish whether its former owner was a mouse or a vole (a cross section of the hair discloses which species of vole), as are the spicules of a tiny feather sufficient to trace the family of a bird. Seeds betray a meal of fruit (many fox droppings are a solid mass of blackberry pips), as do plastic, string and silver paper indicate a feast of scavenge. Soil laden with chaetae indicate a meal of earthworms, and an orange rubber ring reveals that the fox has eaten the discarded testicles of a lamb (these bands are used to castrate lambs). Furthermore, fox faeces tend to be laden with a telling assortment of teeth, claws, beaks and bones.

Sleuthing in this way I have analysed the contents of more than 10,000 fox droppings. The pie diagrams show the overall pattern of diets in four of the areas mentioned in this book (the pies are divided in proportion to the percentage of the volume of droppings made up of remains of each type of food). Summaries of this sort are only superficial portrayals of what any given fox actually ate (and they ignore seasonal patterns). However, they serve to illustrate that the diet in all four areas differed markedly.

There have been very many studies of fox diet (probably because it is one of the few things about foxes which is superficially straightforward to study). In some areas rodents predominate in the diet, in others birds are the mainstay, and in others carrion. In Oxfordshire, earthworms and scavenged human scraps (depicted by a bird table below) were high on the menu of urban and rural foxes alike (both were uncommon in Cumbria). Domestic stock is depicted by a chicken symbol below. Foxes everywhere seem to take mammals (especially voles, lemmings, mice and rabbits) wherever the opportunity arises, and fruit is a universal favourite, whether it be blackberries, bilberries, rose hips, apples, plums or grapes.

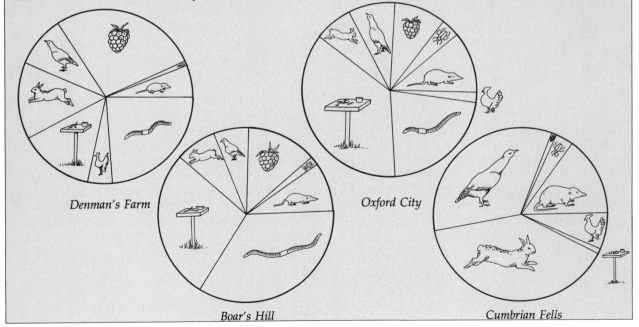

Denman's Farm

Oxford City

Boar's Hill

Cumbrian Fells

Niff picking blackberries during a leash-walk.

Box 20, p. 140). None of these was found uniformly scattered throughout each territory, either from place to place, or from time to time. Such a diversity of foods, each differing in the pattern of its availability, has forced the fox to become a professional opportunist. As predators they are Jacks of all trades (and seemingly masters of most of them too!). The immediate consequence of this lifestyle is that nightly the fox faces conundrums such as what to hunt and how long to hunt it for (*see* Box 17, p. 118). No wonder they have become obsessive hoarders in order to capitalize on any unexpected surplus.

There are also longer-term consequences of not knowing exactly where or when the next meal will come from, and therein may lie part of the answer to why foxes sometimes live in groups (*see* Box 20, p. 140). I think this patchiness of the food supply may also provide a second

answer to why the fox territories on Boar's Hill are not smaller: perhaps the answer lies in the foxes having to gamble on the whereabouts of food which may move around from season to season (e.g. baby rabbits in spring may be in different places to windfall apples in autumn) or night to night (e.g. scraps of a roast joint may be in one garden on Monday and another on Tuesday) or even hour to hour (e.g. worms may surface or retreat at each shift in wind direction). To accommodate such uncertainties, the architecture of territories must anticipate such shifts and keep sufficient options open to cater for the worst conditions. Unless the foxes were to risk going hungry, territories could not contract below the size which afforded an adequate guarantee of encompassing a good patch every night. For foxes on Boar's Hill, the richest foraging patches were the large gardens of detached houses with

overgrown orchards. Each fox territory contained an intriguingly similar number of such households—the average was 23, which occupied about ten hectares of residential habitat in each territory. Therefore, where people's residences were widely spread out, the territories were larger (up to 72 hectares), but where they were packed close, the territories were small (less than 20 hectares). Although each of these territories supported four to six adult foxes, I suspect that the reason they were not smaller was that they could not get any smaller (while retaining a realistically defendable shape) and still guarantee sufficient food for even a single pair.

With a patchwork of richer and poorer hunting grounds in each fox group's territory, an obvious question arises: do all members of the group have equal access to the richest pickings?

To judge by members of the dog fox Roger's group the answer was no. In their territory (in the interstices between several extremely well-provisioned gardens) lay Sands Field—a paddock rich in earthworms. There, in late July 1974, I first met Snowflake Vixen, a dark-featured cub with a preposterously large white tag at the end of her bushy brush. She was about four months old then, and was foraging for worms in the southern section of Sands Field. Snowflake was One-Five Vixen's daughter and, almost certainly, younger sister to Joyce and Whitetip Vixens. At less than 20 hectares theirs was the smallest group territory I knew of at that time, which made it all the more surprising to discover that Snowflake frequently spent entire nights in an area smaller than a football pitch. As a sub-adult she scarcely strayed from Sands Field and when

she did so, it was generally for a brief excursion to a near-by garden to scoff windfall apples. By early November, Snowflake Vixen was the only cub of the year remaining in the group's territory.

It so happened that during November and December of that winter, the weather was ideal for a high availability of earthworms. Night after night I watched her skirting a horse-dunging patch little bigger than a room. When I totted up the scores, I had seen Snowflake, hunting for worms there over four times more than her elder sisters Whitetip and Joyce. Furthermore, One-Five Vixen and Roger hunted only rarely in Sands Field. Snowflake's tendency to steer clear of her elders doubtless reflected the fact that almost every night during those mid-winter months she was harassed and sometimes attacked by the older vixens in her group.

A typical example occurred four days before Christmas when I spotted her in the lee of the spinney in Sands Field. Interrupting her worming to stare downhill, into the wind, Snowflake suddenly spun around and dashed towards the hedgerow. At that moment I spotted Whitetip Vixen racing up the field. Snowflake gained the hedge an instant before Whitetip, and the two vixens crashed together into the vegetation, whence shrieks of submission erupted. Was Snowflake's taste for worms solely due to her being ousted from the main foraging areas in the territory? The possibility that only subordinate foxes ate such lowly fare could be dismissed since I had seen Roger and One-Five Vixen gorging on worms in gardens. The difference in status lay not solely in what they ate, but in where they ate it. The most dominant group members spent

18. WHY ARE FOXES CAT-LIKE?

There is much about foxes that reminds people of cats—their agile, floating leaps when at play; their low-creeping stealth, each hind-foot silently placed in exactly the spot carefully tested by the preceding forefoot; the twitch of the tail before the pounce; the compact, fur-cushioned paws with partly retractable claws, and the elegant touch-sensitive whiskers on muzzle and wrist; and the vertical slit of the pupils (unique amonst canids). These features are so strongly reminiscent of cats that it is common to hear people state that foxes are mid-way between cats and dogs. In terms of their ancestry, this assertion is wrong. Foxes are full members of the dog family (*see* Box 1, p.10). However, dogs and cats started their evolutionary careers with the same raw material because, about 40 million years ago, both families descended from a common (and rather cat-like) ancestor—the Miacidae. Why, then, are foxes so much more cat-like than other members of the dog family? The answer is convergence, an evolutionary process whose principle is echoed in the idiom 'There is only one way to do a thing, and that is the right way'. Convergent evolution occurs when two unrelated species develop similar characteristics because both adapt to the same tasks. In the case of foxes and small cats, the task is catching rodents.

The most refined element of the fox's rodent-catching arsenal is the 'mouse-leap'. First, the fox pin-points the sounds of its hidden victim (foxes can locate sounds to within 1 degree, and their hearing is especially acute at the low frequencies at which rodents rustle in the vegetation—3.5KHz). Then it springs, sailing high above the quarry, beating its tail to steer in mid-air, before plummeting down to land up to five metres away, and smack on target. In a marvellous analysis, entitled 'The fox as a guided missile', Canadian biologist David Henry has shown three ways in which the fox and its behaviour are designed to refine the mouse-leap. First, they take-off at an average angle of 40°, close to the theoretical optimum of 45° for maximum distance (they aim lower for short jumps, and much higher, 80°, if they need to land with extra force to break through a crust of snow). Second, relative to their other dimensions, foxes have longer hind legs than other members of the dog family, which allows them to increase the time (and therefore the propulsive force) for which they thrust upwards. Third, they are much lighter weight than other dogs of the same size (domestic dogs or small female coyotes of fox length are twice the weight). This streamlining involves losing weight from the stomach (wolves regularly eat 20 per cent of their body weight, a fox can scarcely squeeze 10 per cent of its body weight into its small stomach), and from the skeleton. Not only are foxes' leg bones disproportionately slender, they also weigh 30 per cent less per unit area of bone than expected for a fox-sized canid. The mouse-leap is the very essence of foxiness, showing that although they are jacks of all trades, they are masters of mousing.

Rodents may be the fox's speciality, but they can

also be its burden. In northern latitudes, voles and lemmings are the mainstay of fox diet, but the populations of these prey undergo violent periodic fluctuations. The result is that foxes that depend upon these prey find themselves tossed mercilessly on the waves of the vole cycle: one year a fox's territory may be swarming with voles, the next year they may be scarce. To survive, the fox must squeeze through this bottleneck in food availability. The result is that many aspects of their reproduction and, with a lag of one year, the changing number of foxes reflect the numbers of voles.

The existence of regular cycles in the numbers of foxes at high latitudes was first documented in 1942 by Oxford zoologist, Charles Elton. In the fur trading records of the Hudson Bay Company, he found that the fox-trappers' harvest showed two periodicities: (i) a four-year cycle north of the tree-line, and (ii) a nine or ten year cycle south of the timber-line. The cycles were dramatic. For example, only 12 fox pelts were traded at the outpost of Fort Providence in 1921, whereas the number was closer to 1,200 in 1925, only to fall to another trough in the early 1930s. Where foxes have no alternative prey, a crash in rodent numbers forces an unpromising choice: to migrate or to starve. Under these circumstances, the evidence is that fox populations are highly mobile (which must revolutionize their social lives). Mass migrations are recorded. For instance, trappers' records showed, in the autumn of 1942, that foxes were abundant at York Factory trading station, but 550km inland at Island

Lake they were scarce. When the lake froze and foxes could move, they disappeared from York Factory and became abundant at Island Lake. A consequence of the northern four-year cycle and southern nine-year one is that, in one region, fox populations may be high, and food declining while in a neighbouring region populations are low, and food increasing. Migration from the crashing population may explain why, in such years, trappers record an influx of atypical furs.

In northern Scandinavia, vole populations undergo three to four year cycles. There, Jan Englund found that as vole numbers increased so, one year later, did the sizes of fox litters, the proportion of vixens bearing litters, and the proportion of young foxes in the population—all these are indications that the voles directly dictated the foxes' breeding (and therefore limited, directly, the foxes' numbers—*see* Box 15, p.93). Further south, where voles also cycled but where alternative prey were also available to buffer the foxes from these fluctuations, Erik Lindström found that fox territories remained the same size throughout the vole cycle, but fox group sizes tracked vole numbers. A pair of foxes occupied each territory alone during vole troughs (and their litter sizes were correlated with vole abundance). When voles were abundant, some of the breeding pairs' daughters remained as adult group members, but generally these females did not breed. So, the breeding female's reproduction was limited by the voles, whereas that of the additional females (who owed their existence to the voles) was limited by their social status.

much more time in those parts of the territory where several options were open—in gardens where scraps, fruit and worms were all abundant. By comparison, although Sands Field could be bountiful, foxes foraging for worms there had all their eggs in one rather flimsy basket.

Snowflake's encounters with her elders emphasized the importance of scent in fox family life. A typical occasion was the night in November when I was in Sands Field watching Snowflake as she harvested worms. Suddenly she looked up, startled, and crouched flat to the ground. About 40 metres to the south I spotted Joyce standing stiffly, sniffing towards the immature vixen. The wind favoured Snowflake and Joyce looked uneasy. A fox finding itself upwind during such an interaction must be in a similar predicament to somebody conducting an argument with the sun in his eyes. Joyce advanced, her brush in an uneasy curl; she seemed uncertain whether to press her advantage directly, or to circle in order to cross the wind. Snowflake pressed flatter and flatter to the ground, her ears plastered back, her mouth gaping but silent. As if clinging to the absurd hope that Joyce had not seen her, Snowflake shimmied along the ground to cower behind a nearby fencepost. Joyce advanced. When she was only five metres from Snowflake a whiff of the young vixen's scent visibly infused her with confidence. I could hear Joyce sniffing, and puffs of frosty air hovered around her nostrils in the infra-red light. She stood erect and walked stiffly past her cringing sister. One metre downwind of Snowflake, Joyce paused and stared at her. Without shifting her gaze, Joyce cocked her leg. She flaunted four more urinations in the space of 30 metres. Apparently, Joyce had made her point: the stiffness seeped from her limbs and her attention turned to searching for worms. Snowflake remained motionless, not even turning her head to look back at Joyce. Three minutes passed before Joyce abandoned her foraging and trotted off. Only then did Snowflake stand up and begin to forage again.

The association between social success and odorous ostentation is well known within wolf packs, and even a domestic dog will cock its leg with greater panache when a rival is watching. Deluded in the belief that I was the first to discover this phenomenon in foxes, I was suitably humbled to be pipped at the post by an illustration in the *Smithfield Decretals*, a collection of papal decrees now lodged in the British Museum. At least one 14th-century artist was well aware of the importance of scent as the medium of gossip among foxes. One such picture, dated 1340, probably illustrates a Latin poem called 'Ysengrimus' of 1150 in which the fox acts as a physician to his traditional enemy the wolf. In fact, when I went to Italy to study fox–wolf interactions I found that the reality behind this literary tradition is that given the chance wolves tend to kill foxes—another discovery in which I had been pre-empted by 800 years! To return to the picture. The wolf, distinguished from the fox only by its scrawny tail, sits below a tree and has just thrust a full urinal beneath the fox's nose. Clearly a meek character, the fox is visibly disarmed at this humiliating vulgarity; as its nose lingers over the scent, its long elegant ears are folded back in submission, and its lips appear drawn taut. These expressions could have been traced from Snowflake's face as she sniffed gingerly at the dominant vixen's scent. In contrast, everything about the wolf's expression is assertive. Doubtless, in an age when rural allegory touched people's first-hand experience, the artist could draw upon observations of foxes (and in those days, wolves too) to bring life to the fable.

Fox urine is clearly an important feature of the vulpine lifestyle. Expression of social superiority in face-to-face encounters may be one function of scent, but foxes scent mark in many other circumstances too. I became intrigued to know what secret messages were encoded in that acrid bouquet. It is common to catch the whiff of fox in the same places, day after day. Indeed, as an anecdote within a scientific paper published in 1965, Niko Tinbergen recounted the story of a discarded leather boot, found on the sands of Ravenglass, which was regularly annointed afresh with fox urine over three years. Sometimes a fox squats to urinate for half a minute or more, and one could believe that the purpose is purely excretory. On other occasions, though, I have seen foxes marking with urine at extraordinarily high frequencies. Indeed, it was not at all unusual to see foxes, of either sex, sprinkle a few drops of urine as often as once a minute, although others seem not to mark at all. When just

19. WHAT IS THE FOX'S SCENT?

Foxes can communicate with scent, can hunt by scent and can be hunted by scent. The smell which most people associate with foxes is their urine. Among many functions, urine marks may signal occupancy of a territory (the odorous equivalent of bird song). In Canada, David Henry discovered that foxes used urine marks as a form of 'book keeping'—they sprinkle urine on empty cache sites as a reminder to themselves not to waste time exploring these sites subsequently.

In addition to urine there are at least five other specific sources of fox odours. The most obvious is the tail gland, visible as an ellipse of dark guard hairs on the top surface of the tail, about 7cm from the root. Parting these guard hairs reveals a patch of glandular skin about 3cm long by 1cm wide, from which sprout sparse yellowish bristles smeared in sebum. It is often called the violet gland, since the fragrance is reminiscent of these flowers. In dog foxes the gland is more active during the breeding season, and its size certainly varies between individuals, but otherwise its function is unknown. However, foxes arch their tails, and lash them, during many social interactions and these actions probably expose the gland and waft the odour in the other fox's face (they probably expose the anal glands too—see below). The tail gland is very conspicuous as a blackish ellipse on the woolly grey fur of young cubs.

Also at the fox's rear end are the anal sacs. These are paired, bulb-like reservoirs which open through 2mm diameter ducts that are clearly visible on either side of the anus. Each sac has a capacity of 0.5cc and contains an acrid smelling, milky fluid. The sacs contain a rich flora of bacteria. Indeed the smell is produced by compounds which are the secondary products of bacterial fermentation of sweat-like secretions and sloughed skin. Droppings are another source of fox odours, and anal sac secretions are dripped onto some droppings but not others. They are also squirted out when foxes are frightened and during fights (including territorial disputes). Nobody knows what messages the sac odours convey, nor do they know the function of another set of glands in the skin around the chin and angle of the jaw.

Foxes also have scent glands in the pinkish skin between their toes and pads; these have a pleasant, sweet smell. While absolutely nothing is known about the role of this oily secretion, a bloodhound (and so presumably a fox) can follow it for about 20 minutes after a fox has passed. Indeed, if a 5kg scent-free weight is dragged across grass a bloodhound can follow its line after two hours due to the odour of the crushed vegetation. The persistence, and therefore value as a signpost, of the scent of wounded grass may be one reason why wolves, dogs, and a puzzlingly small minority of foxes scratch the ground with their hind feet after urine marking (another reason may be the visual 'arrowhead' of scratch marks pointing to the scent).

It is the scent of the foot glands that hounds follow and which prompted the famous Jorrocks' remark 'Constant only in its inconstancy! There's nothin' so queer as scent, 'cept a woman!' In fact the vagaries of scent are largely explained by the temperature differential between the ground and the air. Since hot air rises (and carries odours with it), so conditions are best for tracing a scent line when the temperature of the ground is higher than that of the adjoining air. By analogy, the earth breathes, and it is easier to smell its breath when it exhales than when it inhales. Therefore, huntsmen and, presumably, foxes find it easier to track their quarry in a fog but difficult when spiders webs on the ground are coated in hoar frost. Indeed, since night air temperatures are generally cooler than ground temperatures it must be easier to hunt and communicate by scent at night—as do many mammals.

The result of the different insulating properties of grass, woodland and open plough, together with the effects of shade and wind, must make each fox's territory an ever-shifting patchwork of contrasting scenting conditions. Although we are 'blind' to the shifting undulations of the olfactory landscape, they must be starkly apparent to foxes, so exposing a topic of which our ignorance is unblemished. For example, does a trespassing fox chart a route through poor scenting terrain? What underlies the huntsman's observation that pregnant vixens leave little scent? Certainly stories abound of foxes exploiting poor scenting conditions to evade hounds—rolling in mint, running through a field of livestock or through water or back on their tracks or along a fence top. Of course there are many possible explanations for such observations, but the possibility that foxes really are attempting to throw their pursuers off the scent is an intriguing one. However, the advantage cuts both ways—bank voles avoid places smelling of fox!

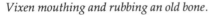
Vixen mouthing and rubbing an old bone.

Vixen urine marking dog fox.

a few drops were sprinkled, I called these token urinations, in the belief that they functioned as a sign or symbol. But a symbol of what? Once again, I relied on Niff's help to tackle this question.

Niff's first reaction to a scent mark was totally unexpected. She was ten weeks old then, and we were taking a walk around the meadow at Hamels. Suddenly, the cub began to shriek submissively, and dashing up to a tussock of grass, prostrated herself beside it, her tail lashing frantically, before rolling on her back and squirting little pulses of urine into the air. I guessed that her excitement had been caused by a wild fox's scent on the tussock. So, later, I took a few drops of fox urine from my supply in the deep freeze (collected from captive foxes or the bladders of fresh road casualties) and sprinkled it on a path. Then I walked Niff along the path and, sure enough, she fell into similarly rapturous writhings when she came upon the scent.

In the following weeks, as Niff cultivated more characteristic vulpine inscrutability, she grew out of submitting to scent marks. However, she continued to take the greatest care to sniff out tussocks of grass, molehills, tree stumps and other sites where foxes typically leave token urinations. When five months old, however, there was a dramatic change in her behaviour. Until then, the 9th August, she had always squatted to leave a large puddle of urine, and had done so, seemingly as the urge took her, irrespective of the site and without preliminary sniffing. From that day on, she began to token mark, seeking out visually conspicuous sites to anoint with a few drops of her personal perfume.

Did the pattern in which token marks were deployed hold some clues as to their function? From the outset, I mapped the locations of every one of Niff's marks. Indeed, I continued to do this with Niff and other hand-reared foxes for the next two years. Armed with a quiver of bamboo pea stakes I stuck one in the ground near each token site as I followed on Niff's heels. Each stick

Vixen depositing a token urination.

bore a reference number, and a strip of reflective tape, the latter being necessary because many of the walks were taken by night. Soon the countryside was sprouting hundreds of pea sticks and as their numbers multiplied, those on Boar's Hill who had entertained doubts about my sanity became convinced of the need for institutional care. At first, as the pattern of scent marks developed day by day, I was thrilled at the completeness of the data. Soon, however, it dawned on me that I had created an *enfant terrible*—a mass of data so prolific and so complex that the task of analysis became horrendous.

As winter advanced, Niff took to making upwards of 100 token urine marks during every walk. Over the winter, between November and March, Jenny and I documented 112 walks during which she established 615 marking sites, most of which were visited several times, and some of which were visited on almost every walk. Biologists tend to pay automatic, but perhaps rather glib, lip service to the importance

of odours to wild mammals. Certainly, everybody believes that foxes have an acute sense of smell. But now my appreciation of just how great a role scent played in foxes' lives was revolutionized as I pored over the case histories of 1,283 token urinations!

Once autographed with her scent, a tussock of vegetation took on magnetic quality for the vixen. So much so that after only 18 walks from the day she left her first token, she had already anointed half of the sites that she would mark during the rest of the year. On our walks, Niff would race from odorous signpost to signpost with the unflagging enthusiasm of an addict seeking the next instalment of a soap-opera. Wild foxes also travelled and marked through Niff's range. Sadly, excluded from their correspondence, I watched her quiver as she read these messages.

Out of these token marks patterns emerged both in time and space. The numbers of Niff's token marks peaked just before she came on

Foxes, like most mammals, are haloed in social perfumes. Dominant adults sprinkle their urine as odorous tokens on mounds and molehills along their trails (bottom), and most fox droppings are found atop visual promontories (and sometimes daubed with the secretions of anal sacs, mid-left). During many social interactions foxes wave their tails, doubtless wafting the odours of their tail gland towards their adversary (mid-right). Prey (and foetid material) may collect urine marks and droppings, and may be rolled on, but it is also often rubbed with the cheek and neck (top right), Vixens frequently chew and salivate upon vegetation which they 'mouth' especially during the period before mating (top left).

heat, then dropped during only six walks from eighty to two tokens per walk on the day she mated. There was also a distinct change in their pungency—in the mating season the odour was much stronger than it was by the time her cubs were born. During December and January, the peak token marking months, other perfumes were added to the marking sites. With obvious excitement Niff would slide her muzzle and cheeks along the upright stalks of saplings and shrubs. At its peak this rubbing behaviour was interspersed with 'mouthing' when she slid the stalks through the angles of her jaw, leaving a visible smear of saliva. Sometimes these bursts of marking became almost frenzied as she urinated, rubbed and mouthed again and again on a site, seemingly locked in a compulsive vortex of marking, unable to drag herself away from the ever more potent aroma. The record was eight returns to re-mark a site within a few minutes.

Niff's tokens were deposited, almost invariably, on visually conspicuous sites, as were her droppings. The marks were not restricted to the border of her range, but, rather, were scattered wherever she travelled. Therefore, they accumulated at the greatest densities in those places which she visited most frequently. Since she generally walked around fields, rather than across them, this resulted in concentrations of marks studded in a ring around the field edge, like an olfactory fence. The majority of her marks were alongside fox paths, and when she was travelling off a trail, across country, she marked only three per cent as often as she did on paths. This dramatic concentration of tokens on well-trodden paths was presumably the best way to ensure that her messages got to their intended readership.

Perhaps the most intriguing aspect of Niff's marking pattern was that she marked only in some areas. It was as if she had a mental map that charted the borders of a 'marking range' within which she sprayed copious billets-doux, but outside of which nothing would induce her to mark. The edge of her marking range was most clearly defined at the gate between Keble's and Lotty's Fields. There, Niff would token mark along the Keble's Field side of the border hedgerow, and even in the gateway itself, but never on the Lotty's Field side, even though she would walk through Lotty's and beyond.

As time went on, I noticed that Niff sometimes terminated the outward leg of her walk by a marked change in direction. I always noted these 'turning points' and soon realized that the gate between Keble's and Lotty's Fields was an important one. Her behaviour raised two related questions: how was Niff's reaction to a scent mark affected by its whereabouts, and how did Niff's whereabouts affect her reaction to a scent mark? To answer these questions I sprung a game of olfactory musical chairs on Niff—I dug up and moved her favourite marking sites! This was easier to do than one might think, because these sites were often isolated and clearly defined. For example, there was the place where Niff had swung off the path night after night to token mark a tussock of grass which grew amidst the leaf litter in Dixieland Wood. On the 24th November, I carefully excised this tussock and, without handling it or otherwise contaminating it with scents, carried it to a new site some 50 metres further down Niff's woodland trail. There, in a flat and featureless stretch of the woodland floor, I planted the tussock. At both old and new sites I did everything I could to disguise my gardening, scattering leaf litter over the scarred soil.

That night, Niff's walk began conventionally, and she had left several dozen tokens before arriving at the place from which I had pilfered her marking site. As if on automatic pilot, she swung off the main path to the spot, three metres to the side, where she customarily marked. There is no doubt that she was taken aback. She looked around, cast from side to side with her nose, and then, with the vulpine equivalent of a shrug of her shoulders, continued on her way. She was loping down the path when she passed the transplanted tussock. Two or three strides later she caught the scent and drew to an abrupt halt and back-tracked cautiously. Doubtless it was my imagination running riot, but her expression seemed to say 'Oh no! Not another experiment!' Of one thing there is no doubt: she doused the transplanted tussock in urine, and emphasized her point with a carefully positioned dropping.

Exactly the same things happened when I repeated this experiment at a similar site. So, for the next 57 walks I shifted these two tussocks to and fro. On 35 of these walks the mobile sites were within Niff's marking range, whereas on the remaining 22 trials they were in Lotty's Field and therefore outside her marking range. The results were gratifyingly consistent: within her marking range, she invariably left tokens aloft the transplanted sites (but only rarely on the visually featureless leaf-litter at the place from which they had been transplanted), whereas outside her marking range she never marked them. On the first occasion when she encountered a transplanted tussock in Lotty's Field she had elected to walk there without coaxing. She scented the tussock from about two metres away, and dashed forward in a frenzy of sniffing. Her nose 'hoovered' the ground for an explanation of this astonishing state of affairs. After prolonged sniffing she moved on, completing a circuit of Lotty's. I left the tussock there for 15 walks and, although she sniffed it regularly, she never marked it. When I moved it back to its original site, which had not been marked for 16 walks, Niff found it, sniffed at it for almost half a minute, and token marked it repeatedly. Before the next walk I moved it back to the same place in Lotty's. It remained there for the next six weeks, often sniffed but never marked.

Niff seemed to remember many of the places where she had, or had not, left token marks, but could she distinguish her own marks from those of other foxes? I began to create artificial scent marks, using the urine of other foxes. I made these marks within and without Niff's marking range. Those inside were sniffed briefly, and marked in much the same way as she re-marked her own sites. Indeed, by applying a stranger's urine to a log, molehill or clump of grass that Niff had not previously marked, I could cause her to adopt it as a regular token site. However, her response was different when I sprinkled a strange vixen's urine in Lotty's Field: she sniffed cautiously, wheeled around and, at a fast trot, retreated back to Keble's. On the next day I placed the foreign vixen's urine in a different site, and again, with brush curled anxiously, Niff retreated from it. Thus, while her own transplanted tokens aroused her interest, they did not seem to affect her route, whereas the smell of another vixen's urine caused her to hurry home. Obviously, by responding differently to these odours, Niff demonstrated that she could distinguish between the odours of her own urine and that of others.

Investigating experimental scent stake . . .

Conducting experiments of this sort in the countryside has the advantage of a natural setting but, in comparison to the laboratory, it also involves a greater number of complications. For example, I do not know the effect of wild fox scents on Niff's behaviour, although it may have been more than coincidence that part of her marking border coincided with the territorial borders of two wild fox groups. Despite the obvious difficulties of interpretation, Niff's behaviour generated plenty of ideas to explore with wild foxes. For example, did the self-inflicted border to her token range indicate that urine marking by resident foxes is a behaviour confined to their own territories? On the few occasions when I saw foxes trespassing in Boar's Hill territories they did not token mark. However, it was during my fieldwork in Israel that I made the observations most relevant to this question. On the 27th December I spotted Thin Vixen as she approached the feeding site at Ein Gedi. The male, Big Dog, was already eating there, and

. . . and removing the experiment.

these two members of the Ein Gedi group greeted briefly. Thin circled the feeding site and trotted off to the south, leaving a token mark on a prominent pebble just 'her side' of the border track, before continuing on for a sortie of 250 metres into the Masada territory. As she jogged along she swerved frequently to left and right to sniff shrubs and boulders. These were typical token marking sites and, indeed, I had seen some of them marked by Masada foxes, but Thin merely sniffed them. She spent just over six minutes trespassing, during which time she marked not at all. However, as soon as she crossed the border back on to home ground, she paused to leave a token mark on a large stone. During the next minute, she left three more tokens in her own territory. A few moments later I caught sight of Big Tag, a vixen from the Masada group. She was in view for about a minute and a half, travelling through her group's territory, during which time she token marked three times. However, during the numerous

occasions when Big Tag, or other members of the Masada group, made incursions into Ein Gedi territory to raid the feeding site, they never once urine marked.

The fact remains that we have few good answers to the key question—what messages do scents communicate between foxes? Myself and others have seen quite a lot of scent marking, and biochemists can even name some of the compounds that make up a foxy smell. These chemicals are the alphabet in which the language of smell is written, and the pattern of scent marking I have described shows something of the text, but we lack a dictionary to make a translation. Lamenting the noselessness of man, Kenneth Grahame in *Wind in the Willows*, called scents 'fairy calls from the void', for which 'we have only the word smell, to include the whole range of delicate thrills which murmur in the nose of the animal night and day, summoning, warning, inciting and repelling'. Until we can decipher these messages we can scarcely claim to understand fox society.

8 | FOX FAMILY PLANNING

JENNY AND I had a somewhat unusual honeymoon, not least because a clutch of weanling fox cubs demanded that it be limited to only 48 hours. After the wedding we set out for a far from exotic destination: Winersh, a village in Cambridgeshire. The next day we were to meet Mr Spring, a gamekeeper who, for more than a year, had kindly been sending me parcels containing the anal glands of foxes killed on his beat. His letters were a mine of fox-lore, and now we were to meet their author. Springy, as everybody, including his wife, called him, was a countryman of the old school. His paradoxical admiration, almost affection, for foxes was characteristic of many who spend a lifetime trying to kill them. As he led Jenny and me through his beats, the history of each spinney gave it a character as distinct as that of a nation. There was the place where, early one morning, Springy had spotted a fox meandering towards him. The fox, preoccupied with its cares, had not seen the wiry gamekeeper slip into the ditch beside the path. Indeed, as it trotted by, it did not see him until the instant after he had grabbed it with his bare hands! As each softly spoken reminiscence reached its climax, mild profanities crept into the narrative, but each was promptly neutralized by a doff of the cap to Jenny and a quickly interjected 'Begging your pardon, Ma'am!'

With questions piling up about birth control in Niff's group I had laid plans to establish further captive groups. Mr Spring had telephoned on Easter Monday 1975 to say he had an orphaned litter of eight newborn cubs—the very same cubs that were responsible for curtailing our honeymoon. Twenty-four hours after that telephone call Niff's old green box was once again at the foot of the bed, my eardrums reverberating to

an eightfold chorus of warblings. The cubs were four days old at most. Every two hours, day and night, they required feeding from an eye-dropper, followed by a thorough rear-end massage. The trouble was that it took us the better part of two hours to coax a filling of milk into the whole family. So, by the time that the last in line was finished, it was almost time to start again on the first! The odour of milk powder still lingers in the nostrils of my memory. The cubs' wrigglings and splutterings showered milk over all participants, and we could do no more than clean them superficially with a damp flannel, for fear that they might catch chills if bathed thoroughly. So, a congealed sludge of Lactol milk substitute permeated our clothes, the cubs' fur, and almost every crevice of the cottage. They were so small and frail that their chances seemed slim, and all the more so when one little male died almost at once. There was no question of leaving them alone for any length of time. So, when Jenny drove to visit her parents, she did so with a carful of cubs and the paraphernalia of motherhood: drapes, towels, brushes and Thermos flasks full of boiling water (to replenish their hot water bottles and to mix their milk *en route*). Every two hours throughout the journey, a lay-by had to be found in which startled motorists gawked while the milk-spattered family fed on Jenny's lap as she sat on the tailgate amidst a cacophony of warbling.

From the outset the cubs differed from one another. First, they looked different: three of the five vixens had varying numbers of white patches on some of their toes, and they also differed in the extents of the white tags on their chubby tails. The two little dog foxes were distinguished by their colour, and so came to be known as Red

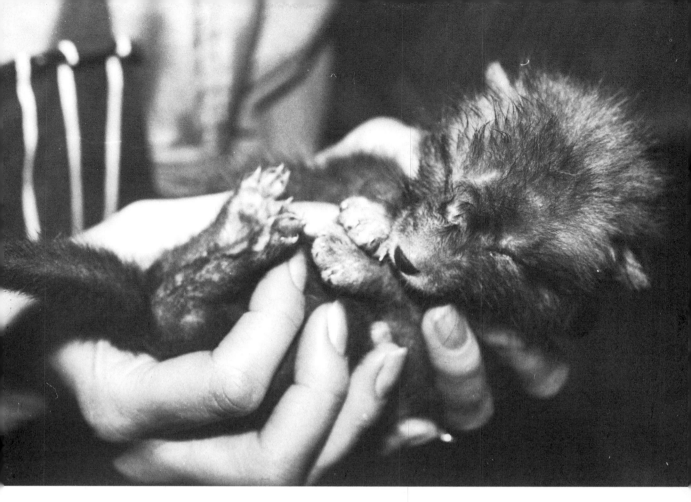

Dog and Grey Dog. Almost as soon as their eyes opened, it became clear that the cubs also differed in character. By far the most affable was the vixen Big Ears. She was the biggest vixen, limitlessly playful, and the most cooperative when it came to inserting the milk dropper into her mouth. By the standard of even the brightest puppy, she was a regular tear-away—a bundle of lightning reflexes; but by fox standards she had a lumbering good nature. Whitepaws, her sister, was quite the opposite, shunning play with humourless reserve. Sickly and Pseudo-sickly were like two peas in a pod: bland-faced cubs only distinguishable because Sickly always looked the closer to death's door and had a peculiar paralysis of the hips (from which she eventually recovered). Last of the vixens was poor Wide Eyes. From the outset she had a frenzied but futile friendliness for the other cubs. Squeaking and whimpering, Wide Eyes would stumble in infantile uncoordination towards her sisters. At best they greeted her with disdain; more often they locked their pin-prick teeth deeply in the soft skin of her tummy, and shook so hard that they threw themselves off their own wobbly legs.

The two male cubs died through my lack of foresight. In the absence of a mother's comforting nipples, the five sisters remorselessly sucked at their brothers' genitals, and rapidly induced infections that I was too late to halt.

I built a wire door across the stairs to confine the vixens to the hall and kitchen. They shredded the lino, and stripped off all the wallpaper to a height of two feet. They leapt up and bit the curtains, and then swung from them, gripped with self-inflicted vertigo and seemingly anxious not to lose face by letting go. They sat on the draining-board—five faces, jostling to peer out of the window. And, if anybody should approach the front door, there would be a fearful scrabbling of claws on stainless steel as all five leapt from the sink and dashed to hide behind the cooker where they became hopelessly wedged until we rescued them.

We quickly realized that many of the traits

we had once thought to be Niff's personal quirks were common to these cubs too. There was the destruction of anything made of leather, the wild-eyed determination to dig at loose corners of carpet, the desire to lick inside human ears, and the agonizing toe-killing game. The latter was particularly in evidence because the telephone was in the kitchen. If a night-time phone call lured one, barefoot and sleepily unwary, into the kitchen, five sets of jaws would close in, each selecting its particular toe. I'm sure the irresistible quality of toes is that they scuttle, mouse-like at ground level. With several jaws full of playful teeth, poised to crunch their 'prey', the imperative to keep still generally outweighed my enthusiasm to reach the telephone.

From the time they were only eight weeks old, and playing like kittens, I set about unravelling the cubs' relationships. Firstly, I noted who initiated play with whom and secondly, I documented the outcomes of their squabbles over food. Since the rumbustious family devoted almost every waking minute to either riotous play or squabbling, it was easy enough to make these observations. During May, I noted 225 occasions when one vixen cub launched a playful onslaught on another, and of these, Big Ears initiated over half. Next in line, with half as many playful attacks to her credit, came Pseudo-sickly, then Sickly, Whitepaws and, finally, Wide Eyes.

By this stage, life was really grim for Wide Eyes. The attacks on her by the others were so savage that she was constantly cut and bleeding. It was a daily struggle against infection to keep her alive. I have no doubt that the others would have killed her if we had not intervened, sometimes at great cost to our own fingers. They attacked Wide Eyes as they attacked a piece of meat, without inhibition in the force with which their teeth clenched on her skin. To say that she ranked lowest during play is not strictly accurate—she did not rank at all. Her position was like Groucho Marx's when, in *Memoirs of a Mangy Lover*, he described himself as underneath the bottom rung of the social ladder—a ladder which it would take her three years to scale.

When the vixens scrambled for access to a dead chicken, feathers flew around our kitchen. In this case it was Whitepaws who most frequently claimed the prize first. Indeed, she was five times more likely to get sole possession first

Fox Loo

than was Big Ears (the most confident vixen at play), but Whitepaws' ability to grab the chicken and stand over it warding off her sisters was not enough. While the other vixens snarled and spat over the chicken, Big Ears would unhurriedly shoulder her way to the top of the queue, and when she got there she was almost unassailable. So, if I changed the question and asked not who secured the chicken first, but rather who ate from it first, then the tables were turned: Pseudo-sickly, Sickly and Wide Eyes never ate first. Whitepaws and Big Ears had similar scores, with Whitepaws ahead by a whisker. Despite their roughly equal scores, these two vixens could hardly have been more different in their approaches: Big Ears was larger, more powerful, but tolerant. Tolerance was precisely what Whitepaws lacked and, for her, losing seemed to be unbearable; none of her attacks was anything less than furious. If another cub had the food then Whitepaws would attack again and again, relentlessly committed to winning at all costs.

This same difference in personality showed up in play: only once out of 116 play attacks that Big Ears launched did she fail to bluster through to a mock victory, amidst much frivolous pushing and shoving. In contrast, it seemed that Whitepaws took play far too seriously: almost half of the 21 playful attacks that she initiated floundered due to her lack of playfulness. Even in play, Whitepaws either lost her nerve or her temper, with the result that she ended up backing off with the ignominy of the spoil-sport.

While the cubs grew, we set to work on building a second enclosure at Hamels. This time there was no tennis court to modify, so it was necessary to start from scratch and sink the wire to a depth of a metre. John Gee lent me his JCB digger, and three days of excavation with this most satisfying piece of machinery completed the trenches. With the experience of the tennis court behind us, the work went swiftly, and when it came to wire twiddling we were helped by two volunteers, Nick Hough and Malcolm Newdick, who were subsequently to become founder members of the Oxford Foxlot, but more of that later.

During this hive of activity, the five vixens were living in another of the growing number of garden sheds we had adapted as temporary fox quarters. They had long since grown out of the need for feeds of milk, but this had been replaced by an even more time-consuming demand: we were trying to accustom all five of them to walking on a long leash, like Niff, and since they were such handfuls, each required a separate walk. Five adolescent foxes to walk or, more accurately, to run each day is no small feat, and Jenny did most of it.

As the vixens grew, their relationships stayed remarkably unchanged. By August, when they were just over four months old, their access to food showed a clear 'pecking order': Whitepaws, Big Ears, Pseudo-sickly, Sickly and Wide Eyes (with a 16-fold difference in the score of dominance between Whitepaws and Wide Eyes). It was time to set in train the next experiment. Not only was it necessary to confirm the observations made on Niff's group, I also wanted to shed further light on the mechanism of fox birth control. I selected Whitepaws, Big Ears and Wide Eyes as the three vixens whose relationships seemed to illustrate extremes, and introduced them to the new enclosure. Mean-

Digging a trench to sink the wire for the new enclosure.

while, Sickly and Pseudo-sickly, now in rude health despite their names, were selected—because of their similar status—to participate in an even more ambitious experiment scheduled to begin a year later (to which I shall return in Chapter 11).

In the autumn of 1976 Whitepaws, Big Ears and Wide Eyes were introduced to Smudge, Niff's hand-reared son, whom we had carefully groomed for this role in the new enclosure. By this match I hoped to test three propositions. First, if avoidance of incest were the only restriction on fox breeding then Smudge should mate with all three vixens since he was unrelated to any of them. Second, and alternatively, if the vixens' rungs on the social ladder determined which of them would breed, then Smudge should mate only with Whitepaws, the most dominant of the sisters. In this case my third proposition was that one or both of the non-breeding vixens would help rear the dominant's cubs. It had taken us two years of preparation to get to the starting point of this experiment so it was a black day indeed when, a fortnight later, vandals broke the padlocked door of the enclo-

sure and the whole group escaped. There followed a desolate evening of whistling but as hope was fading, Big Ears emerged from her hiding place. Further rattlings of the tin of chocolate drops and Whitepaws, Wide Eyes and Smudge appeared from the undergrowth. With great relief, and a large expenditure of chocolate drops, they were all bribed back to the enclosure.

Between the 6th and 25th January 1977, courtship was in the air. Until then Smudge's life had been cluttered by these vixens—they were forever throwing themselves, squirming, at his feet and, as often as not, tripping him up. Amongst the vixens, relationships were much the same as they had been almost since their eyes had opened. Wide Eyes still had to watch her step and was thoroughly subordinate to both Whitepaws and Big Ears. From day to day the latter two were amicable enough, save over food when Whitepaws exerted her dominance. All three vixens were copiously submissive to Smudge. But now things changed. Whitepaws became assertive in her dealings with Smudge, while Big Ears remained lavishly submissive to him. Smudge, for his part, became preoccupied with Whitepaws. He would be dozing quietly

when it would seem as if she flashed into his thoughts, and he would jump up and trot around the enclosure until he found her. Then, instead of the fawning welcome he might normally have expected, he was met with a sharp rebuff. In contrast, when on the 15th January Smudge trotted up to the spot where Big Ears and Wide Eyes were curled up together and sniffed amicably at them, the two sisters melted under his gaze. Both vixens immediately rolled on their backs, lashing tails, ears flat back, gaping submissively as they squirmed towards him, until Wide Eyes was nibbling at his teeth and Big Ears sniffing his scrotum.

A few days of harsh rebuffs were sufficient to engender a distinct caution in Smudge's flirtatiousness. No longer would he risk having his nose snapped at by thrusting it confidently at Whitepaws. Rather, he paused a metre from her, shifted his feet uneasily, and dropped his forelimbs to the ground while his haunches remained aloft and poised for a rapid retreat. From this solicitous, if undignified posture, Smudge stared at Whitepaws. Soon, however, her irascibility reached such a pitch that the mere sight of Smudge's pleading gaze was sufficient to provoke an attack. Yet, such was her capriciousness, that on other occasions she would spend many minutes delicately grooming his lips.

By 23rd January Smudge was following Whitepaws' every move as assiduously as his father had trailed Niff two years before. Four times that day I saw Whitepaws deliberately walk in front of him and sprinkle a few drops of urine for his delectation. When Whitepaws snoozed in a den, Smudge sat above, waiting tense and alert for hour after hour until she emerged. Relationships between Whitepaws and her sisters became very frayed. Whitepaws launched savage and unprovoked attacks on Wide Eyes, and both Wide Eyes and Big Ears skulked near by, seeking opportunities to fling themselves at Smudge's feet. His response was simply to step over their prone bodies and continue to prowl along behind Whitepaws. On the 25th January (one year to the day after his own conception) Smudge mated with Whitepaws.

Almost at once the mood returned to a more tolerant stability. Whitepaws was no longer aggressive to Smudge, and he reverted to ignoring all three vixens except when he wanted to play.

Soliciting play was a frustrating business for Smudge, since the vixens were paralysed with submission as he bounced around them. The vixen of his choice would roll on the ground, squirming and squealing in deference as Smudge darted back and forth. Sometimes he would launch 'mouse leaps' on his reluctant playmate—soaring into the air to land with a painful thud on her ribs. On other occasions he tried to drag them to their feet. This involved grasping the prostrate vixen by the neck and heaving her head off the ground. The result could look murderous, as the vixen was dragged back and forth by the throat. Amongst the vixens there was a great deal of amicable mutual grooming. Each vixen initiated grooming with each of the others, but Whitepaws did so the most often. However, the fact that a vixen groomed another did not necessarily mean that it was she who had initiated the event. Indeed, it was more often the case that the other vixens sought Whitepaws' attention. For example, on 15th February, Big Ears spent a full ten minutes pushing her head beneath Whitepaws' nose, in a clear attempt to solicit grooming. When

Whitepaws responded, Big Ears shut her eyes and sat in a trance while her sister groomed her. When Whitepaws paused in this coiffure, Big Ears nudged her until she started again.

During her pregnancy, Whitepaws was tolerably amicable towards both Big Ears and Wide Eyes. For example, on 27th February the vixens were dozing in the winter sunshine. Whitepaws lay beside Big Ears and meticulously groomed her head and ears until the two vixens fell asleep with Whitepaws' forelegs wrapped around Big Ears' neck, and their heads resting on each others' flanks. When Whitepaws awoke she sought out Wide Eyes' sleeping place and woke her by pawing at her head, whereupon she groomed her thoroughly. At one stage in this process, Whitepaws moved about a metre away, token marked, then returned to Wide Eyes, who gave a shudder of submission, and then stretched out while Whitepaws continued to groom her. The very next day, Wide Eyes crept submissively towards Whitepaws, and on this occasion it was the subordinate vixen's turn to thoroughly groom her sister's head and neck,

Penalties of motherhood—sores around the teats caused by over exuberant cubs.

while Whitepaws stood transfixed and ecstatic, her eyes closed and ears held slightly back. Then Big Ears arrived and began to groom Wide Eyes, who in turn closed her eyes and quivered until Whitepaws nudged her into the grooming again. What little aggression there was during Whitepaws' pregnancy was largely directed at Wide Eyes. For the most part, though, the mood was calm, and relationships generally friendly.

Two changes took place almost immediately after Whitepaws gave birth on 19th March. First, Smudge began to carry food to her at the earth, and he also made many caches in the immediate vicinity of the earth. Second, while remaining amicable to Big Ears, Whitepaws launched the most extraordinary vendetta against Wide Eyes.

Smudge was almost comical in his husbandly diligence. Before eating a scrap for himself, he gathered as much food as he could wedge into his gaping jaws, and lugged it to Whitepaws' earth. There he would warble at the entrance. If she did not emerge, he would use his nose like a billiard cue to poke the lumps of food through the entrance and into the den. Smudge's devotion to duty seemed inexhaustible—the more food we provided, the more he carried to the den.

The result of this glut was a distinct food shortage for the other two vixens. Big Ears could venture near the earth and pilfer occasional morsels, but Wide Eyes dared not show herself for fear of attack by Whitepaws. However, on 24th March Smudge was ferrying back and forth with food while Wide Eyes was cowering under a bush watching with mounting agitation as the food was carried past her. As the last chicken was carried towards the earth, Wide Eyes bolted out and threw herself to the ground beside Smudge, but he trotted past her. She dashed along beside him, casting nervous glances towards Whitepaws' earth and squealing at Smudge. He paused to rest: the chicken was so big that he could barely carry it. When Smudge next moved forward, Wide Eyes writhed on the ground in front of him and tripped him up so that both foxes and hen tumbled to a heap on the ground. He was about half-way to the earth by then and Smudge righted himself, looked first at the earth and then back at the squirming Wide Eyes. He continued to look back and forth for the next 15 seconds. At last he trotted off, leaving Wide Eyes with the food. What was it about Wide Eyes that provoked such rough treatment from Whitepaws? It took several years before this question could even be phrased in sensible terms.

While Whitepaws was preoccupied nursing her cubs a special relationship developed between Smudge and Big Ears. It stemmed from their shared trait of playfulness, and involved a particular clump of grass. The two foxes would pounce back and forth around this tussock, stalking it, playing king-of-the-castle and generally squirming about on it. Soon the tussock was battered and the grass trampled and torn, but it became a symbol of their play. Indeed, when Big Ears wanted to play, she would walk, not directly to the dog fox, but to the clump, where she would stab and pounce at the vegetation while glancing surreptitiously over to Smudge to ensure that her antics had caught his attention. He, it seemed, could not resist such an invitation.

All the adults took a great interest in the suckling cubs. Of course, Wide Eyes was forced to keep her distance, but Smudge and Big Ears visited the cubs again and again, and excitedly sniffed at them. Whitepaws did not appear to resent this attention at all. The cubs began to squabble amongst themselves over scraps when aged only 20 days, sucking ferociously on the meat with their gummy jaws. Would the non-breeding vixens bring them food?

Until 22nd April only Smudge and Whitepaws behaved towards the cubs in a parental manner. However, on the 22nd, Big Ears moved into the earth, together with Whitepaws, and thereafter shared all maternal duties save nursing. Big Ears retrieved cubs that strayed from the earth, she groomed them, ate their faeces and, from 28th April onwards, she brought food to them. While Big Ears' role as a babysitter increased, Whitepaws became less attentive and Big Ears was frequently left in sole charge of the cubs, circumstances which threw her into unaccustomed conflict with Smudge. Smudge passionately enjoyed playing with the cubs, and they too revelled in their father's high jinks. For some reason, in her new-found matronly role, Big Ears was uneasy with their games—disapproval was made forcefully plain to all concerned. The result was that Smudge would skulk

20. WHY DO FOXES LIVE IN GROUPS?

Charles Darwin coined the expression 'survival of the fittest', meaning that individuals that are better fitted, that is better adapted, to prevailing circumstances are more likely to survive than are those individuals that are less well adapted. For example, wolves which cooperate when they hunt moose would be more likely to survive than those which lacked the capacity to cooperate. If cooperation amongst the wolves was a hereditary characteristic, then it would become increasingly prevalent where they depend upon hunting moose, because cooperators would survive to produce cooperative progeny, whereas non-cooperators would perish. This is how evolution works, and the yardstick of success (the measure of fitness) is the number of surviving descendants an individual leaves. When biologists ask why animals behave in a certain way, this is often a short-hand way of asking what evolutionary advantage such individuals have (in terms of probable numbers of descendants) in comparison to other individuals which behave differently. (An animal behaving in a way which maximizes its descendants is said to be maximizing its fitness.) So, the question, why do foxes live in groups, really enquires why each individual that joins a group is more likely to survive and leave more descendants than if it opted for a different lifestyle.

Fox groups are normally families of one dog fox and several, related vixens. A young vixen faces the alternatives of joining her parents' group or of dispersing in the expectation of establishing a territory of her own. To maximize her fitness she should behave in a way that takes account of the risks and the benefits associated with each alternative. For example, if her chances of survival as an emigrant, or her chances of winning a breeding territory, were very low, whereas her chances of inheriting her mother's territory were quite high, then it might be to her advantage to stay at home, even though we know that in fox society that might involve postponing her own reproduction due to her subordinate status. In contrast, if her chances of securing a territory of her own elsewhere were high, then tolerating such as postponement would be disadvantageous.

The question arises of whether she has the option of joining the family group. This will depend partly on the food supply—if there is no spare food in the territory there will be no room for her unless she and her parents undertake the costs of expanding its borders (and these cost will have to be taken into account too, and weighed against the advantages of her membership). However, I suspect that there are many habitats in which the nature of the food supply is such that the smallest territory that will provide sufficient food for a pair will also provide sufficient surplus to support additional group members (*see* Box 16, p.117). For example, to ensure that they have an adequate chance of eating every night, and from season to season, a pair's territory might have to include a pasture, a warren, an orchard and a garbage tip, and these may yield sufficient worms, rabbits, apples and offal to support additional group members at minimal cost to the pair. This is just one example of circumstances in which the pattern of food availability may create an opportunity for groups to form. Whether the foxes take that opportunity will depend on the balance of costs and benefits to each individual involved, and this balance would be affected if additional group members behaved cooperatively—and sometimes they do.

Additional vixens in a fox group cooperate, to varying extents, in defence of the territory and in rearing the dominant females' cubs. They are therefore more than sitting-tenants in the territory, and this may reduce the risk of their being evicted. But why do they expend so much effort feeding cubs that are not their own? The answer probably lies in the theory of kin selection, formulated by W.D. Hamilton. From an evolutionary point of view, individuals have a vested interest not just in the survival of their own offspring, but also in that of other blood relatives. This is because relatives share part of their genetic heritage (a vested interest captured in the maxim that blood is thicker than water). An individual has half its genes represented in its offspring (the other half coming from the other parent) and, on average, in its full siblings. But, on average, it shares only a quarter of its genes with its nieces and an eighth with its cousins (a fact which prompted the geneticist, J.B.S. Haldane's famous remark that he would give his life for two of his brothers or eight of his cousins).

So, if by acting as a nanny, a non-breeding vixen can improve the survival of her kin, she is thereby promoting the survival of her own genes—a sort of breeding by proxy. The greater the helper's contribution, the more it offsets the disadvantage she endures due to not breeding herself. Indeed, if her help could double the survival of her younger sisters, then the outcome would, on average, be the same as if she had bred. The opportunities for such cooperation can make group living advantageous for all concerned.

Helping her kin can enable a non-breeding vixen to compensate for some of her lost reproduction, but why does she tolerate that loss at all? The answer is probably that she has no choice: the breeding vixens' domination prevents the subordinate from breeding (it

is generally to the dominant's advantage to monopolize all the resources of the territory, and the energies of the dog fox and others, for the benefit of her own cubs). Of course, the subordinate vixen may be the dog fox's daughter, so one might argue that avoidance of in-breeding explained their restraint. However, in theory a limited amount of in-breeding is not disadvantageous, and in practice foxes do not seem to avoid it.

In this connection, Dennis Voigt records an interesting story: in Ontario, he radio-tagged two cubs, a brother and sister. From August onwards the young dog began a series of exploratory excursions, before he finally dispersed in October, setting up a 900ha territory some 10km away. Meanwhile, the vixen dispersed in a different direction, but in November ended up in the same territory as her brother, where, the following spring, they reared cubs.

What is the mechanism of reproductive suppression amongst foxes? There are several possibilities: vixens may fail to produce eggs (to ovulate), they may fail to mate or conceive, they may abort or resorb their embryos, or they may fail to rear their cubs. All of these phenomena certainly happen, but those which are the crucial mechanisms for social suppression of reproduction is unknown. One possibility is that dominant vixens actively obstruct the male's access to subordinates, and this certainly can happen. However, in my enclosures the dog foxes generally took no sexual interest in subordinate females. Perhaps these vixens did not come into reproductive condition. However, almost all wild vixens (presumably including non-breeders) do come into breeding condition (i.e. they ovulate), so perhaps the effect of subordination is to switch off the scent signals that would normally advertise their receptivity, rather than switching off the reproductive system itself.

Similarly, in two studies in Sweden (by Jan Englund and Erik Lindström), almost all vixens ovulated, but many showed no sign of pregnancy. In contrast, in Freik Niewold's study in Holland, in an area where foxes lived in groups, most vixens became pregnant, but many did not rear cubs. There are plenty of puzzles in this topic. For example, a two-year old vixen and her two yearling daughters were killed together in the same earth in Gwyn Lloyd's Welsh study area, and all three were in the late stages of pregnancy. I suspect that the mechanism of suppression, and whether it is exerted at all, varies with circumstances, perhaps in a way determined by the stability (and polarization) of the social hierarchy within fox groups.

in the vegetation, waiting for Big Ears to fall asleep, whereupon he would quietly warble to the cubs who would sneak off to gambol with him. Soon their exuberance led to squeals and snirks that awoke Big Ears who would vigorously reprimand Smudge. On these occasions he never made the slightest sign of submission in the face of Big Ears' remonstrances, but simply withdrew.

As the cubs were weaned. Whitepaws relented somewhat in her vendetta against Wide Eyes who, for her part, was as keen as Smudge to play with the cubs. Once again, the group was becoming amicable. On 5th May, Smudge, Whitepaws and Big Ears were all busily carrying food to the cubs. That evening, Wide Eyes was allowed to play at length with the cubs, who literally swung from her tail as she cavorted with them. However, Whitepaws' mood towards Wide Eyes could still be mercurial. On 6th May Wide Eyes entered the earth, apparently without noticing that Whitepaws had gone in there before her. A fight broke out and Big Ears, along with the cubs, were all attracted by the commotion and ran in too. Almost at once they all came

tumbling out as Whitepaws ejected Wide Eyes who ran to the far end of the enclosure, where Whitepaws caught her and continued to attack. Big Ears also joined in briefly, taking sides with Whitepaws. However, this reprimand was mild compared with Wide Eyes' earlier thrashings.

On 7th May, Wide Eyes also began to give food to the cubs, warbling to attract them to her so she would not have to venture too close to the earth. Wide Eyes' social rehabilitation was swift, and by 10th May she was actually venturing to carry food to the cubs at the earth, and three days later she had the temerity to rebuke Smudge for playing with them too rumbustiously. On the 15th May, Wide Eyes, as a fully fledged baby-sitter for the first time, slept alone with the cubs. Thereafter most of the care of the cubs devolved from Whitepaws, who largely ignored them, onto Big Ears and Wide Eyes, and while Big Ears became increasingly tolerant of Smudge it was now Wide Eyes who sternly subdued his frolics with the youngsters.

So, as the summer of 1977 passed, Niff had once again ruled the reproductive roost in the tennis court and the inmates of the new enclosure had also gone a long way to answering my three questions. Smudge had not mated with all three vixens. He had sired cubs by Whitepaws, the socially dominant vixen of the trio. The non-breeders had been assiduous nannies to Whitepaws' cubs. They played with them, groomed them, lay with them (sometimes splitting the litter between them), retrieved them when they strayed and fed them.

At the very outset of this book I explained that one aim of the study was to find out why some foxes live in groups. In 1977, with the combined results from my field and enclosure studies, I felt close enough to some answers to submit my doctoral thesis for examination—a daunting experience but one which, happily, I survived. In a nutshell, my arguments were at two levels. There were both ecological and sociological reasons why foxes might sometimes form groups. At an ecological level there were some habitats (but perhaps not all) where an unpredictable or patchy food supply facilitated the formation of groups. In such a habitat a yearling vixen faces a decision (although probably not a conscious one) of whether she would be better off staying at home to join the family group or emigrating to establish her own group. 'Better off' in this context means maximizing her chances of survival and breeding. Both strategies have their pros and cons. For example, emigration involves travelling across unfamiliar and possibly dangerous terrain, it requires finding a suitable territory, and probably fighting for it. It is easy to imagine circumstances where emigration is very unlikely to be successful. Weighed against these risks are the consequences of staying at home, always assuming that family competition for the available food supply leaves this option open. Several sociological considerations would be relevant to a vixen facing this option. If she stays at home, at least for as long as her mother is alive she will probably have to endure low status and therefore relinquish the opportunity to breed until she is older than might otherwise have been the case. However, this disadvantage would be offset to some extent by the security of staying at home in a proven and familiar territory, of contributing to its defence, and the possibility of inheriting the matriarchy one day, and meanwhile having a secure base from which to 'house hunt' for a vacant territory. Most significant of all, I suspect, may be the opportunity of helping rear cubs which are her close relatives (and even of adopting them if the mother dies).

These are the sorts of factors which must be weighed in the balance—factors not so different from those that might affect a young person's judgement on whether or not to join the family firm. The weight attached to each factor will vary from individual to individual, depending on their circumstances. Some foxes live in groups because the benefits are likely to outweigh the costs.

With my thesis behind me I was fortunate to have secured a fellowship at Balliol College, Oxford, and so began the Oxford Foxlot—a motley crew whose story began with an unorthodoxy with which it has resolutely continued. An unexpected knock at the door announced one of the first arrivals, Pall Hersteinsson, an Icelander who has the sort of congenial quick wit that makes him instantly likeable. He was a postgraduate at Cambridge University and being a field-man at heart, he had somehow become embroiled in a doctorate on the nervous reactions underlying the conjugal clasp reflex of the *Xenopus* toad, a topic for which he had very rapidly exhausted any enthusiasm he originally had. One evening, dejectedly reflecting on his disenchantment with amorous toads, he switched on the television and, by chance, saw our film *The Night of the Fox*. Instantly he knew that this was his vocation—hence his arrival on my doorstep. To cut a very long story short, Pall left Cambridge, came to Oxford, and persuaded the Icelandic government to finance a study of Arctic foxes.

After sundry misadventures on light aircraft and rough seas, he set up the Foxlot's most northerly outpost on a wild and remote corner of north-west Iceland. When I joined him there I realized that the red fox's bad press in Europe was nothing in comparison to the venom with which the Arctic fox was regarded in Iceland— when tuning into the national radio station we would hear hourly government announcements vilifying the Arctic fox as a sheep killer. The broadcasts reminded citizens of the law, dating from AD 1295, that it was a crime not to kill a fox if the opportunity arose.

As Pall and I sat on a cliff watching by the

21. HOW LONG DO FOXES LIVE?

Red foxes have a potential lifespan comparable to that of a small dog—up to 14 years in captivity. In the wild the oldest fox I have known died 'naturally' at nine years old. However, in most wild populations only a minority of foxes survive their first year, and most (generally about 95 per cent) die before their fourth birthday. This heavy death rate is generally due to man or rabies.

How do biologists tell a fox's age? A simple, but rather unreliable method is to look at the tooth wear—the teeth of older foxes having blunt, worn cusps. The wear on the front, incisor teeth give the best clue. In a first year fox, each central incisor has a serrated appearance (two little notches split the crown of the tooth into three cusps). As the fox ages, these serrations are worn away. They are barely perceptible by the second year, and generally completely smoothed when the fox enters its third year. One difficulty with this approach is that tooth wear probably varies between habitats (e.g. foxes eating a lot of earthworms may incur heavy wear due to chewing soil). Dead foxes can be aged much more reliably. There are several methods, but the best is to count annuli (rings) in the cementum of the teeth. This is a complex technique but, in short, foxes' teeth lay down growth rings, rather like those of a tree. When the tooth is cut into fine sections and prepared with appropriate stains, these rings are visible under a microscope—one ring for each year of the fox's life.

One difficulty in studying the age structure of fox populations is that the research generally involves dead foxes, and they are not necessarily representative of the survivors. For example, if the foxes were killed by a method selected for young, inexperienced foxes then yearlings would be more common in the sample of foxes dying than in the population of foxes surviving (e.g. there is evidence that juvenile foxes are more prone to road accidents and to rabies). Despite fears of such bias, it is clear that the life expectancy of foxes differs greatly between populations. For example, in one sample of 69 foxes over 12 months old killed in my Oxfordshire study areas, 23 per cent were aged five years or older. However, the great majority of these older foxes (78 per cent of them) came from Boar's Hill, where they had been killed by cars, but where traffic was light and where foxes were completely undisturbed by people. Such elderly foxes were rare (2 of 23 adults) in the remainder of the sample which was shot or snared on nearby farms where intensive effort was put into their control. A further 15 adult foxes (most killed by cars) were collected nearby in Oxford City (where the traffic was heavy). Of these, only one had survived five years.

These samples are small, but they serve to show that where mortality is higher the average age of those dying is younger. This is clearly illustrated by the fact that the proportion of juveniles (less than one year old) amongst those dying increases with the severity of attempts to control them. For example, one scheme in Central Iowa paid fox-trappers a double bounty over seven years. The result was the youngest, most bottom-heavy, fox population so far recorded (84 per cent died as juveniles).

In Ontario, foxes are killed by both fur-trappers and rabies, and 80 per cent die as juveniles. In Denmark, trappers were paid a bounty to kill foxes in an attempt to control rabies, with the result that 75 per cent of foxes died as juveniles. The mortality pressure in Oxford City (largely due to traffic accidents) was high compared to the sheltered and prolonged lives of foxes on nearby Boar's Hill, but it was low relative to the intensity of these other studies (63 per cent of the City foxes dying did so before their first birthday). The Oxford City death rate was comparable to that calculated (from much bigger samples) in several European studies—for example, in mid-Wales (where Gwyn Lloyd studied foxes killed principally by sheep farmers) and in London's suburbs (where Stephen Harris studied those killed principally by cars or shot by pest-controllers).

So, as a rough estimate, and excluding on the one hand areas with either rabies or organized bounties, and on the other hand sanctuaries like Boar's Hill, juvenile foxes in most areas have a life expectancy of about 1.5 years. Furthermore, most of them can expect to die, directly or indirectly, at human hands (across several studies, 40 to 60 per cent of foxes ear-tagged by biologists were subsequently returned by hunters and motorists, thereby providing minimum figures for the proportion of fox mortality generally due to man). Before they die, they can expect plenty of close-shaves: a large proportion of skins taken from rural foxes carry lead-shot, and in London, Stephen Harris found that one third of adult foxes had healed bone fractures (and therefore an increasingly debilitating tendency towards arthritis).

We might expect these death rates to have a marked effect on fox society (imagine a human society in which few survive into their thirties). Nonetheless, as a rough approximation, fox populations can sustain more than 60 per cent annual mortality, so only the most intensive control is likely to reduce their numbers (see Box 31, p.207).

light of the midnight sun, chocolate brown foxes trotted along the shoreline below. The dramatic white form of the Arctic fox was rare on this coastline (*see* Box 22, p. 148) and while watching the foxes we formulated similar questions to those which had directed the red fox study. What did they eat? How did their food supply affect their movements and social lives? In particular, did the Arctic foxes also form groups and have helpers? The fox below us, who came to be known as Brunn, picked his way through a pile of rotting seaweed, and gobbled up the kelp fly maggots burrowing therein—the Arctic fox's equivalent to their red cousins' predilection for earthworms.

Over the years, it became clear that these foxes got most of their food by beachcombing, a food supply which was very patchy for depending on the drift of the tide some coves were rich in edible flotsam and jetsam, while others were barren. We concluded that it was the dispersion of these bountiful beaches that determined the territory sizes (which varied in area from 7 to 17 sq km). We found that Arctic foxes were living in groups, generally one dog fox, a breeding vixen and a non-breeding vixen. After hours of observation, Pall confirmed that the non-breeding vixens were indeed helping at the den, bringing food to the breeding vixen's cubs. So it turned out that another supposedly solitary species of fox was actually rather sociable. However, the story of non-breeders in the Arctic fox groups had an interesting twist. After one breeding season as helpers, they dispersed and set up their own territories as breeding vixens. For them, therefore, the weighing of the odds on how long to stay in the 'family firm' had a rather different answer to that for the red foxes on Boar's Hill. I suspect that one reason for the difference was that so many Arctic foxes were killed by government hunters that a dispersing vixen had a better chance of finding a vacant territory.

Meanwhile, twists were also developing in the story of baby-sitting vixens back in Oxfordshire. During the summer of 1977 the *status quo* had stabilized in Smudge's enclosure, with a clear rank order among the vixens: Whitepaws, Big Ears, Wide Eyes. However, as summer turned to autumn, Big Ears would no longer stand aside in the face of Whitepaws' aggression,

nor would she any longer show signs of subservience to her sister. At the same time, Smudge became more friendly with Big Ears, and Whitepaws noticeably avoided disputes with her. By the time the mating season arrived again there were two 'top dogs' among the vixens, and for the first time in the enclosures two vixens were mated: Big Ears on 24th January, Whitepaws on 3rd February. Before his cubs were born Smudge took ill. Smitten by a bacterial disease, leptospirosis, he wasted away. By the 4th of March we were running a relay of hot-water bottles to his den, and on the 5th he died. With no dog fox to feed them, how would the nursing vixens fare?

Big Ears' cubs were born on 28th March, whereupon, like Whitepaws the previous year, she began a vendetta against Wide Eyes which was to rage for ten days. At the same time, Whitepaws became unusually amicable with Wide Eyes, but highly submissive to Big Ears. Wide Eyes, in her turn, began a series of savage attacks on the one yearling vixen remaining from Whitepaws' previous litter (the other youngsters having been removed from the enclosure in autumn). Then, on 11th April, Whitepaws gave birth to four cubs of her own. Immediately, she became what can best be described as a nervous wreck, seemingly forgetting her diligent and successful qualities as a mother the previous year. Big Ears, in contrast, although her only previous experience had been as a helper, was now an exemplary mother. She would visit Whitepaws' earth, but at her approach Whitepaws shrieked in submission, grabbed a cub in her mouth, and fled with it.

The cubs soon succumbed to this treatment and on 19th April the last one died, and Whitepaws emerged from her earth carrying the corpse. She ran to Big Ears' earth, and found that Big Ears was away. Carrying the dead cub into Big Ears' earth, she quickly re-emerged and dropped the cub outside. During the next ten minutes Whitepaws visited Big Ears' cubs ten times. Meanwhile, Big Ears returned, but showed no animosity towards Whitepaws, who submitted lavishly to her. Big Ears then made three separate trips to Whitepaws' earth, exploring it thoroughly, whereupon she returned to her own earth in which Whitepaws was lying with the cubs. Big Ears greeted Whitepaws and then wandered off, leaving her bereaved sister to

nurse her cubs. Thus, within an hour of the death of her last cub, Whitepaws was yet again transformed, this time to a diligent wet nurse. Her anxiety had vaporized and been replaced by an air of calm competence. In the following days Big Ears and Whitepaws lay side by side, each vixen grooming the cubs that nursed from her sister's teats. Within a week Whitepaws too began to attack Wide Eyes.

With no dog fox to feed them, the two nursing vixens were forced to leave Big Ears' cubs in order to eat. Once the cubs began to chew solid food both Big Ears and Whitepaws fed them. Eventually their aggression to Wide Eyes subsided, and then she too provided food for the cubs. It was almost as if by relenting in their attacks they 'allowed' her to feed the cubs.

These remarkable events of 1978 showed how a vixen's family life was governed by her status, and not necessarily by her ability or experience. But why had this reversal of status

between Whitepaws and Big Ears happened at all? This question was all the more pertinent considering the stability of Niff's position as matriarch in the tennis court. In the hope of answering this question, another of Niff's sons, called simply Fox, was hand-reared to fill Smudge's role as mate to Big Ears and her sisters.

When Fox was introduced to his harem in the autumn of 1978 he found a very different state of affairs to that left by his deceased brother: Wide Eyes no longer collapsed in rag-doll submission as her sisters approached, and in the New Year it was she whom Fox doted upon. For the first time in her life, Wide Eyes token marked, whereas both Big Ears and Whitepaws were demoted to the prolonged squats of their cubhoods. After a lifetime of subjugation, Wide Eyes in power was a martinet. Furthermore, Fox tended to back her up—when Wide Eyes thrashed an underling, Fox was more than likely to add a few forceful nips of his own. Whitepaws

in particular was left in no doubt about the new situation when, on the 25th February, Wide Eyes trotted over to her: Whitepaws squirmed low in deference whereupon Wide Eyes turned around and splashed a token urination across her muzzle. Whitepaws lay frozen in humiliation while Fox trotted up, sniffed at the scent, licked up a few drops and jogged off after Wide Eyes.

On the 3rd March 1979, just before her fourth birthday, Wide Eyes bore six cubs. The vixen who had started below the bottom rung was now at the top of the social ladder. But the weather was cold and wet and soon only two cubs survived. Otherwise everything went as normal: Fox diligently ferried food to his nursing mate, Wide Eyes was implacably brutal in her attacks on her yearling niece and on Whitepaws (now number three in the pecking order). Then, 31 days after her birth, the vixen cub died, followed two days later by her brother. I'm really not sure of the circumstances of their deaths, but the little dog fox had a broken leg and wounded chest. We left his corpse in the den, and the adults continued to tend it. According to schedule, Big Ears began to lie with the dead cub, and Fox and Wide Eyes brought it food. Nine days later Wide Eyes was still calling it, and Fox was endlessly carrying food around and looking for a cub to give it to. Big Ears even took to trying to carry her yearling daughter.

On 15th April I introduced a five-week-old orphan cub. I had two ideas in mind. First, I wondered whether they would adopt the orphan and second, if they did, I hoped to salvage the season's data on helping behaviour. At that time, Big Ears would normally have been at the peak of her endeavours as a helper. She was immediately besotted with the new cub and hurriedly stuffed it into the den. The orphan was less than enthusiastic about her plans for its upbringing, and after a brief tour of its quarters, waddled into the open again. Big Ears stuffed it back through the

22. WHAT COLOUR ARE RED FOXES?

Although red in name, foxes can be far from red in colour. Throughout most of the species range, red foxes are certainly coloured as variations on a reddish theme, but individuals vary greatly through shades of brown to yellowish-grey. However, in the northern parts of the range there are two other colour phases of red fox. The silver fox has no reddish hairs; instead they are black or black with a band of white. The presence of this white band determines whether the fox will appear black or silver. The silvering effect may extend over part or all of the body.

Silver, red foxes and red, red foxes are the same species, and may even be littermates. The genetics underlying these differences in coat colour are complex, and can lead to various intermediate varieties. One such mixture is the cross fox which has red flanks, shoulders and cheeks, and a silver or black back and neck. The darker line along its back intersects with the dark band around the neck to form a cross, hence the name cross fox.

The Hudson's Bay Company has kept records of the colours of fox skins traded by trappers from the Canadian barrenlands since the early 19th century. From 1825 to 1850, between 19 and 25 per cent of the red fox skins traded in British Columbia were silver, as were 16 per cent of those from Labrador. In the course of about 100 years these proportions fell to between 5 and 7 per cent, and have continued to fall.

What caused this dramatic change in the appearance (and therefore the genetic constitution) of these northern red fox populations? Several ideas have been advanced, although none is wholly convincing. One idea was that the great value of silver foxes (four to five times that of reds) and cross foxes (two to three times that of reds) caused hunters to concentrate on catching them and on transporting their skins. However, such selectivity could easily operate only where foxes were shot, since leghold traps are unselective. Only 5 per cent of the hunters' catch was secured by shooting. Furthermore, the decline in silver foxes continued even after their value slumped to that equivalent to red foxes (due to the production of large numbers of better quality silver foxes in fur farms). So, it seems unlikely that selective hunting of the silvers accounts for their decline. Another idea is that the northern progress of human settlement has improved the habitat for foxes, leading to a migration of more southerly, red, red foxes, whose red genes have swamped out the local silver genes.

These explanations for the decline in silver foxes beg the question of why the silver phase flourished in the first place, and why they did so in greater numbers further to the north. The fact that the red and silver forms lived in balance in the same populations shows that both had advantages, so neither could usurp the other. For example, perhaps the silver fox has adapted to hunting (or avoiding being hunted) in forest, and the red fox is at an advantage in clearings.

Another relevant factor is that the northern fox populations are subject to four and ten year cycles in their numbers, and there is some evidence that silver foxes occur in greater proportions during troughs in these cycles. The possibilities for speculation are legion, but the fact remains that the tide seems to have turned against whatever advantages the silver foxes enjoyed two centuries ago.

Another fox colour conundrum is why do only some red foxes have white tags to their tails (it is not, as often claimed, a prerogative of males). A biologist seeing such a marked characteristic as a powder-puff tail-tip is bound to think it is there for a good reason. The biologist noticing that the same characteristic is absent from other foxes will suspect that it costs sometimes outweigh the benefits. For example, as a guess, a big white tag certainly accentuates and makes conspicuous tail movements in poor light. Tail movements are a crucial part of fox communication. Perhaps the advantage of the tag is to reduce ambiguity in the semaphore of tail signals—a visual beacon in the dark, roughly analogous to the olfactory flag of the tail gland (see Box 19, p.125). However, the same beacon may also attact attention to a fleeing fox (or disclose its whereabouts to prey), putting those with a conspicuous tag at a disadvantage. The fact is that nobody really understands why the colours of red foxes (or of the tips of their tails) vary.

Arctic foxes also occur in two colour morphs, known as blue and white, and both change colour from winter to summer—giving four possible colours of Arctic fox. The white fox is white in winter, and brownish-grey in summer. The blue fox is light brown with a bluish sheen in winter, moulting to chocolate brown in summer. Both these seasonal changes make sense in terms of camouflage adapting to seasonal circumstances. But why do the two morphs exist at all? The answer seems to be that white Arctic foxes are adapted to inland regions where snow settles, whereas blue Arctic foxes are adapted to coastal regions where it does not. This explains why the proportion of blue foxes in the population is greatest on smaller islands (which have a higher ratio of coastline to interior than do larger islands). Pall Hersteinsson proved this point nicely in Iceland where, overall, one third of Arctic foxes were white. However, the proportion of white foxes varied within Iceland—in coastal areas it was as low as 8 per cent, and in inland areas it was as high as 59 per cent.

entrance; it stumbled out again. Sixty-seven times Big Ears pushed it into the den, 68 times it came out. After an hour and half of this Big Ears was panting hard and no longer picking the cub up, but exhaustedly butting it in the general direction of the den. At this point Fox turned up with some food for it. By nightfall Big Ears and the orphan had struck a deal: it would stay near the den, but not necessarily inside. Wide Eyes was generally disinterested in these proceedings. By the next day both Big Ears and Whitepaws were tending the orphan, and three days later Fox, Big Ears and Whitepaws were all busy feeding it but it was not until 27th April that Wide Eyes was seen to feed it.

So, the adoption had been a complete success and the helpers' behaviour had followed a very similar course to that of previous years, despite a sort of musical chairs in each individual's social role. Wide Eyes retained her dominance and by the following clicketing she was token marking on everything (including us) at a rate of eight times a minute until she mated each day from 5th to 8th February 1980. Her pregnancy appeared to go normally but we never found the cubs. Perhaps they were still-born.

In the summer of 1979 we hand-reared four more cubs and installed them in a third enclosure. These four were litter-mates, two dogs (Friendly and Retiring) and two vixens (Sandy and Dark). I chose this combination in order to shed light on several questions and, in particular, to seek further evidence of whether foxes avoided inbreeding. I also hoped to discover how two males in one family (a rare but real possibility in the wild) would react to any resulting cubs. The story of the third enclosure is too long to tell here, but in short Friendly mated the dominant vixen, his sister Sandy, and when her cubs were born both he and Retiring Male fed the nursing vixen. Once the cubs were weaned both dogs and both vixens fed them.

Eventually, in spring 1980, we began the last and most ambitious phase of the plan: to transfer the whole experiment into the wild, and thereby to lay to rest the fear that the enclosures gave unnatural results, but more of that later.

I had launched into these experiments to discover why only a third of the wild vixens resident on Boar's Hill were breeding. The vixens in our three groups of foxes produced a dozen litters over the years, which was slightly under a third of their potential productivity—but why was this so? I think the answer is that within social groups of foxes only one or two dominant vixens breed while those of lower rank are effectively sterilized by their status. But what of Niff's reproductive monopoly in contrast to the shifting reproductive prerogative between Whitepaws, Big Ears and Wide Eyes? My hunch is that the dynamics of dominance are such that the inequalities of age and maternal status made Niff's (and Toothypeg's) matriarchy unassailable even into their dotage. Among the three sisters, the status differential was less fundamental. One might even speculate that the loss of condition wrought by nursing a litter contributed to the mother's subsequent loss of status. Whatever caused them to tumble from their throne, the fact that they did so is the important point, since it shows that the chances of becoming dominant vary not only with the size of the group, but also with its composition—and this might affect a vixen's decision as to whether or not to join the 'family firm'.

Finally, what of the annual onslaught by breeding females on the lowest rankers? In the absence of any very clear-cut answer it is all too easy to dream up explanations of the sort that biologists dismiss as *Just So* stories. The possibility that these low rankers pose a direct threat to the cubs cannot be completely dismissed remembering the mysterious deaths of Wide Eyes' cubs. However, all the evidence suggests, on the contrary, that the victims of the dominant's spleen actually seek to tend the cubs. I favour the idea that the arrival of cubs signals increasing demands on the territory's larder and the risk that there will not be enough to go around. Anticipating such a risk, it might be a prudent time to shed hangers-on or to reinforce the *status quo* in anticipation of such evictions. This notion, however, begs the question of whether subordinate group members are indeed evicted in times of food shortage, a question to which I will return. In the meantime, I will address my original question about how fox behaviour varies between habitats. To answer this I must go back in time to Niff's cubhood and our trips to the north of England.

9 | A Fox In Sheep's Clothing

CARRIGILL IS, for all practical purposes, at the end of the road. In the shadow of Crossfell's windswept heights a clutch of grey stone cottages, their once regular lines now wrinkled and warped, cluster around the *George and Dragon* pub. It was there that I had a memorable introduction to the hill countryman's hatred of foxes.

After a long drive north Jenny, Niff and I arrived weary and stiff in Carrigill, and stopped to seek directions. We were looking for the rough track to Moor House which, at 600 metres above sea level, is the highest Nature Conservancy Council Field Station in Britain. It was 1975, my project was still in its infancy, and I was looking for a new study area. The idea was to choose an environment as different as possible from Boar's Hill, in order to tackle the question: do foxes behave differently in different places? The bleak grouse moors of the Cumbrian fells seemed to fit the bill. Furthermore, this would be the place to explore some more practical issues, such as the fox's reputation as a blight on sheep and grouse. We drew up outside the *George and Dragon*. Niff, then still a youngster, emerged from her accustomed place under the driver's seat, clambered onto my knee, and thrust her nose out of the window to sample air alive with the sounds of bleating sheep and a gurgling stream.

Leaving Niff in the car with Jenny, I went in to ask for directions. Inside was a storybook scene: pint pots glistened in the light of a wood fire, and at the end of the dimly lit bar an old man in a cloth cap and worn tweed jacket supped drowsily at his beer. At his feet a Black Labrador dozed, its lead looped loosely around the leg of its master's bar-stool. A friendly greeting was followed by a few simple directions, and a pleasant enquiry as to what had brought me to these parts. In my innocence I trotted out a quick answer—foxes, radio tracking, research—the words hit home like bullets. Too late I heard the low whistle of expelled breath, heard the disgusted grunt from the drowsy drinker, saw the landlord's lips tighten and his expression of friendly indifference harden to mistrust.

Before I could make amends, a whiff of Niff's scent, which permeated my clothes and had already banned me from the secretary's office in Oxford, thudded into the sleeping dog's nasal membranes. Its eyes flew open, it sniffed loudly and all vestiges of dozy dogginess fell away as it adopted an expression unnervingly like the landlord's. With a snarl the dog lunged at me, tightening its leash around the legs of both the stool and its master, which, together, crashed to the floor. Mercifully, the combined weight of man and stool were sufficient to anchor the snapping dog while I beat a hasty retreat.

The pockmarked gravel road to Moor House wound across a peaty landscape as bleak as any in England. Ten kilometers from anywhere, the research station nestles in this windswept wilderness. People who have lived for long at Moor House are said to be recognizable by their splayed stance and forward tilt to their walk. We were greeted warmly by Robert Williams, the Nature Conservancy Council's resident scientist, and his rough-coated collie. Robert and I launched into an exchange of foxy yarns while the collie conducted a thorough olfactory exploration of my trousers. Its wagging tail slowed, faltered and stopped; its worst suspicions were confirmed—a two-legged fox! A furore of barking and some rather indelicately placed nips set the seal on our relationship, and for the coming days Niff, Jenny and I arranged our movements to avoid further

23. DO FOXES KILL A 'DOOMED SURPLUS'?

One idea about foxes as predators is that they tend to select infirm prey, because they are the easiest to catch. If these weak individuals would not have survived to breed anyway, then they (probably along with many healthy ones) could be part of what is called a 'doomed surplus' in the prey population. Indeed, in a natural population that is stable from year to year, the same number of individuals must die each year as are born. In this sense the equivalent to the entire annual production is surplus. Thinking of gamebirds, a common misapprehension is that the gamekeeper has nothing to lose from foxes which feed on this surplus so long as they do not bite into his breeding stock.

The case of grouse shows why that interpretation would be incorrect. I collected 231 fox droppings from the soggy heather and cotton grass moors around Moor House, and discovered that grouse made up some 60 per cent of the bulk of remains therein (grouse constituted a much smaller percentage of the volume of droppings on adjacent fellside, where rodents and rabbits predominated). Were these foxes selecting unhealthy grouse? They certainly had the opportunity to do so since Moor House grouse population, like most others, was afflicted with an intestinal parasitic worm called *Trichostrongylus tenuis*. This parasite weakens the grouse, causes them to lay smaller clutches, and can kill them. By comparing the remains of grouse killed by foxes and those killed by sportsmen, Peter Hudson of the Game Conservancy has shown that those killed by foxes tended to be more heavily infected with worms. A reasonable interpretation is that foxes were selectively killing the sickly grouse (another possibility is that they were selectively not eating them).

How did the foxes make their selection? It seems that healthy hen grouse stop producing smelly caecal droppings when they are incubating eggs. Heavily parasitized hen grouse, whose blind-guts (caeca) are bulging with worms, cannot suppress their odours in this way. In a field trial Hudson showed that a trained

encounters with our new enemy. By day we walked the fells, gathering fox droppings, searching for active earths, looking for good trapping sites. I was laden down with bait and lures— tasty dead chicken, fox urine, extract of anal gland, even a suitably greening dead cat. All to no avail. Not only were these foxes thin on the ground, they were wary and the landscape was as difficult as could be. Nonetheless, I was learning about fell foxes, finding 'feetings' (pawprints) in the peat hag, faeces on sheep trods, and neatly snipped off grouse feathers on the heather. Niff had a wonderful time, weaving along the network of paths, her brush whisked into violent contortions at the whim of the wind. She learnt quickly. Soon I noticed that she almost always headed into the wind, and so disliked it up her tail that she took pains to seek the shelter of slack ground. She also chose to scan her surroundings at frequent intervals, and would run to boulders or rises from which to chart her route; and she took to rolling in sheep dung—not all sheep dung, but particular bits that had some special and mysterious appeal. Often, as Niff wove through the heather she would stop and point, sniffing intently as her ears flicked back

and forth. Circling until she cut the wind full-face, and then at a high stepping trot she would move forward until a grouse rattled away in front of us. Sometimes she caught their scent from the best part of 50 metres downwind. Occasionally, even with me clumsily in tow, she caught and ate an enfeebled, worm-laden bird that flopped across the heather too weak to take off (*see* Box 23, p.152). Niff's self-taught apprenticeship as a fell fox was watched bemusedly by rugged little Swaledale ewes, whose powder-puffed noses and startled expressions destined them to a lifetime of looking as if they had been caught red-handed (or white-nosed) in the milk churn. Sometimes a ewe would stamp her feet at Niff and, once, one stretched forward and the two unlikely acquaintances sniffed noses, but for the most part they ignored each other.

Despite several trips back and forth between Moor House and Oxford, I failed to catch foxes on the fell. The prospects looked bleak and, doubtless, the project would have foundered, had Edwin Dargue not entered my life. South of Carrigill, crossing the hunchback of England at Crossfell's 900 metres, the moor slopes down towards Dufton and there, at Bow Hall, furthest

dog had difficulty smelling healthy hen birds, whereas the parasitized ones stuck out like odorous beacons, which was probably why they were caught by the foxes. This selectivity may explain why on moors with more gamekeepers and therefore, perhaps, fewer foxes to weed out the sickly birds, a greater proportion of grouse had serious parasite problems. Furthermore, bags of grouse were bigger on moors where fewer foxes were shot by the 'keepers. These two correlations might seem to suggest that foxes are good for the health and numbers of grouse. Hudson concluded, on the contrary, that the reason grouse abound where fewer foxes are shot is that these moors are the ones where most 'keepers are employed and thus they have already killed so many foxes that there are few left to shoot. He believes that where foxes abound they keep grouse numbers below that at which the parasite becomes serious, but in so doing they keep the birds below the maximum numbers that would otherwise be available to sportsmen (the bag records of grouse tend to be greatest where the population density of 'keepers is highest).

Disentangling cause and coincidence in such findings is always tricky, but the fact is that it is irrelevent whether or not most grouse eaten by foxes were doomed to die before the next breeding season. It would be relevant if the aim were to maintain a natural balance between predator and prey. In fact, the aim is to maximize the yield of grouse to shoot, and so the fox and the sportsmen are in competition for the same doomed surplus. Most managed grouse are not in any normal sense natural populations—they are cash crops, farmed and harvested just like a field of wheat. As long as the aim is to maximize the yield, then the fox on the moor will be as unwelcome as the cornflower in the cereal field. In these circumstances, foxes could only hope for absolution in the eyes of gamekeepers if they restricted themselves to grouse doomed to die before the 12th August.

up the fell of the surviving farms, Edwin shepherded his flock of Swaledales. The Dargues of Bow Hall had wrung a living from the fell since the earliest parish records, and probably long before. Edwin, hewn from the ruggedness of the moor, had the physique of a tank and hands that, ungloved, could wrench winter turnips from beneath a blanket of snow for hours on end. Furthermore, he had to do so: it was the hall mark of the Dargue's farm that when it rained everywhere else, it snowed at Bow Hall.

On Dufton Fell, Edwin was Mr Fox. As both shepherd and gamekeeper on the grousemoor, he had been pitting his wits against foxes since his uncle, known to everybody as 'The Boss', had taken him as a small boy to every fox hole he knew on the fell. Doubtless, many years before, the Boss' father had, in turn, taken him to those same holes. Since his boyhood, never a Spring had passed without Edwin scouring the fell for

sign of whelping vixens. His tuition in foxing had been completed by master gamekeeper, Alec Mason. By the time I arrived on the scene Alec was old and infirm, but his reputation was still vibrant. He had been a 'keeper of the old school, teaching Edwin to discard his hob-nailed boots and stalk foxes in barefoot silence across the sharp, clattering flints of the scree slopes. The motives for our shared pursuit of foxes could hardly have been more different—mine to capture, radio-collar and release, his to eradicate—but the skills of our trades were remarkably similar, and the thrill of foxes was irresistible to us both. In no time at all I had moved into Edwin's house, and the very heart of fell-side foxing.

I had first met Edwin because he was the subject of a documentary film about shepherds and sheep dogs, being made by my close friend, Lary Shaffer. Doubtless their familiarity with Lary's filming antics eased my entry into the shepherding community. I found myself in the company of men whose very names were redolent of the windswept hill—men like Joe Threlkeld and Palmer Swinbank—all of them were shepherds who saw that radio-tracking had one good use: it would, after all, lead you to a fox and thereby hasten its demise. What most of them could not stomach was the release of a fox that had once been captured. My argument that the situation would be no worse than it had been, that a number of radio-collared foxes was neither better nor worse than an identical number of uncollared ones, sparked either rage or gawps.

As I have stumbled, cajoled and ranted through many hundreds of discussions of what seemed to me to be an illogical and paradoxical objection to radio-collaring foxes, I have come to understand that logic is often not the trump card that ingenuous academics suppose it to be. I think the problem is that for many shepherds and 'keepers a fox in the hand is already dead, by definition, so that to release it unharmed is, in effect, to create another fox and thus, to the hardened fox-hater, to commit a nightmarish variant on reincarnation. Without Edwin's patronage, not to say protection, I would not have stood a chance of studying foxes on the fells.

Edwin took me to the fell, showed me his best fox holes, pointed to the tracks in the plantations, the scats on the rabbit warrens. Here was the stonebed where Alec Mason had waited for many long, long nights to shoot a vixen; here was the cliff where you could peer over and sometimes surprise a fox sunning itself on the ledge below; here was the gully where Maurice Bell's Wensleydale Foxhounds had jumped that old fox; there was the place where Jo Wear's Ullswater hounds had nailed the vixen who had lost her cubs and turned to lamb worrying. Not forgetting the pure white fox, the bob-tailed fox, and the cubs in the peat hole and many others. Soon the barren sweep of the hill was studded with foxy anecdotes.

I had put in a fair few miles of walking on Dufton Fell, and a routine was developing. By day I trailed the hills, looking for signs of foxes, trying to catch them, and getting nowhere fast. At tea time I'd make my way back to Bow Hall and recount my futile but enjoyable adventures to a good-natured audience over delicious cakes and huge pots of tea. There, I'd drink in the warmth of the fire and the enthralling stories of the last days of a vanishing era. The stone-floored room was oblong and tall, with meat hooks and sides of bacon hanging from the ceiling. Most of us sat on a bench around a long schoolroom dining table, while 'The Boss'—old, ill, but still the patriarch—sat separately on his Windsor chair, its wooden arms worn smooth by a lineage of roughened hands.

The Boss stared at his slippers, wore patched dungarees, had tousled grey hair that sprouted at reckless angles and startlingly boyish blue eyes. He did not say much, but what he did say was thoughtful and good-natured and commanded everybody's attention. Then there was Edwin's other uncle, Joss, perpetually ribbing Edwin and glowing with pride for his handsome fell ponies, and there was Joss' wife Elsie, a cheerful farmer's-wifely woman, who slaved over the brown enamelled coal range to provide the mountains of food that were consumed at six sit-down meals daily. And Joss' schoolboy son, Frank, who had seen more days of hard work than many men twice his age. Folded at the end of the table were the rangy limbs of Big John, the Boss' son. And there was Edwin, his character as jaunty as his cap which somehow retained its grip while perched almost vertically on the side of his head. We talked of foxes and lambs, of terriers and hounds, of scab and staggers and louping ill.

And all the while I was learning a new language, for the Westmorland brogue, amply smattered with thee's and thou's, turned school to skial, cake to kiark, freezing to starving, food to bait, very to gaily, clever to canny, slippery to slape, holes to oils, and used a form of address that sounded disconcertingly like 'sister' as a friendly greeting for grown men! (In fact it was 'Sees'ta', a contracted version of 'See'st thou?' and used as an exclamation 'Look!')

More than a month of failure to catch foxes had slipped past by the time that Edwin, his best friend, Arthur, and I stood at Scordale Beck. The grey walls of the valley hung eerily above us, a dipper bobbed in and out of the torrent, and Wick, Sparrow and Nancy milled around our boots. These three mildly named working terriers were the scarred representatives of a warrior race. The risks of the Border terrier's trade are encapsulated nowhere better than in the breed's standard, which states that part (only) of the terrier's face may be missing—in the show ring such missing parts may be assumed by judges to be perfect. Edwin and Arthur had decided to take me in hand and had offered to help me catch

foxes. The only available method in that rocky landscape was to bolt the fox into a net, a distinctly worrying prospect since the baiting-type terrier which confined itself to haranguing the fox was unknown and unwanted in these hills where men were men and terriers 'hard'. The muscular necks and wiry fur of our three accomplices did little to reassure me. I remembered the story of how an earlier generation of 'keepers used to select them: each of a litter of pups was picked up by its upper lip and shaken; those that squealed went to the bucket, those that retorted with an infant snarl were kept. However, on this occasion Edwin and Arthur had chosen the most inexperienced, and therefore least hard, terriers they could find. So with their chains clacking, we set off up Scordale.

On the north slope, we clambered over scree and rock, through tall bracken, and into a small woodland of wind-stunted hawthorn trees. The gradient was so steep, that as we climbed up each man's face came close to the heels of the man in front. Puffing, panting and bantering we climbed towards Mason's Holes. I looked at the map and, sure enough, Mason's Holes were marked—it's a fair reflection of local obsessions when fox holes are marked on the Ordnance Survey map.

Mason's Holes had a multitude of openings, nestled amongst a landslide of boulders the size of beer barrels. The dogs sniffed gustily at the entrances, their bodies stiffened, tails whirring—there was a fox at home (or at yam, as the dialect had it). The openings were far more numerous than our nets, so many had to remain un-guarded. Wick, judged to be the milksop of our company, was slipped in. Many minutes ticked by as we heard the echoes of his claws scraping on rock in the distant labyrinth, until he reap-peared, looking somewhat puzzled, from a hole 15 metres or more down the bank. Next Nancy had a turn; she too seemed sure that a fox was somewhere close, but failed to find it. Again and again the dogs tried until, suddenly, there was a furore of barking, a clattering of stones, and 7 kg of dog fox rocketed from one of the few holes draped with a net. In an instant he was grabbed, disentangled, speedily equipped with a radio-collar, christened Mason, and released back into his lair. At the sight of Mason making his exit unharmed, realization of just what a dreadful thing they had done dawned on the faces of shepherds and terriers alike. However, my jubi-lation saved their spirits and we moved on to search for other earths.

All day we trailed on, up Swindale Crag, across the Slape Stones to the holes called Fox Yards, to the rock holes on Roman Fell where many a terrier had met its end, and up to the peat holes on Murton Fell. Not so much as a sniff of a fox rewarded our efforts until, in the afternoon, we cut back to the south slope of Scordale and reached Amber Holes. Amber Holes, like all the others, had been 'dogged' with fierce terriers for decades, probably for centuries. The best holes were visited every month, some every week during lambing, and yet generation after generation of foxes chose to lie up in the very same spots that had been the undoing of so many of their ancestors. Meanwhile, other holes, just as homely to the human eye, remained scorned by the foxes. What it was that drew foxes to these special dens I do not know. At Amber Holes we were in luck again. Deep in the hillside the terriers found another fox, and cornered it in a passage just below where we stood. Through chinks between the boulders we could glimpse

flashes of red fur, but nothing would induce the fox to bolt into our nets. It began to rain, and we began to quarry. A heavy metal crow-bar was at hand, doubtless discarded years before during some previous foxing expedition. Levering and pushing we shifted boulders to the side, prising an access to the fox. It was heavy, skin-raking work, made all the more so as the rocks became slippery with rain. Dusk began to fall, the fox shifted position. Reaching an arm's length through the boulders, I grabbed at its scruff as it passed within reach, and soon the second fox of the day was fitted with its radio and released. This one, a vixen, was named Amber.

The light was fading as we walked home-ward, down Scordale Beck. I was overjoyed with our success, but as we neared Hilton village, and the pub, Edwin and Arthur grew more downcast at the prospect of explaining what we had been doing. Their laughing banter took on the nervous tension typical, as I recall, of jokes told while waiting outside the headmaster's study prior to being caned. Out of the darkness, we stood blinking in the smoke-laden light of the pub. We were dripping wet, smeared in mud, and accom-panied by a leash of swarthy terriers—there was only one thing that we could have been doing. A welcoming chorus of 'Aye lads! How'ster ga'in on? What'ster bin de'in, thun?' met us. Edwin jumped in with both feet—we had been busy setting free a couple of foxes. Riotous mirth greeted this preposterous joke. The tension visibly went out of Edwin's massive shoulders. Yes, we had spent the day liberating a couple of our long-tailed friends up Scordale—more laugh-ter. Edwin was in full throttle now: 'Yon canny lad'—gesturing at me—had stuck little bleepers on them so that we could call them if we wanted them. The other shepherds were getting into the spirit of the joke now—one wag jibed 'Sees'ta, thou'll tell us next yon cuddly la'l boogers 'ad ne-ams!' 'Aye', said Edwin, 'Dog called Mason, bitch was Amber', Well, we had a fair old evening toasting Mason, Amber, their unborn cubs and their ancestors. When we came to leave, Edwin and Arthur were beside themselves with merri-ment: they had committed heresy, confessed, and nobody had believed them!

Slowly I began to learn how to radio track in the fells, following radio signals as they ricocheted from cliff faces at misleading angles.

Edwin Dargue out foxing.

At once it was clear that Mason and Amber had enormous ranges in comparison to the lowland foxes I had known. The comparison was kept all the more vivid because the necessity to maintain routine observations in both places forced me to drive between Oxford and Cumbria every few weeks. Problems seemed to leap up to await me at either end: I sped down the motorway to find that in Oxfordshire the batteries in Blackears' transmitter had expired, and that a 'keeper had killed another of our foxes. Up north again, I was summoned by the Commanding Officer of Warcop Ministry of Defence firing range—some of his soldiers had shot Mason on the fell, and smashed the radio-collar for fear that its signals would trigger their rockets. They had killed Mason three kilometres onto the fell from his holes—more than four times the diameter of a typical territory on Boar's Hill. At least Amber's radio was functioning well, but she was leading me a merry dance around the 'slape' stones on Roman Fell, where following her over the scree

by moonlight was a harrowing experience. The bitter truth was that Amber was sometimes almost untrackable because of the danger. It seemed unlikely that she would provide adequate information to answer the obvious questions: why were fell foxes' ranges so big, and were they, like those in Oxfordshire, defended territories? Then our luck changed: we caught Pussghyll Dog.

Pussghyll Dog was a beauty. He weighed a good 8 kg, had a large white tag to his brush, and a broad, intelligent-looking face. His teeth were magnificent, worn and mature, but not chipped, and he was soon bleeping on Channel 7 of my radio receiver. As soon as we released him he ran off to some gorse in Pussghyll, and hence earned his name. However, as time went on, it transpired that this refuge was on the very edge of his range. By night, in howling winds and punishing temperatures, Pussghyll Dog led me six kilometres along the fellside, and as far again over the moors. For the most part he steered well

clear of any human habitation, quite the opposite of the Oxfordshire foxes whose movements hugged human settlements. He would circle Bow Hall, visiting the gully opposite to explore the whins where rabbits abounded. Occasionally I would see him, through the hot-eye, loping through the bushes, sprinting whenever a rabbit chanced in his path. Soon every rabbit would be underground and Pussghyll would move on, up through Harthwaite, to the field-house where there were more rabbits, then on up the hill. At the summit, his route would either cut through the steep valley to the allotments at Keisley, or else would wind on upwards, through Burthwaite 'lotment to High Cup Nick (allotments being the last band of enclosed second-rate land below open fell). I used to dread the latter route. High Cup Nick is a spectacular glacial valley, cut savagely into the Pennine whinsill, with rocky flanks that drop 300 metres in a few stones' throws. By day these slopes were negotiable down sheep trods at a tendon-rending scramble. By night, I was scared stiff of them.

Pussghyll Dog would skirt High Cup, his low-slung form dodging the worst of the ice-laden wind which sliced through my moleskin breeks. Around the top, he led me over the place where the track crossed the treacherously slimy stones of a waterfall, onto the fell top with its rabbits and grouse, past the flyblown corpse of a ewe to add another to the accumulation of his scats that were her puzzling epitaph, and back around High Cup crag to the Old Man, a chimney of rock perched above the cliff. Pussghyll Dog would then drop down into the valley and head towards Harbour Flatt and the allotments to the south, leaving me too timorous to risk the descent, and having to retrace my steps. An hour and a half later, with luck, I would pick him up again, skirting Murton Pike to Cringley Holes and around to the whins below Mell Fell, bordering precisely on Scordale Beck, just the other side of the stream from Amber's hunting ground. It was a huge distance, encompassing some 1300 hectares of appalling radio-tracking conditions—an area roughly 70 times that occupied by Roger and his group on Boar's Hill. Clearly, in regard to their movements, the hill foxes were behaving differently from their lowland cousins.

A further two months passed before I radio-collared my next fox, Gaythorne Vixen, and yet another month before her neighbour, Muddy-ghyll Vixen, came my way too. They both lived south of Appleby, on the grassy moors and limestone pavements known by the belligerent sounding name of Orton Scar. My first encounter with Muddyghyll Vixen was successful only by the skin of its teeth—my skin, her teeth! I was with Boots at the time. Boots (whose nickname had stuck from days as a bootboy at Appleby Castle), was otherwise known as Gordon Shaw— a man whose increasingly spherical frame belied a very considerable toughness. He was a railway ganger when not busy as a mole catcher, ferreter, terrier man and pheasant rearer. Any fox that trod the moors from Hoff to Orton was on his patch, and living on borrowed time. Yet Boots took me under his wing.

After his wife Irene had stuffed me with scones, we plodded the fields. Boots used an ancient pair of curling tongs to dip juicy earth-worms into strychnine and poke them into mole holes. We made detours to look for signs at fox earth after fox earth. On one such trip we came to a little valley in Muddyghyll Plain. At the top of the slope a wizened tree had hunched its back to the wind, and clung precariously to the soil with spidery roots. A freshly dug tunnel led between these roots, and the loose dirt bore clear fox pawprints. A sniff at the entrance was rewarded by a warm fug of fox. The nets were draped over the entrances, and Boots' Nip was slipped in. A few seconds later a fox launched into the net with such force that it pulled the retaining peg free from the ground and landed at our feet. In the split second that it took us to move, one rear leg, then another, thrust clear of the net. As I lunged towards the fox, I realized that it was rolling away from me and rapidly emerging from the net. The fox and I leapt, neither of us could hold our balance on the steep slope, and side by side we tumbled to the bottom. By the time we got there we were two metres apart, and the fox was completely free of the net which draped from one of its ears. I pounced, there was a scuffle, and I found that in grappling for the fox's neck I had fumbled and thrust my fingers firmly into its

open mouth! The fox was so nonplussed that its jaws snappped shut only the instant after my hand whisked free. So it was that Muddyghyll Vixen was radio-collared, and I impaled myself on her teeth, providing Boots with the funniest sight that he had ever seen.

These two vixens also travelled enormous ranges, 1,000 hectares apiece. Gaythorne Vixen moved so fast across such a mosaic of farmsteads that she could be tracked only by car. I raced between vantage points as she circled west from Gaythorne Hall, through the small pastures behind Maulds Meaburn, and on towards Crosby Ravensworth Fell five kilometres south. There her route skirted the old Roman settlement at Ewe Close and down Wicker Street to Coalpit Hill and Robin Hood's Grave. As she loped back to the east and skirted Marksclose Wood, I had the excitement of simultaneously hearing her radio signal from my left and Muddyghyll's from my right. At Linglow Hill their ranges came together along a neatly drawn border.

In contrast to Gaythorne, Muddyghyll Vixen was almost impossible to track except on foot, and her movements led me stumbling far across the ankle-twisting cubes of limestone strewn across Asby Scar. In the company of startled sheep and curlew calls, Muddyghyll Vixen and I felt our ways along the sheep trods, along the leeward sides of tumbling dykes, and through the maze of trails which the power of erosion had etched on the scrag-edged limestone. Her route led between rabbit-grazed lawns where, by day, I found her droppings on the warrens, together with the occasional sign of a successful kill. As the wind whistled and fluted in the crags, Muddyghyll would find a basin of slack ground, a hollow beneath the fur-ruffling force of the wind. There, she would curl up to sleep. Several 100 metres behind, and learning from her, I too would seek out a hollow. Sticking my dipole antenna on a nearby vantage point, a technical monument alert among the stony tumuli, I would curl up on a grassy couch soothed by the unvary-ing bleep in my headphones which signalled her continuing immobility. With back to the wind and goose-pimply snug, I would doze until a change in note of Muddyghyll's signal would alert me to her awakening. Dawn might find us on the other side of the moor, looking down over Sunbiggin Tarn, where hordes of black-headed

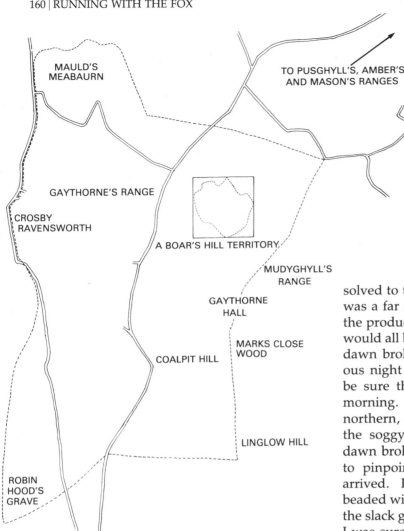

MAULD'S
MEABAURN

TO PUSGHYLL'S, AMBER'S
AND MASON'S RANGES

TERRITORY BORDERS

0   1KM

GAYTHORNE'S RANGE

CROSBY
RAVENSWORTH

A BOAR'S HILL TERRITORY

MUDYGHYLL'S
RANGE

GAYTHORNE
HALL

MARKS CLOSE
WOOD

COALPIT HILL

LINGLOW HILL

ROBIN
HOOD'S
GRAVE

gulls wheeled and called in raucous satisfaction at having survived another night.

Having radio-tracked five hill foxes I concluded that they were maintaining territories, but what of social groups? Various clues pointed towards group sizes of at least three adults in several territories, but without more radio-tagged animals I lacked solid proof. Certainly, in Pussghyll's territory two litters of cubs were born. Indeed, barren vixens were regarded as a rarity by the shepherds (although they may have been less likely to find them due to concentrating their attention on breeding dens).

Just at the time when I was tracking Muddyghyll and Gaythorne Vixens, the filming of our television documentary was in full swing. Despite the obvious practical difficulties, we re-solved to try for some footage of the hill foxes. It was a far from trivial achievement ensuring that the production team, soundman and cameraman would all be at Orton Scar and ready for action as dawn broke on the agreed morning. The previous night I radio-tracked Muddyghyll Vixen, to be sure that I would know where she was by morning. Luckily, she finished the night at the northern, and most accessible, tip of her range, the soggy allotments east of Linglow Hill. As dawn broke I stalked downwind of her, anxious to pinpoint her whereabouts before the crew arrived. It was a glorious Spring morning, beaded with dew and alive with bird song. Using the slack ground, I slunk down a stream bed until I was sure of Muddyghyll's position.

Just as I began my retreat, the radio signal fluttered, and I knew she was on the move again. To my horror, I realized that Muddyghyll Vixen was making her way towards me. Moment by moment the signal grew louder; there was nowhere for me to hide and, anyway, it was already too late. I was sure that she was wandering up the same stream bed in which I was crouching. I hunkered down in the peat hag, where the side of the bank was eroded. Padding lazily along the water's edge, Muddyghyll Vixen appeared not 30 metres from me. In her mouth hung the corpse of a young rabbit. Twenty metres from me she paused. The scene was idyllic—the rust-red vixen, the moorland backdrop, the condensation spiralling as her warm breath was stung by the cold, wet dawn. But all this and no cameraman. Furthermore, at any instant Muddyghyll would spot me and take flight to some distant, inaccess-

ible crag, taking with her our hopes for an upland sequence in the film. She gazed straight at me, turned wearily, and padded up the bank and out of sight. Miraculously, she had been oblivious of my presence.

Half an hour later, in the lee of Marksclose Wood, dark clouds were gathering, and a fine but unpleasant drizzle trickled down our chilled necks as I discussed strategy with the BBC crew. Conditions worsened by the moment and the only hope was to abandon the tripod, spare film magazine and assistant. Hugh Maynard stalked forward with me in the hope of getting a hand-held shot of Muddyghyll, using my shoulder as a support for the heavy camera and long telephoto lens. There would, at most, be only one chance, and on this our whole sequence depended. As the drizzle turned to splashing raindrops, Hugh's mood became blacker than the leaden sky. It was now or never. I was wired up to the radio-microphone to record the sounds of our progress. Pointing the antenna in Muddyghyll's direction I crept forward with Hugh a pace behind, leaving the rest of the crew to listen to, and record, our whispered blasphemies as we squelched closer and closer to the vixen. Forty minutes later the radio signal was deafening in my headphones. We had done well to get this close undetected and were grateful as the wind continued to blow squarely in our faces. Pace by pace we edged forward. Hugh began to film my back; zooming out so that his view widened over my shoulder and along the antenna beam as I scanned for the signal. Any minute Muddyghyll must be seen, but Hugh had only one magazine of film, and he was fearful of 'running' too soon. 10, 20, 30 agonizingly silent paces forward, and still no sign of the vixen. Hugh's back was giving way under the strain of holding the heavy camera at the ready. The signal could not have been louder if the transmitter had been in my hand. We were on top of the transmitter and the air was so drenched in radio signals that the antenna had lost its directionality. Perhaps we had walked past the fox, perhaps she had slipped her collar, or gone to ground, or perhaps that rabbit had been poisoned bait and she lay dead nearby. We did not know what to do, so Hugh started filming, and I took one last pace forward. A split second later Muddyghyll Vixen leapt up smack in the middle of Hugh's viewfinder.

For a few seconds he filmed her as she jinked in a wild dash away from us, then she was lost from sight. Moments later she appeared again, racing down a slope below us. Hugh wedged the camera on my shoulder, pulled to maximum zoom and began filming just as the distant fox leapt astride a stone wall and paused in as beautiful a moorland panorama as one could imagine. The clouds parted just above the vixen and a shaft of sunlight pierced the drizzle, suffusing the scene with rich, warm light. Off the wall and into a field of sheep, she ran in a wide arc through the flock and into the distance. It made a stunning sequence.

As lambing time approached, the farmer's thoughts turned with increasing unease to the risk of fox attack. Edwin and I nurtured a special dread: what if one of our radio-collared foxes was caught slaughtering lambs—then we really would be in trouble. My fears of the impending carnage were doubtless heightened by grim boyhood memories: my Uncle Iain's normally jovial features furrowed as we stared down at a lamb, its entrails trailing like bloated worms from a gash in its flank. They were certainly the first entrails I had seen, and that lamb was probably my first close encounter with death. I remember its burial vividly as it was stamped into the muckheap with a curse about foxes for an epitaph. Spring on my uncle's farm in the southern uplands of Scotland was childhood bliss for me, a bliss tarnished only by queasy regrets of the farmyard deaths. The worst occasion struck while Uncle Iain (who had a spell-binding way of making a cigarette appear to travel in one ear and out of the other), Rags the collie, and I were making a circuit of the farm to fetch in Mary the milkcow. We rounded a stone dyke to find the dismal sight of a couped ewe (that is, one struck irrecoverably on her back, trapped by the weight of her own water-logged fleece). As she writhed and bleated in panic my gaze was locked, in horror, on two wet, black holes in her face—hooded crows had pecked out her eyes while she lay stranded. With memories of those empty sockets, my uncle's fury, and the crack of the ensuing shot, one could hardly do other than sympathize with the sheep farmer's loathing of predators. But are the culprits as guilty as they appear? In the case of the hooded crows, appearances have turned out to be deceptive. In a

24. DO FOXES KILL FOR FUN?

The idea that they kill for 'fun', or 'sport', or even simple malice is as widespread as foxes themselves, but is it true? There is no doubt that a single fox may wreak havoc in a farmer's hen coop or a gamekeeper's pheasant pen, killing every poult in sight. Does this prove that foxes are motivated by vicious bloodlust? The answer is no.

Foxes are not unique in killing more, sometimes much more, than they can eat at the time. This phenomenon, known as surplus killing, is widespread amongst the 200 or so meat-eating species of the Order Carnivora. Wolves, coyotes, dingos and jackals do it; lions, tigers and lynx do it; mink and wolverines do it, and so, too, do mongooses and hyaenas. Even leopard seals do it, lying in wait beneath an ice floe to ambush penguin after penguin. Furthermore, although domestic stock are often the victims (indeed, the cause), this is not invariably so; surplus killing is a natural phenomenon and happens in the wild.

What function could this behaviour serve? It seems that surplus killing is triggered by abnormal behaviour on behalf of the prey, not the predator. Hans Kruuk was the first person to make sense of this when he studied predation on black-headed gulls by red foxes. Conventionally, these gulls nest upon tussocks of vegetation in marshland, so that each nest is surrounded by its own moat. However, in one colony the gulls behaved oddly and nested on sand dunes. For the most part these dune-nesting gulls avoided fox predation by taking flight, but on a few nights each spring they were massacred. On these nights the foxes' paths through the colony could be plotted by the trails of dead gulls, killed on their nest and discarded. Careful sleuthing revealed that these massive surplus kills only occurred during nights when high winds swept the coast and storm clouds obscured the moon. Hans Kruuk discovered that in such treacherous weather the sitting gulls refused to take flight, presumably because to do so was more risky than sitting tight. So, the fox trotting through the colony found itself confronted with the same bizarre phenomenon as the fox in the poultry house or release pen: prey that fail to run away. Under these abnormal circumstances, the fox does what foxes normally do, namely grab the opportunity. If only these particular gulls had followed the practice of all other black-headed gulls, and nested in a marsh, then their habit of sitting tight on stormy nights would have paid off. If Hans Kruuk's proposed mechanism is correct then the root of the problem lay not in vulpine bloodlust, but in the gulls nesting in the 'wrong' place.

The fox's normal behaviour can therefore be inappropriate when the prey's behaviour is abnormal. As a result, this can lead to the wastage of prey (disadvantageous to the fox as well as the poultryman). Under this explanation surplus killing has no function—it arises from the misfiring of a trait that is useful in another context (like modern man's tendency to take too much sugar). In this case catching prey requires snap decisions and split second timing. Under normal circumstances a fox adapted to snatch additional prey will be at an advantage, as long as it has a way of storing the food for future consumption. Indeed, foxes behave in precisely this way, making caches of surplus food (see Chapter 4). The unsatisfactory feature of this explanation is that it requires belief in maladaptation in creatures which otherwise epitomize predatory adaptation (a belief which could, mistakenly, be interpreted as a whitewash on the fox's character).

Questions about the mechanism of the function of surplus killing may one day be answered, which distinguishes them from questions such as whether foxes take pleasure in killing, which are philosophically unanswerable. The sensation we recognize as pleasure is, like any other trait, presumably the product of natural selection, and in humans I guess it arose as a device which gave immediate rewards to individuals that behaved in ways that promoted their survival and Darwinian fitness (for example, eating and mating). Since predators must kill to survive, it does not strike me as unreasonable to suppose they enjoy killing (assuming they are subject to emotions recognizable to humans). I have watched foxes surplus killing. Certainly their postures and expressions were neither aggressive nor frantic. If anything they looked playful, or perhaps merely purposeful. The fact that we can never know what, if anything, a fox feels about killing does not affect the fact that it is nonsensical to judge them on human cultural values. Words like evil, vengeful and wicked are all too often provoked by the fox's predatory behaviour, even when no surplus prey are killed. Such words may have occasional relevance to discussions of human morality, but none whatsoever to fox behaviour.

survey in 1962 shepherds in Argyll estimated that crow attack cost them £60,000 annually. When biologist David Houston began a study of the problem he found that lamb mortality there was indeed high at 15–20%. Furthermore, 48% of lambs found dead showed signs of damage by crows. Yet post mortem examinations showed that four out of five of those mutilated lambs had actually been pecked after death, and that three-quarters of those few that had been pecked while alive had already been in the terminal stages of starvation. In fact, the birds had actually been responsible for the deaths of only 1.4% of the lambs which at first impression one might have thought they had killed! Houston's study showed how in Argyll circumstantial evidence had led the farmers to jump to the wrong conclusion: the reality was that with existing shepherding practice, of 1,700 lambs born in his study area, two more might have survived had it not been for crows! Even the attacks on couped ewes were not all they seemed: because rumen gases cannot escape when a sheep is on its back, couped sheep will suffocate within about 12 hours if not righted. Therefore, those not rescued

quickly are doomed whether or not crows attack them. There is a great deal in common between hooded crows and red foxes—both can behave in ways which we judge distasteful or brutal, and both are burdened by dreadful reputations—so the crow's acquittal raises the possibility that the verdict on the fox might be fallible too. How much damage do foxes do to lambs, how much difference to this does fox control make, and is the control cost-effective?

With such questions in mind, I started to watch the ewes by night as they grazed the low moors of Orton Scar. These were Dalesbred sheep, a lovely breed whose black noses are punctuated with vivid white exclamation marks. As Spring advanced and the ewes became acutely tubby, so too Gaythorne and Muddyghyll Vixens grew heavy with cub. Most of the ewes were gathered in to lamb in the small pastures that hugged the valley bottoms. They and the foxes were in nightly contact; occasionally a flock would split as a fox passed between them, but for the most part I could seen scant reaction from either party. Once their offspring were born I feared this disinterested tolerance would change:

the foxes would have cubs to feed and the ewes would have lambs to protect. As I waited for the births I was torn by the need to keep tabs on the Oxfordshire foxes too. The compromise was frenetic commuting up and down the backbone of England. So it was that in the small hours of one morning, I found myself at the Tebay Transport Café, gazing wearily into the somewhat unwelcome rainbow that shimmered on the oily surface of my mug of tea. Soon I was chatting with the massively tattooed Glaswegian drivers of southbound articulated lorries. Their harsh banter gave way to astonished fascination with my journey north to keep a date with a pregnant fox. Three nights later some of us met again at the Tebay Café; this time I was heading south and they north. The announcement that Gaythorne's cubs had been born brought broad grins and a congratulatory chinking of already chipped mugs; the good news, they promised, would be relayed to the other drivers at cafés around the land.

Gaythorne Vixen• girth birth on the 28th March, and Muddyghyll's cubs arrived almost a fortnight later. Just as Gaythorne's cubs were born, the peak of lambing was upon us and her range was adrift with animated, bleating snowflakes. Before and after their few days' confinement following whelping, the two vixens moved nightly among the ewes and lambs. Each night Muddyghyll crossed the moor and slipped into the fields beside the Asby road. Occasionally I glimpsed her through the hot-eye, trotting busily about the field. I saw her sprinting after rabbits, for the lambing field was also pock-marked with rabbit warrens. At other times her distant shadowy figure pulled and pawed at indistinct shapes on the ground where a torch-light inspection revealed a bloody stain on the grass beside a glistening sliver of membrane: Muddyghyll was eating afterbirths.

On some of the occasions when I saw the vixens among the sheep they were eating after-births, but they also scavenged beside lambs which were far from newborn. Clearly, the foxes must be after something else too. At last I got a good view: Muddyghyll Vixen was eating the lamb's dung. On reflection it does make sense:

25. DO FOXES KILL SICKLY LAMBS?

Any animal below par, sick or enfeebled is less able to escape predators. Furthermore, because it pays predators to take the easiest option, they have a sharp eye for such weaklings and select them out. Do foxes selectively kill sickly lambs and, if they do, does this mean that they are not pests to sheep farmers? A team of Australian scientists shed light on this when they studied a flock of Merino ewes in which lamb mortality was at 25 per cent. They examined the dead lambs for evidence that they had been killed by foxes. In this context the reader should be alert to the different impressions sometimes given by expressing data on predators as a percentage of deaths or of births. For example, of those Merino lambs, 26.7 per cent of dead lambs showed signs of mutilation by predators, which is to say that 6.6 per cent of lambs born showed such signs.

The scientists examined these mutilated corpses and found that just half of them had been weak, with minimal fat and possibly doomed anyway. Had there been no fox predation, an estimated three extra lambs in 100 would have survived. I have re-analysed

Moore's and his colleagues' data on the reasonable assumption that lambs which survived had been healthy and those that died had not. From these data it emerges that foxes killed 3.8 per cent of the available healthy lambs and 16.7 per cent of the available unhealthy ones (i.e. those which subsequently died anyway). This almost five-fold selectivity seems to be good evidence that these foxes were seeking out weak lambs. Another Australian study, this time by Alexander and his colleagues, actually watched foxes foraging in a large lambing paddock. Foxes were frequent visitors to the paddock (sometimes five at a time), and they were principally involved in eating afterbirths. Neither ewes nor lambs showed any fear of foxes, but it is commonplace for prey to appear nonchalant when they 'know' predators are not hunting them. However, they were very fearful of a stray collie that also visited, and the observers did see a fox backing away when approached by a lamb! Clearly the foxes in this study were not always so timorous since 2.7 per cent of lambs born were killed by them despite being healthy, and a further 4.4 per

cent were killed while starving. Alexander and his colleagues saw one healthy lamb killed: it walked towards the passing fox which grabbed it by the neck; the fox ate the lamb's head and tail.

In Scotland, Ray Hewson assessed the fat around the hearts and kidneys (scant fat tending to indicate poor condition) of predated lambs. On average the lambs killed by foxes were in better condition than were those that died of starvation and illness. However, there was no evidence as to whether they were as healthy as those that survived.

What other factors, aside from bodily condition, might affect a fox's selection of lambs? An obvious answer is size: most Blackface lambs killed by foxes are less than 4.2 kg (most are killed when less than five days old). Twins may be at greater risk since the mother cannot defend them both simultaneously (the argument is further complicated because on some hill ground twins place such a burden on the ewe that the loss of one may increase the survivor's chances). It is argued that the practice of mating small upland ewes with larger breeds of downland rams (to generate

heavier lamb) leads to difficult, prolonged labour and greater risk of fox (and crow) predation (all the more so if twins are involved). Much may depend on the mother's care too, which is affected by her own condition. On the open hill, lambs of gimmers (ewes breeding for the first time) suffered higher mortality than those born to more experienced mothers (overall, 32 versus 9 per cent). Experienced mothers tended to stick closer to their lambs than did gimmers, which not only indicates a poorer mother-infant bond, but also an increased risk of predation.

If one was to risk a generalization from such scanty evidence, it is that foxes tend to select disadvantaged lambs, but do not invariably do so. However, the question of whether foxes select infirm victims, while biologically interesting, is increasingly irrelevant in practice as one moves from the hard hill to lowland farms where easier shepherding conditions and sophisticated husbandry mean that non-viable lambs can be less common. Even the most unpromising weakling can be cosseted all the way to market.

the milky faeces of young lambs are rich in undigested fats and proteins. Of course, foods like afterbirths and lambs' pellets show up the weakness of diet studies (like mine) that rely heavily on examination of fox droppings—such meals leave few detectable remains. That April I found only 12 fox scats in Muddyghyll's and Gaythorne's ranges; every single one of them was crammed with rabbit fur (a couple contained vole fur and beetle remains too). One thing they did not contain was any trace of lamb's wool. Perhaps this was reflected in the ewes' unruffled reactions to the vixens. Some drifted slowly from the section of the field where a fox foraged. Others seemed quite unconcerned. Several times I saw an old ewe stamp her feet irritably when Muddyghyll Vixen strayed too close to her lamb.

My apprehensions grew when, in late April, Gaythorne moved her day time harbourage to an earth in the middle of a lambing field. One day, in a hollow on Linglow Hill, I found a mutilated lamb, its tail and part of a hind leg chewed off. The holes in its neck seemed to be the puncture wounds of a fox's canine teeth, and the splashes of blood and bruising beneath the skin confirmed that this lamb had been alive when the fox had struck. Then I noticed its feet—sticking like a wrapping of cellophane to the underside of the hooves were dried birth membranes—this lamb had never walked. An incision with my penknife revealed an empty stomach—it had not sucked either. Perhaps it had been a weakling—born alive, cleaned by its mother, but perhaps doomed from the outset. Or perhaps it had been the first of twins, and had been killed before being fully cleansed while its dam was preoccupied with her second birth. Both suggestions are plausible. In the territories of the two vixens on Orton Scar I found a total of four dead lambs that had been partly eaten by foxes, and two of these showed no sign of bleeding and so had presumably died before the fox took them. Of course, I may have missed some other corpses, but I think it is fair to conclude that no great carnage occurred in those two territories that year.

Meanwhile, the Swaledale ewes on the high fell were lambing about a fortnight behind the Dalesbred flock at Orton, and so the focus shifted to Pussghyll Dog's territory. Edwin was in his element, striding among the newborn, a lamb swinging by the forelegs from each hand as he sorted out one maternity problem after another. Newborn tails were 'ringed' with tight elastic bands that cut the circulation so that a few days later a shrivelled remnant dropped off to provide the foxes with a morsel to scavenge. The scrotums of ram lambs suffered a similar fate—less than a generation ago the shepherds simply bit them off! Edwin, as often as not with his forearm in up to the elbow as he delivered a lamb, whistled shrill instructions to his dogs—he had followed the old school and filed a gap between his front teeth so he could whistle commands without withdrawing his fingers.

A fox killed a seemingly healthy lamb in the allotment behind Bow Hall and left it uneaten; there were dead ewes in Burthwaite Allotment, but they too remained untouched. I began to puzzle over two questions, which may or may not be related: why are so few lambs killed by foxes, and why do foxes not eat more lamb (or mutton)? After all, the hills and fields throng with tasty, defenceless, woolly morsels. Considering the number of foxes in most areas, if most of them killed lambs habitually the losses would be astronomical. Since they are not, I presume that most foxes rarely or never kill a lamb. There are three actors in this plot: the foxes, the sheep and the farmers, and the behaviour of all three can affect the outcome. The ewe's defence of her lamb may be critical (and will be affected by a host of factors—see Box 25, p.166). The farmers' husbandry may be more or less diligent and may reflect forces that unwittingly set the scene for fox predation. For example, British hill farmers are paid a government subsidy based on the number of sheep they keep, not on the number of lambs they produce—inevitably the result is overstocking; with sheep surviving on a subsistence knife-edge a slight change in circumstances (such as hard weather) may affect the condition and thus behaviour of ewes and lambs, and this may in turn affect fox behaviour. On some hill farms almost half of newborn lambs' deaths are due to depleted fat reserves, that is to say, lambs are born starving due to their mothers' poor condition. From the foxes viewpoint, the brevity of the period when lambs are small enough readily to fall prey to them (mostly 1–5 days but up to a couple of months) may be part of the answer. Remembering how fear of the unfamiliar caused the foxes at our Boar's Hill feeding site to reject mice it is possible that it takes them a while to realize that lambs are food (that realization might depend on whether they had been fed lamb as cubs). Of course stories abound on what turns a fox to lamb-killing (and on why they strike only some properties and some years). Vixens bereft of cubs, barren vixens, and dog foxes whose mate has been killed are all favourite scapegoats in an anthropomorphic search for the most likely culprits. A frequent suggestion is that the culprits are 'rogue' foxes. The idea that one fox among many is the 'rogue' gains credence since bouts of lamb-worrying often stop when a particular fox is killed. In Edwin's clearest case no more lambs were lost after the last of the three vixens was killed; in a similar story from Wales it stopped after 76 foxes had been killed. The fact is that lamb-worrying always stops eventually, and shepherds almost always kill foxes during lambing. Thus it is inevitable that one fox or another is almost certain to be killed shortly before the lamb-worrying ceases. The fact is that almost nothing is known about the fox's behaviour as a predator on lambs.

The second question was why do foxes in some sheep farming areas eat so much sheep meat (mostly scavenged) while in others they seem to eat little of it? In the ranges of my hill foxes, dead lambs and sheep were often left to rot uneaten. Nonetheless, they were clearly visited by foxes, who deposited valedictory droppings on the corpses. Of those few lambs from which the foxes had eaten at all, most had only been nibbled—a tail chewed off, perhaps the liver gone—but almost always less than a square fox meal had been eaten. Meanwhile, amidst this plenty I saw the radio vixens in strenuous pursuit of rabbits, dodging amongst lambs as if they were obstacles rather than free food. Furthermore, live lambs might be killed while dead ones were readily available.

I began to suspect that one explanation was that lamb or mutton carrion is not a preferred food. This suggestion would be compatible with the fact that lamb carcasses often accumulate uneaten at breeding earths (as do moles and other un-preferred food, while favoured food like rabbits and voles rarely remain uneaten). Therefore I suspect that one of many factors which may

Fox droppings on sheep skull.

underlie local differences in the amount of lamb eaten by foxes is the availability of an alternative prey. When I discussed this with Dr Ray Hewson, a biologist studying foxes in Scotland, he told me that foxes scavenge lots of Blackface lambs on the West Coast where there is scant alternative. In contrast, in areas with similar sheep and husbandry practices further east foxes eat mountain hare, grouse and rabbits (which are plentiful) and only rarely do they scavenge lambs although they are readily available.

On return to Oxford I set about testing whether foxes like fresh lamb carrion. In late May I was able to present Niff, her family, and eight wild-born cubs which we were rearing, with freshly dead lambs on five occasions. In short, the result was that all these foxes either refused to eat the lamb, or did so only when there was no alternative and they were extremely hungry. However, I have no explanation for why foxes everywhere seemingly relish both sheep afterbirths and, especially, the withered tails and testes that drop off 'banded' lambs, and I am fully aware that whether or not foxes like eating lamb is of small recompense to the farmer who loses a

26. DEAD LAMBS AT DENS—ARE THEY INCRIMINATING?

A grizzly collection of dead lambs at a fox's earth seems to be incriminating evidence, but is it proof that the occupant killed them? The answer is no, and nor is it a measure of the damage foxes do. First, foxes are scavengers as well as predators and so some of the lambs may have been dead already. Second, some lambs killed by foxes may have been in such poor health they they would have perished anyway. I conducted a questionnaire survey of about 400 lowland sheep farmers in England, asking how many lambs they believed they had lost to foxes annually, and what was their evidence. Forty-six per cent believed they had never lost a lamb to foxes and from 62 to 74 per cent that they lost none in the three years of my survey. The most serious damage was estimated at more than 30 lambs killed in one year, but each year over half the cases of lamb worrying amounted to one to five lambs. Overall the average farmer thought he lost about two lambs per year to foxes (in a similar survey of hill farms in Wales Gwyn Lloyd found that farmers estimated an average of 0.5 lambs killed by foxes per year). However, when asked for their evidence that foxes were the culprits, 83 per cent cited seeing a fox among the sheep, 80 per cent found dead lambs mauled by foxes and 46 per cent found dead lambs at earths. Fifteen per cent of the farmers reported ever seeing a fox attack a lamb. None of these lines of evidence really helps with the important question, which is: how many viable lambs are killed by foxes?

The number of dead or dying lambs likely to be available to foxes varies greatly with shepherding practice. In harsh mountain areas, ewes lamb on the hill and up to 25 per cent of their lambs will die in the first few weeks. On better quality moorland the ewes may be gathered in to lamb on inbye land in valley bottoms and there the mortality is 10 to 20 per cent. In the most favoured lowland farms they lamb indoors with individual attention from the shepherd—mortality 5 to 10 per cent. In each case the stocking density, the breed of sheep, its maternal behaviour, condition, tendency to produce twins, and size of the lambs will all be different—which is why generalizations about foxes and lambs are ill-advised.

In a survey of fox dens in Scotland there was wide regional variation in the proportion with lamb carcasses (9 to 78 per cent). In the west Highlands, where other prey were scarce, the remains of Scottish Blackface lambs were found outside about 60 per cent of fox dens. At first this figure seemed horrifying. However, Ray Hewson autopsied dead lambs in that region and estimated that foxes probably killed less than 3 per cent of the crop (his bleakest local estimate was 5.2 per cent). Many of the lambs accumulated at fox dens had been dead or dying when the fox collected them. In that region sheep and lamb mortality were high and there was little alternative prey, so sheep carrion was the mainstay of foxes and golden eagles (although these foxes ate less sheep in years when voles were more abundant). In some months (March to May) there was sufficient sheep carrion to support completely all the foxes living in the area—up to 157kg per sq km of sheep carrion was available annually—but there was a 'bottleneck' in this food supply at other times and then the foxes depended on voles, whose numbers varied yearly. Hewson's study emphasizes that sheep can be an important part of fox diet without foxes being an important factor in sheep survival.

No sensible person would deny that foxes sometimes kill lambs, but this does not answer the three crucial questions. First, how much does fox predation contribute to lamb mortality? On the hard hill in Scotland the answer seems to be that foxes kill about one in 15 or 20 of those lambs that die. Second, does fox control reduce these losses? Lamb survival on the Scottish Isle of Mull, where there are no foxes, was no better than on the nearby (and otherwise similar) mainland where foxes occur and were hunted. This implies that fox control on that area of mainland was either irrelevant or very effective! Ray Hewson found that in four different upland habitats, the number of foxes killed from October to March varied from year to year and place to place. However, killing more foxes in winter did not reduce the number of fox breeding dens in the following spring, nor the numbers of complaints about lamb worrying. This tells us that in these four areas, within the limits of current practice, whether a greater or smaller number of foxes was killed in winter was irrelevant to lamb losses, and it suggests that breeding populations of foxes were limited by their food supply, rather than by game-keepers and shepherds. However, it does not answer the critical question of what would happen to lamb losses if no foxes were killed.

The third question is whether fox control is cost effective. If the answer is restricted purely to economic considerations, and remembering that much upland sheep farming is based on financial subsidy, and that in the Highlands 15 or so lambs may die of malnutrition for each one killed by a fox, then the economic arguments for intensive blanket fox control must, at least, be doubtful. These answers, however, are restricted to the bleakest of sheep-farming country. Elsewhere there is even less evidence on which to speculate.

healthy one. Nonetheless, I thought it worth delving briefly into this topic in order to emphasize its many uncertainties and to illustrate why someone asking whether foxes are a significant predator upon lambs should not expect a simple answer (*see* Boxes 25, p.166, 26, p.170).

A related, and similarly vexed, question is why do foxes kill prey which they then waste. One suggestion is that they react to prey as a kitten does to a ball of wool—prey-like movements trigger predatory behaviour which may have little to do with the need or desire to eat. This line of thought was originally developed by Hans Kruuk to explain the mass slaughter that has earned foxes a reputation for killing for fun. There is no way of proving whether or not foxes enjoy killing, but if their reflexes are indeed primed to leap before they look this could result in wasteful killing (*see* Box 24 p.164). Perhaps such knee-jerk predatory responses explain why some lambs are killed but neither eaten nor cached.

Finally, there is the question of whether lamb deaths due to foxes, aside from being irritating, are economically significant. Edwin could recite a dreadful dirge—Bow Hall lost 40 lambs in 1964, and that year their neighbours at Harbour Flatt lost a further 40. Losses of this magnitude amount to financial ruin, and burn scars that can span generations. It is hardly surprising that the fact that such losses have not recurred has done little to quell either the fear that they might, or the belief that they would have done except for vigorous fox control. In such an atmosphere it is hard to identify, far less to evaluate, the facts, and they will certainly vary regionally, and even locally. No precise answer can yet be given to questions as to how various forms and intensities of fox control affect losses of either lambs or money. However, there is a straightforward way to resolve the debate: a comparison of lamb losses between farms where foxes are controlled and similar farms where they are not controlled (the comparisons would have to be conducted over large areas, repeated for the different shepherding systems in different regions, and continued over several years and then reversed). Anybody unfamiliar with either the depth of feeling against foxes in sheep country, or the strength of the cultural imperative to kill them, might be surprised that such an experiment was not done years ago. In many upland areas, asking a shepherd not to kill foxes to test the effect on lamb mortality would be asking something almost unthinkable. Nonetheless, it would be an exciting and worthwhile experiment.

The fact that not all foxes kill lambs and that foxes are difficult to kill both militate against the efficiency (and thus acceptability) of blanket fox control. Is there any selective method to weed out the trouble makers? One approach is 'on call' hunting. This is routinely practised by packs of foxhounds in upland areas. At the first sign of lamb-worrying, the farmer calls the huntsman who brings his hounds to the lambing field at dawn, and attempts to find the scent line of the culprit. However, several foxes may visit a field of sheep, so the selectivity is diminished by the risk that the pack will follow the wrong one. Of course, on-call hunting is only selective in a restricted sense, since the pack will hunt (according to a prearranged fixture card) whether or not it is called to cases of lamb-worrying. There is no doubt that the on-call facility is widely used. For example, one pack in Wales was called out 52 times in the spring of 1986 to deal with suspected lamb-worrying by foxes. Some lowland mounted packs of foxhounds provide a service to farmers who complain of lamb losses by sending one of their staff to kill the culprit if they can find it. Some hunt servants of the old school might spend many sleepless nights with spotlamp and rifle in the attempt to kill a lamb-worrier. This may well be the most selective method of control currently practised, in so far as the hunt servant seeks to weed out only the rogue foxes in order to placate the farmer, while leaving as many foxes alive as possible in order to provide sport for the hunt. This brings us to the nub of the matter: the fox is simultaneously a pest, a sporting quarry and a furbearer. It is this combination of traits which entwines advocates of the control, the chase and the harvest of foxes in a mesh of paradox, and throws all three into conflict with those who think foxes should simply be left alone. Furthermore, since foxes are conspicuously sentient creatures, questions about their management, whether as a pest or a resource, flounder in an ethical morass from which science alone cannot rescue them.

Lamb-worrying has led me to the controversial spectre of fox hunting—a pastime enjoyed by men with a gun and a dog or spotlamp in most of the Northern Hemisphere, but which involves a pack of hounds and mounted followers in Great Britain, and parts of France and the USA (*see* Box 6, p.20). The legendary ingenuity with which some hunted foxes evade doom verges on the uncanny, and generally belittles the most exhuberant fishing stories. My own contribution to this repository comes from an occasion when the Blencathra Foxhounds met at Mungrisedale in Cumbria. It was New Year's Day and biting cold as Jenny and I watched the pack pick up a fresh line. The racily built fell hounds had fanned out, and set a fast pace onto the fell. Johnny Richardson, the Huntsman, and Barry Todhunter, his aptly named Whipper-in, fell into the lung-rasping lope of men who earn their daily bread striding after hounds over the roughest country —days that can be 40 kilometres long. The fox's scent was broken and the hounds cast widely. Now and then, a young hound gave tongue excitedly, chased a phantom scent, and lost it. Each hound's voice was different, and the older hounds seemed to pay little heed to the exuberant young voices. Then, out of the mist and far ahead, a deep booming bell of a voice rolled down the valley. Johnny Richardson breathed the old hound's name, and set his cap in the direction of the distant call. That hound kept his mouth shut until he had something to say. His was the voice of experience, and every hound in sight tensed at the sound of it, abandoned whatever stale scent it had been tracing, and sped into the thickening mist. As hounds and huntsmen were lost from sight, we cut down a small beck to lower ground and by the time we reached the lower slopes sunlight had burnt through the mist to reveal a glorious winter's day. We sat on a boulder and waited.

Below us a stream trickled along the green valley bottom. To the north it flowed beside a spinney, and from there it drained along a tattered wire fence which separated a reedy bog from a pasture. Far in the distance we could just hear the voices of hounds. Then, through binoculars, I spotted their quarry running towards the spinney. There were no hounds in sight, and the fox moved at a steady lope—a magnificent animal, flame red and with a powder puff tag to his brush. He disappeared into the trees just as the first hounds hove into view. They had run

27. WHAT IS FOXHUNTING?

Foxhunting in its traditional English sense arouses such censure, enthusiasm or curiosity, that it merits description. My sole intention is to provide an accurate description of foxhunting, and to identify, without moral judgement, some of the many perplexing issues it raises.

The origins of foxhunting lie in the Middle East in the 4th-century BC or earlier (*see* Box 6, p. 20). Today, much of Britain is divided into the territories or 'countries' of 206 registered hunts (the average territory being 730sq km) and I have surveyed 81 hunts in order to produce a profile of their activities. The average pack of foxhounds hunts for 2.5 days per week during a 7 month season. Hunts have an average of 120 paid up riding members (subscribers), and on a given day might be followed by 50 riders and between 20 and 100 cars. The pack hunts over farmland (about a third of farmers are active in the sport, while 2.2 per cent discourage or ban the hounds from their land). The season is split into cubhunting: averaging 25 days in September and October to 'enter' (i.e. give experience to) young hounds (and young foxes), and to promote the dispersal of foxes, and hunting: averaging 70 days between November and late March. On each hunting day the pack operates in the vicinity of a given 'meet', returning to that district two or three times each season, more often where foxes are plentiful. In traditional packs an 'earthstopper' may travel the neighbourhood before dawn blocking fox holes – this is to prevent foxes spending the day under ground, thereby making it easier to find them and prolonging the chase. As the 40 or so hounds scour the vicinity they 'move' (i.e. put up) foxes (between one and four being moved on an average day with an overall average of 3.5 foxes seen to be moved per day). Some of these foxes are then hunted – on average 2.5 per day.

Pursuits generally last less than an hour. Near Oxford, one sample of pursuits averaged 17 minutes, but one fox may be hunted more than once, and one pursuit may involve swopping foxes. An average of 0.63 foxes are killed per day and the most successful hunts average two or three per day. More foxes are moved (and about twice as many killed) during cubhunting than during the remainder of the season. About half the tally comprises foxes killed by hounds, and the remainder are shot having been dug out (with the aid of terriers) after going to ground.

Using data from 81 hunts over 22 years, I have calculated that nationally, the average pack kills between 50 and 75 foxes per year, of which about half are killed during cubhunting (the most successful hunts averaged total kills of between 200 and 300 per season). This works out at about 0.17 foxes killed per sq km of hunt territory per annum (with a maximum about five-fold greater). Since hunting is primarily restricted to farmland, which constitutes about 80 per cent of the countryside, this toll corrects to roughly 0.15 foxes per sq km or 1 fox per 6.7 sq km of farmland per annum.

One cannot mention foxhunting without prompting the question of whether it involves suffering. Violent death (for mammals at least) probably involves pain and fear (the two comprising a workable definition of suffering – although the existence of natural opiates which deaden pain – as described by wounded soldiers – complicates its assessment). Therefore, the underlying question is whether a given level of suffering is acceptable (the same question can be asked about other methods of killing foxes, such as snares, leg-hold traps, firearms and poisoned gas). To answer this, one must balance an assessment of the suffering (and other negative factors) against an assessment of the benefits (just as a vet might do in assessing the benefits of a painful treatment). Since we cannot know what it feels like to be a fox, assessing their suffering is difficult. Comparisons with how we would feel about being hunted have the obvious shortcoming that we are different to foxes. In evolutionary terms, the fox is a close relative of the domestic dog. The two species are physiologically and behaviourally very similar. Therefore, it would be reasonable to suggest that they have a comparable capacity to suffer. Objective measurement of this capacity is either very difficult or impossible. In making a guess, it might be wise to consider that the moral costs of an underestimate are greater than those of an overestimate. On the other hand, there are obviously circumstances under which causing suffering in such creatures can be widely acceptable – few people object to killing stray dogs or foxes during rabies epidemics (and few express concern over the poisoning of millions of rats annually). An onlooker might judge foxhunting (and other methods of killing foxes) solely on the criterion of suffering. However, for those intimately involved, the balance of acceptability is shifted by other considerations, notably the perceived need for fox control, employment, profit and a general category I will call enjoyment. While these considerations may diminish the relative importance somebody attaches to the suffering of wild animals, they do not, of course, affect the level of suffering itself. A game manager may decide that the prospects of doubling his partridge crop, and hence his profit, are among the factors which outweigh his remorse at the death, mostly by strangulation in snares, of several dozen foxes each year. The game shooting industry is probably largely responsible for the frequently unpleasant deaths in the order of 100,000 foxes annually in Britain, but against these must be weighed the fact that this industry provides the major incentive for habitat conservation on farmland. In Britain, in 1982, it was estimated to generate the equivalent of 12,000 full-time jobs, more than £200 million worth of consumer expenditure and a game 'bag' valued at £17 million. There is an argument that game shooting is the greatest hope for the conservation of on modern farms, but that predators of game are the sacrifice required to secure that end.

Similarly, in a survey of over 800 farmers I found that those who were enthusiastic foxhunters had removed 35 per cent less hedgerows than the average farmer during the 1970s (apparently because of their desire to produce good fox habitat). Some might judge that an average of 170 metres of extra hedgerow per keen hunting farmer (about 20 per cent of farmers) compensated for the suffering of some 15,000 foxes killed annually by packs of foxhounds. Others might judge that the enjoyment of the 200,000 people who are estimated to participate in hunting compensates for that suffering. Yet others might judge that not even the sum of hedges and enjoyment (nor even the employment of farriers, the 2,600 full-time jobs, the revenue to the exchequer, etc.) make any suffering acceptable. It would be difficult to perceive such judgements as straightforward, and they are further complicated by the questions of whether, if hunting stopped, the same number of foxes, or even more, would be killed by people using other methods (there is also the difficulty of assessing the net difference in suffering between each method of killing by people, or by the 'natural' starvation, disease or predation that otherwise kills foxes). Similar dilemmas are commonplace in mankind's involvement with wildlife, and amongst these, foxhunting is of minor significance to foxes in particular or amongst wildlife issues in general. Such dilemmas are also commonplace in everyday life: people's gastronomic enjoyment outweighs their concern for the consequences of harvesting billions of fish annually, as their enjoyment of their cat's companionship outweighs regret at the deaths of millions of hedgerow birds annually.

Of course, the foxhunting debate defies concensus since different people put different values on each of the relevant factors. There is no common currency with which to equate units of suffering versus units of hedgerow versus units of employment versus units of cultural heritage and rural infra-structure and so forth. Scientists and economists can provide data to clarify the issues, but ultimately decisions will rest on values which are beyond the scope of science.

hard and were strung out in a long line, spattered in mud with tongues lolling and plumes of breath pumping from their open jaws. The first hound was in the spinney before the fox broke from the other side. Now he was running in earnest, down the fence line, along the side of the pasture.

Behind the fox the hounds were thronging out of the wood; they had him in view and seemed to be finding their second wind for the gap was closing dramatically. By the time the fox was level with our vantage point the lead hound was 30 paces behind him and hunter and hunted were straining their haunches in long, muscle-bunching lurcher-leaps along the fenceline. 25, 20, 15 paces; at 15 paces we knew that the fox was a goner. Then, with a violent swerve, he flung himself to the right, through a break in the fence, and into the reeds of the bog. Immediately he doubled back, snaking through the reeds, then ducked into the densest sward and lay still. The hound overshot badly, running well past the break in the fence. Several long seconds dragged by before it sniffed its way back to the spot.

By then other hounds were arriving. They swarmed into the bog, but the scent seemed to have vanished. Even so, as they fanned out, I knew it was hopeless. At any instant one of them must surely stand on the fox, even if they seemed unable to smell or see him. We could see the fox crouching on the bog side of the fence as the main body of the pack raced down the pasture side not many feet from his nose. Some hounds began to cast to the south, in the direction that the fox had been running before he doubled back. The focus of their ungainly lumberings drifted past the fox until the pack was some 20 metres from him. Slowly the fox began to squirm through the reeds, until he stood under the fence looking back towards the wood. He took a pace or two back along the path. For a glorious moment I thought that he was enacting a brilliant daredevil tactic, to slip back through the enemy's ranks, but then he slunk back into the reeds. The pack was in the reeds now, and my sadness at the fox's inevitable death was made all the more bitter by the foolishness of my momentary belief that he was following an ingenious plan.

Then, out of the trees loped one last hound. A straggler, with sides heaving from its marathon exertion, it ran the fence line, passed within inches of the fox's muzzle and rejoined its com-

panions. The fox stood up, crept under the fence, looked right and left to confirm that the coast was clear, and ran like the wind back along his scent line towards the spinney. Did the fox delay his retreat because he was exhausted, or was he waiting for that last hound? A scientist's burden of scepticism makes me doubt the latter, but I confess that is what it looked like. The pack eventually cottoned on, but by the time they began to retrace their steps, the fox was half a mile off making good his escape as he dodged through a field of sheep, no doubt further foiling his pursuers.

As spring turned to summer and cubs began to lark about, Edwin's unofficial amnesty with the foxes could not continue. New rules were agreed: any foxes that I got to first were 'mine' and spared, any others were fair game. They found and killed a litter on Crossfell, and another on Knock Pike. My options were diminishing fast. I knew, having failed to catch her several times, that there was a vixen in the territory to the north west of Pussghyll's range, embracing the rocky valleys of Great Rundle and north east towards Bluethwaite. This vixen was my last sure chance to add another territory to the mosaic of neighbouring radio foxes, and the need to add just one more territory to my scanty sample assumed huge importance in my mind. It was a race against time to catch her before somebody else did. Then, the day came for Edwin and Arthur to scour Rundale for foxes—an onslaught which they had already delayed time and again in deference to my efforts.

All three of us were apprehensive about the outcome as we set out together that day. We trudged from earth to earth, from crevices in the crags to old mine shafts to stone beds. Then at the foot of Brownber Hill, we came to a simple two-holed earthen den, with freshly dug spoil pattered with fox spoor, and a warm reek of fox from within. For sure this was the breeding earth of the vixen that I had been after for so long— here, at last was the missing piece in my territorial jig-saw puzzle. It was a dreadful moment: the parting of the ways. In my mind's eye the success of all these months in the fells hinged on radio-tracking this one vixen. Yet, as the shepherds stood there, shotguns under their arms, terriers straining and coupled at their feet, they were in sight of the young lambs at Bow

Hall, frail white keys to their livelihood. To spare this vixen in their backyard would be heresy. For the first time in almost a year we could not joke our way of this one, and we stared glumly at the earth. At last we struck a compromise. We would try to bolt the vixen, using Wick and Sparrow, the two inexperienced terriers. If we netted her she was mine to radio collar, on the condition that we use the radio to track her down and shoot her at the first sign of lamb losses. If she dodged the nets, they would shoot her; if the young terriers could not shift her, then they would send down Arthur's Jack, and Jack was as hard as they come. It was a deal—we both had our jobs to do.

We draped the nets and first Sparrow, then Wick, then the two together tried to bolt the vixen. She was in no mood to shift. There were cubs inside for sure. It was time for Arthur's Jack. Jack was a dog in his prime. He was hard and scarred, and with the sort of reputation that got him talked about in pubs. Jack was not interested in bolting foxes to the gun—he did the job himself. Jack was slipped in. A fierce growling, then a dull thudding noise, wafted to the entrance of the hillside lair. Jack emerged, tail wagging happily, dropped the mangled corpse of a week-old cub, and darted back in. My world was falling apart. There could be no stopping Jack now. A final hasty deal was struck—I could dig for the fox, and if I got to her before Jack, she was mine. The soil was laden with chert, the burrow ran horizontally into the steep hillside, but it was diggable. I dug as I have never dug before; 12 stone of hill-fit desperation wielding a spade. My spade broke into the tunnel, closer and closer to the thudding sounds of Jack lunging in the confined echo chamber of the burrow. For Jack and me the decisions were simple, but poor Edwin and Arthur were torn between their loyal-ties to a lifelong crusade against foxes and their sympathy for me. I was flagging. 'Move ow'er sees'ta Dave, we'll help th' dig t'old bitch out'. Now it was the three of us against Jack, but as we dug down the tunnel we passed two more infant corpses. We dug a massive wedge out of the hillside. I was head and shoulders into the cavity, steeped in the sound and stench of it. The vixen must have backed into a cavern and held Jack at bay. I was reaching in to grab either the dog or the fox: I could feel somebody's fur, but could gain no purchase. Another frenzied onslaught on the roof of the tunnel and I could just see Jack. With the tips of my fingers I could touch his fur. The muffling of his growl told that his mouth was full of fox, but the thudding told that their was still hope for the vixen. I managed to stretch and squeeze my arm another inch or so into the burrow until I had his neck. Jack had not won his reputation for nothing, so I knew that the only way to get him to release the vixen was to choke him off. Edwin and Arthur pulled me out of the tunnel, feet first; next came Jack, my fingers locked on his windpipe, his eyes bulging; and then came the vixen, Jack's teeth clenched in her throat. We prised Jack's jaws open. We laid the vixen gently on the ground, and she died.

It was a mile or more to home. As we trudged wearily along, Jack trotted at my heels, jauntily carrying a mangled cub in his jaws. That night we were in the pub, every muscle aching, when Edwin concluded an account of our exploits by pointing at me and saying 'that lad chews nails and spits rust'. In the company of the moorland men that compliment was as good as they get, and I was truly glad to have such friends, but it had been a dispiriting way to win my colours—try as I might, I never did manage to radio-collar another fox on the fells.

10 | THE OXFORD FOXWATCH

IN THE LATE 1970s, foxes were sending shudders through Oxford City. More specifically, in the grounds of the University's Astrophysics Department a vixen was burrowing into the mound above the underground chamber that housed a seismograph. Cohabitation with a family of fox cubs provoked the machine into registering a series of spurious earthquakes beneath the town. Meanwhile, in the graveyard of St Cross Church, within sight of my office, a vixen excavating a breeding earth beneath a headstone was indiscreet enough to scatter some rather fusty bones nearby. My insistence that these were not the remains of a university don, but rather of a Sunday roast scavenged from a nearby birdtable, did little to assuage the church warden's feeling that the site of the fox's residence was in questionable taste. At the same time, debate was raging in the Senior Common Room of Worcester College over what action to take concerning the fox who had set up residence perilously close to the College's ornamental waterfowl.

There could be no doubt that foxes were living in the heart of Oxford City, where they were frequently seen in college quadrangles and widely assumed to be living off the offal of academia. Clearly, it would be fascinating to compare the behaviour of these city-dwelling foxes with that of their country cousins. What is more, with the fear of rabies looming large as the disease moved westward across Continental Europe, it was increasingly important to know more about these foxes that lived on our doorsteps. So, I laid plans to study Oxford's city foxes, and set out to find funds for an assistant to help with this task.

The negotiations were at a delicate stage. Two men from the Nature Conservancy Council (NCC) had been through my proposal. We had delved into the practicalities, aired reservations, shuddered at the thought of urban rabies. Now they had to decide whether or not to fund the study. From the window of my office in the Zoology Department they looked out across a mosaic of rooftops, pierced here and there by the Arnold's dreaming spires. My heart sank as the man holding the purse strings shook his head doubtfully and, gesticulating across this scene, mused 'I just can't believe you will find enough foxes here to work on.' Hardly had this death knell to my project left his lips when an outraged shout rang out. Five storeys below us, in the gardens of Halifax House, the University's staff club, the Spanish barman appeared whirling a broom around his head like a berserk polo player. Screaming abuse and making extravagant swipes with the broom, the barman circled the garden with a remarkable turn of speed. Ahead of him, dodging hither and thither, was a small brown fox cub which, after two hair-raising circuits of the garden, took refuge in the inner workings of a derelict spin-drier beside the kitchen door. The men from the NCC and I rushed downstairs and found the barman kicking and cursing at the spin-drier. The cub was far too young to undertake such adventures, and was noticeably disheartened by the outside world's unfriendly reception. It put up a spirited resistance to my attempts to extract it from the spin-drier, but eventually I was able to smuggle it discreetly back to its home in the seismograph mound. After this timely charade the NCC granted funds for an assistant to work with me on urban foxes and in November 1977, Malcolm Newdick joined the Foxlot.

Our first task was to get an impression of the

foxes' whereabouts in the town. To do this we appealed for evidence of foxes through the radio and newspapers, and we quizzed nocturnal cabbies, bus drivers and policemen. We also began the task of knocking on some 14,000 doors and accosting the inhabitants with a questionnaire. 3,469 people agreed to complete the form. Of these, 15 per cent had seen a fox in their own gardens (3 per cent saw foxes in their gardens regularly), and a third had seen a fox somewhere in the city. To a greater or lesser extent, it seemed that foxes were to be seen throughout the town, and in every urban habitat from sports grounds to factories. The survey suggested that Oxford's foxes had distinctly up-market tastes: they were seen most regularly in the gardens of detached housing (especially the larger, more overgrown gardens).

Among the many unexpected reactions provoked by our house-to-house search was that of the character who had never seen a fox but asked if he could have a job in our department because, as he put it, 'Zoology's just up my street, I've always fancied the idea of digging graves for a living.' As it turned out, he was not so wide of the mark, since it was in Botley Cemetery that Malcolm and I struck upon the most abundant signs of foxes. There, beside the Ring Road carrying traffic at a rate of 3,000 vehicles per hour, we found the remains of a dozen or more hedgehogs, their armoured jackets neatly peeled off and nibbled clean. The poor hedgehog is in a bind: roll up and be squashed by a car, or unroll to make a dash for it, only to be nabbed by a fox. Legend has it that foxes persuade hedgehogs to unroll by dousing them in urine. Considering how foxes sprinkle token marks on conspicuous objects, I can imagine the roots of this story lie in somebody seeing a hedgehog being marked. A population of such mobile scent marks could play havoc with the territorial system!

The fox paths led from the graveyard to the overgrown back garden of an unoccupied house, and there an abundance of droppings indicated frequent visits by foxes. We were only three kilometres from the tranquil woodlands of Boar's Hill, but what a different world, within earshot of the roar of the city's traffic. It was in that disused garden, in December 1977, that we captured our first city fox, named Green after the colour of his radio collar. Chatting with people during our house-to-house survey, many believed that foxes survived in towns by confining their activities to parks, graveyards and college gardens. On the other hand, our questionnaires had revealed that foxes were often seen in residential neighbourhoods. But where foxes were seen may say more about people than about foxes. What were the habitat preferences of Oxford's city foxes? Radiocollaring Green was the first step to tackling this question.

Green crossed the dual-carriageway several times each night and introduced us to the peculiar pastime of radio-tracking in the city. There was no doubt that he was at home in built-up districts. The very first night he led Malcolm into the heart of the urban jungle—a housing estate where fox and tracker tiptoed between the densely packed houses. Radio signals bounced in disarray, reflecting off buildings, buzzing along fences, and generally leading the tracker up a maze of garden paths. At first, the occasional insomniac was alarmed by the antenna-topped mini-van cruising slowly up and down the street. Their thoughts flashed anxiously between the prospects of burglary and a raid on unlicensed television viewers. But soon the word spread, and the inhabitants of Green's home range professed that they felt more secure from thieves, knowing that the vulpine vigilantes were patrolling their neighbourhood by night. When we tried stalking on foot we doubtless looked an odd pair: my rural green clothing and muddy wellies were out of place in the town, whereas Malcolm, determined to play the urban role, blended inconspicuously in the camouflage of a cagoule in fashionable fluorescent orange. The first nights in pursuit of Green were tumultuous partly due to our inexperience at dodging territorial urban householders, and largely due to the devastating effect of the concrete jungle on the radio signal. However, it was not long before we devised a technique for radio tracking which rested largely on listening to signal volume through the gaps between successive houses along a street—the fox was behind the house bordered by the loudest signals. In fact, the network of roads and the foxes' familiarity with traffic and pedestrians allowed us to radio track at very close quarters, so we generally knew (and often saw) precisely in which garden the fox was moving.

Soon we had radio foxes throughout east

Oxford and could give a firm answer to the question: which habitats do they favour? By day, the foxes generally laid up in secluded spots where they were relatively free from human disturbance. Indeed, although scrub and woodland together made up less than 5 per cent of the city, our radio foxes spent, on average, three out of four days in these secluded corners, and often lay above ground (although not often so far above it as the dog fox who slept 2 metres up a pollarded willow, within sight of a busy park-and-ride bus stop). Most of their earths were in rural enclaves, but many were in gardens, and almost a quarter of them were under garden sheds (one was beneath a factory, another was in an old coke oven, and another in an air-raid shelter).

Green had been no exception: by night, the city foxes visited every habitat in the town including the most unpromising expanses of concrete. However, the pattern of more than 20,000 radio fixes revealed that they spent most time in detached housing, followed closely by semi-detached housing and then golf courses and parks. Terraced housing came a long way down the list. With such discerning tastes in housing

perhaps a fox in the neighbourhood will become a status symbol in the suburbs! At least they could provide a clue to the pollsters, since our colleague Stephen Harris found that, in Bristol, foxes and Conservative voters congregated in the same parts of town. In any event, the idea that urban foxes confine themselves to rural enclaves in the city is incorrect—in Oxford the majority of their nightly travels were in residential areas.

What was the reason for the bourgeois housing tastes of Oxford's foxes? The answers were food and shelter. Detached and semi-detached properties had reasonable-sized gardens, with easy access to adjoining properties and to the street. In these gardens the majority of householders maintained compost heaps. Compost heaps can be a good source of food: 20 per cent of the people we questioned put edible food waste on them. What was more, 66 per cent of households put food out for birds (15 per cent did so for hedgehogs and 9 per cent for cats), and almost half of these people put this food out in their gardens more than once a week. Our frequent observations of foxes standing on bird tables, digging in compost heaps, eating cat food or hedgehog's milkslops soon confirmed that a large number of people were inadvertently feeding foxes. Perhaps most important were the households (1 to 3 per cent) which deliberately fed foxes in their gardens. Some simply saved household scraps for 'their' foxes; others made frequent trips to the butcher on the foxes' behalves. This back garden smörgasbord largely explained why 36 per cent of the foxes' food was scavenged. Certainly the droppings contained plenty of chip paper, Kentucky fried chicken wrappers, plastic bands and an unnerving amount of broken glass, but the idea that urban foxes live by raiding dustbins has not been substantiated—in Oxford it was rare indeed for us to see evidence of a fox rifling through a dustbin, or even through a plastic waste-bag. The claim that they cause a significant nuisance by ransacking bins is a non-starter. Our survey of the pest status of urban foxes (*see* Box 28) disclosed strikingly few

first-hand complaints of raided dustbins. Foxes were blamed for this by the families of only 12 of 818 Oxford schoolchildren who helped with our survey. A further 1,436 pupils in Portsmouth and 420 in Southampton helped with the survey. Overall, for these three towns, 1.5 per cent of families complained of dustbin raiding. Even this small figure will be an overestimate since the majority of culprits we caught in the act were dogs and cats. That is, of course, not to say that foxes never raid dustbins (for example they are known to do so more often in Bristol), only that it does not hold water as a general complaint against urban foxes. Anyway, raiding robust, heavy, trap-like dustbins is a poor option for foxes whose territories contain hundreds of bird tables and several dozen families who feed them on choice scraps. Furthermore, such gardens are rich in other foods—worms on the lawn, fruit and vegetables, birds and small mammals in the

28. ARE URBAN FOXES A NUISANCE?

Many people assume that urban foxes are pests, but our surveys revealed very few first-hand, substantial complaints. In general, the answer to the question of whether urban foxes are a nuisance is: only occasionally and to a small proportion of townspeople.

In Oxford, we delivered questionnaires to 14,000 households, enquiring about the whereabouts of city foxes, and the problems they caused. Of these, 3,469 families provided answers and 149 (or 4.3 per cent) of those reported that at some time they had been caused nuisance by foxes. People who had complaints against foxes were anxious to voice them, so we believe that very few of those who declined to fill-in the questionnaire had a complaint. On this assumption, about one in one hundred households in Oxford reported that at some time they had experienced some nuisance for which they believed foxes were responsible. In evaluating this figure we must remember that: (i) people reported any nuisance they had ever experienced (some episodes were recalled from 30 years previously), and, (ii) many of those documenting a case of nuisance stated that it was of insufficient importance to constitute a complaint. What, then, were the types of nuisance reported?

The group with most numerous, and most serious, complaints was people keeping livestock in their garden. Just over half of the 40 townspeople keeping

chickens in Oxford had some complaint against foxes. Of the families of 2,674 school children from three cities, 25 (0.9 per cent) reported the loss of hens to foxes, and 21 (0.8 per cent) the loss or rabbits or guinea pigs. Many people kept their pet rabbits in open runs or even allowed them free range of the garden, despite knowing that foxes were in the neighbourhood. We were sometimes surprised by the shock or outrage expressed by people who had lost pet rabbits and yet who knew (and often welcomed) the fact that foxes on the neighbouring farmland preyed upon wild rabbits. Since it is self-evident that prey cannot safely cohabit with their predators, there are in principle two options. First, pet rabbits and guinea pigs can be made inaccessible to foxes by housing them in robust hutches and runs. Second, the risk of predation can be removed by killing the foxes. In practice, the first option is likely to greatly reduce the risk, with minimal inconvenience to people, pets or predators. The second option is unlikely to greatly reduce the risk (because fox control tends to be ineffective), but is likely to generate controversy and expense for people, suffering for foxes and, if successful, an imbalance for the ecosystem.

Probably the most widespread concern was whether foxes killed cats. We found three families (0.1 per cent) in our sample who believed that their cats had been killed by foxes. In a similar survey in Bristol,

shrubbery (*see* Box 17, p. 118). Finally, the garden of a semi-detached property is ideally designed for the undercover activities of a city fox: a garden shed is almost invariably beside the fence, and a tall hedge is grown to obscure it from the neighbours' view. The result is that the fox excavates an earth beneath the shed, its access via the overgrown side obscured from its own household by the shed itself, and from the neighbours' view by the hedge. Small wonder foxes favour such surroundings.

The next obvious question was whether the city foxes, like those on Boar's Hill, lived in territorial social groups. In 1980 Malcolm and I drafted our report to the Nature Conservancy Council, and by then we had already tracked over 50 urban foxes and ear-tagged (which we started doing in 1980) 39 city-born cubs. The adults occupied home ranges averaging about 50 hectares. These home ranges clearly formed a

pattern of groups, but it was not so neatly tessellated as on Boar's Hill. Within a group, each individual's range overlapped about half the area travelled by each other member of its group, and only about 5 per cent of the neighbouring groups' ranges. Overall, this pattern led us to conclude that the foxes were spaced out into group territories, but there were nagging cases where seeing that pattern required the eye of faith.

If there were territorial groups, were their members blood relatives? Detailed case histories go some way to answering that question. Malcolm put tremendous effort into recapturing as adults some of the foxes we had ear-tagged as cubs and fitting them with radio-collars. Knowing their places of birth we could ask: do city foxes disperse from their parents' ranges and, if so, how far do they go? For most dog foxes the answers were yes, and about four kilometres (*see* Box 14, p. 88). In contrast, some of the vixen cubs

Stephen Harris also found 0.1 per cent of families reporting cats killed (about 0.7 per cent of cats in the district per year). Urban foxes and cats meet very frequently and it is commonplace to see them in a close company, often feeding side by side. If there is a squabble over food, the cat generally displaces the fox. Authenticated cases of foxes killing cats generally involve kittens. So, although it is clear that most foxes do not kill cats, some do so. However, this risk must rank very low amongst the worries besetting the urban cat-owner, and certainly is much less significant than the risk of the cat being killed on the road by traffic. Why do foxes kill cats? We examined 1939 fox droppings collected in Oxford City, and found only 0.4 per cent that contained traces of cat fur. Considering the numbers of road-killed cats available as scavenge, one might have expected them to occur more frequently in fox diet. Perhaps those fights that do occur between fox and cat arise because the fox treats the cat as a competitor for food rather than as food.

What, then, of other causes of complaint (we gleaned a total of 354 from a nationwide radio and press survey)? The issue of dustbin raiding is mentioned on p.180. There were some perplexing cases such as the small scratches dug in the grass that would have gone unnoticed on most lawns, but were a major blemish on Oxford's championship

bowling green. The foxes may have been after cockchafer larvae, but more likely they were attracted by bonemeal fertilizer. The only solution was an electric fence. Another unusual one was the car salesman who had to wipe muddy fox pawprints from the roofs of his wares every morning. Another tricky problem arises where foxes set off security alarms while trotting through industrial premises. Other complaints, such as causing the dog to bark, taking eggs from the doorstep, entering the lounge to steal fruit from the table, pulling down the washing line and scattering lawn-mowings did not seem to merit widespread action. Nonetheless, 61 per cent of townspeople we questioned in Oxford expressed the general view that urban foxes should be controlled (47 per cent thought that rural foxes should be controlled). Our surveys, and those of Dr Harris, do not justify this view.

In general, most urban fox 'problems' are more imaginary than real (people often ask whether foxes will attack them—the answer is no), and many complaints are frankly trifling or foolish. Most real problems are isolated cases, and are more likely to cure themselves (often when a litter of cubs grows up and moves away) than they are to be cured by outside interference.

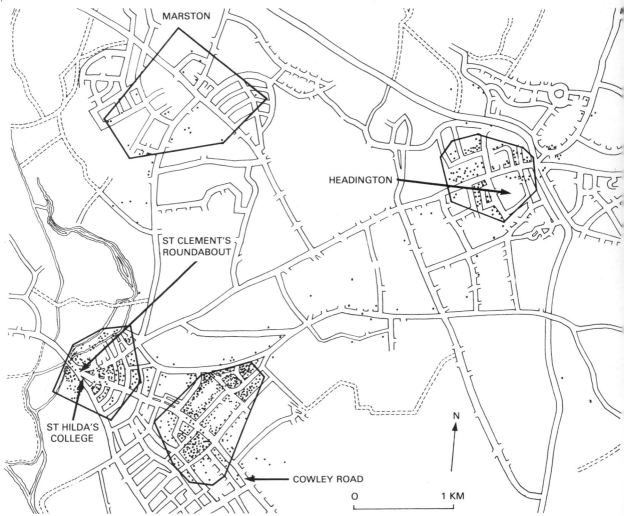

Woteye Vixen's four home ranges in Oxford. Each dot is one radio fix.

stayed at home as adults, and eventually bred in their parents' territories. At this stage we had half an answer to the kinship question—some vixens do stay at home, but do some others join up as members of unrelated groups? One of the vixens which did leave home, Woteye, provided our first case history of a dispersing vixen and an opportunity to tackle this question.

Woteye Vixen was born in 1978 not far from the Cowley Road—the ultimate in urban habitats. When she was six months old, Woteye was captured in the back garden in which she had been born, and was equipped with a radio transmitter. Another member of the Foxlot team, Nick Hough, began an intensive study of her adolescent months. At first, Woteye Vixen was often seen with her brother, as they scavenged together on discarded fish and chip wrappers.

For almost two months, her home range fell within a clearly defined block of streets spanning just over 30 hectares. Her movements were so regular, and followed such consistent routes, that Nick could predict where she would be at certain times of night, and so he lay in wait to watch her. In October she made two short excursions beyond this boundary into adjacent terraced housing, and on 9th November 1978 she made another short foray. Then on 13th November, Woteye set sail on a major expedition, cutting down towards the London Road, heading towards the city centre before veering off into the grounds of St Hilda's College.

From there, she circled the St Clement's roundabout before travelling more than two kilometres north to a new neighbourhood where dawn found her in a district called Marston.

Throughout the next day Woteye lay up in her unfamiliar surroundings, but at dusk, rather than retracing her outward route, she made a bee-line for home, cutting a new path through more than a kilometre of unfamiliar urban terrain until she reached the garden where she had been born. No sooner had she arrived than she was off again, half a kilometre to the west, to St Clement's, where she made herself a shelter inside an old drain. The St Clement's roundabout stands in the shadow of Magdalen College tower, famed for its May Morning madrigals. Five roads lead from the roundabout, flanked by shops, a school and St Hilda's College. in the rush hour, some 2,000 vehicles per hour revolve around the round-about. It was from the centre of this sanctuary that Woteye perused humanity spinning by. From there, as the traffic thinned, she trotted busily through the gardens of terraced houses, behind the Half Moon pub, to the chip shop, carefully choosing her moments to cross the roads. Once she crossed Magdalen Bridge and travelled through the Botanic Gardens to visit the grounds of the former Bureau of Animal Population, where Charles Elton, Oxford's father of ecology, had done his pioneering research. Woteye's new

range, centring on the roundabout, was almost exactly the same size as her previous one.

Nick Hough was on her trail every night, and knew that at least two other foxes lived there too. Would Woteye be able to join their group? Nick saw those two squabbling amongst themselves and, separately, they both attacked her. In late November these two foxes together attacked Woteye and a battle raged down the main streets. The fight culminated in a boxing match in the middle of the St Clement's roundabout, as the traffic circled the combatants. Woteye retired to her drain and remained there for the remainder of the night. The very next night she left the St Clement's range and headed four kilometres north, towards Marston, where she spent that night exploring before returning to St Clement's at a brisk trot just before dawn. Three days later she again headed to Marston and by the end of November it was clear that she had vacated the St Clement's range. We knew little of the foxes at St Clement's, but it seemed likely that at least one of them was a vixen and that their aggression had caused Woteye's move to Marston. However, she spent only five days in this third home range, during which time Nick's sleuthing revealed that

she made an exploratory trip some two kilometres west, to the motor works at Cowley, where she was in the company of an unidentified stranger.

On the 5th December 1978, she moved to Cowley and we suspected that she had paired with the stranger. Once again her movements settled down in a range of some 28 hectares until, a month later, on the night of 4th January 1979, she travelled five kilometres north-west to Beckley. In the small hours of the morning she began to hurry home, Nick driving behind with the radio-tracking gear. Within 20 minutes she had covered the distance and was within 200 metres of her Cowley range when she came to a halt. As dawn broke Nick waited outside a Garden Centre. At first the radio-signal told that Woteye was active within, but later she was still—it seemed that she had found a new lair. Later that day we found Nick distraught—curious to see Woteye's den, he had returned to the garden centre in daylight and found Woteye hanging dead in a snare—he had presided over her death, unaware of her plight only metres from him.

So, we know for sure that Woteye failed in her apparent bid to set up home in the St Clement's territory where at least one other vixen was established. We also suspect, but cannot prove, that there was only a dog fox in the Cowley range where she seemed to settle down. Adding Woteye's story to other similarly incomplete ones, I suspect that the general rule is that vixens do not immigrate into ranges where other vixens are already established. Therefore, where groups exist, they are likely to be made up of close kin.

Tracking radio-collared foxes in the town brought its own difficulties. Imagine, for example, the small hours of one wintry morning, mist wafting up from the Thames and hanging in a greyish dome over the shimmering street lights of the city. Just beyond the railway station, the Botley Road was deserted, save for one lonely parked car. By a dim light that glowed within, the blurred outline of a figure could be seen hunched over the steering wheel, just visible through the steam-coated windscreen. The paraphernalia of aerials on the car's roof identified it as a Foxlot vehicle, and the martyr battling with sleep was Nick Hough. For the last two, bone-chilling hours the soporific pulse in his headphones had conveyed the hypnotic information that a dog fox named Henry was continuing to snooze 50 metres away, in the allotment that ran parallel with the road. The scene was common enough and, depending on one's mood and the degree of frost, lay somewhere between monotonous and serene. It was into this scene that a drunken skinhead swayed, leaning forward with a distinctly distorted sense of the perpendicular. He navigated from one lamp-post to the next, charting a course that took him past Nick's car without so much as a glance. Perhaps it was his bellicose mutterings that shook the fox from his slumber, or perhaps it was just an unfortunate coincidence that Henry happened to wake up then. Whatever the reason, Henry the dog fox began to move through the allotments at that moment, and Nick started the car, slowly drove down the road and stopped at a new vantage point. A few minutes later the skinhead caught up and lumbered by. Again the fox moved, again Nick crept forward, again the shaven-headed youth caught up.

This improbable trio leap-frogged in parallel down the road, doubtless unaware of the influence that each was having on the others' destinies until any residue of sleep was jolted from Nick as a bristly scalp was thrust through the car's open window. 'Why the 'ell are you following me?' Nick could sense the inadequacy of his immediate denial, and so launched into an explanation about Henry the fox, who was walking along in the same direction and fitted with a radio and 'Don't you take the micky out me, sunshine.' Nick had barely started to explain about the radio collar when the knuckles thudded into his cheek. And so it was that another member of Oxford's public was introduced to radio-tracking, the technique which, above all others, has revolutionized field biology this century.

Although a lot of people had caught glimpses of foxes in Oxford, a surprising number were unaware of the nocturnal cohabitants of their gardens. This partition between the human dayshift and the vulpine nightshift persisted because, despite their proximity to people, most of Oxford's foxes maintained a remarkably low profile. There was, however, one memorable exception to this, in the form of a fox called Unipart. His story began for us with a telephone call from a perplexed factory manager—foxes were resident in his warehouse and the shop-steward was restive. Later, as Malcolm and I dodged the fork-lift loaders, and shouted to make ourselves heard over the metallic clunkings of the workshop, the story that unfolded stretched even our credulity in vulpine versatility.

For a long time, it seemed, a vixen had been resident in this industrial complex, and had taken to exploring the warehouse where she thrived on the crusts left by the nightshift. Then, in the spring of 1979 she had been seen trotting through the doors with her cubs. While the vixen had remained timorous as she slipped inconspicuously between crates and girders, one of her offspring grew brazen in his familiarity with the workforce. Soon he took up residence in the warehouse, where he built up a substantial fan club. Now, as we were led through the warehouse, it was clear that we had stepped blithely into an explosive controversy: on one side the workmen, protective of the fox, threw us belligerent glances and some fierce words; on the other side a shop steward, flustered to a thrombotic puce, recited snippets of legislation on the hazards of wild animals in places of work. Both parties were equally mistaken in their convictions that we were there to kill, or remove, the fox. The workforce was enraged at the imagined threat to their mascot, and they were reluctant to believe that we had no intention of harming their fox; the shop steward was enraged because he did believe that we had no intentions of removing it. Diplomatically, we could not win, but in terms of our study, this approachable fox was a coup.

Nightfall for Unipart was a far cry from the image of rural tranquillity. Not for him the rustic scene, but a maze of iron beams criss-crossing in the light of fluorescent tubes, an air-brake hissing near by, cogs grating, and a mechanical hoist clattering. Waking from his slumbers, Unipart was unruffled by the metallic clamour of his surroundings; he would stretch himself, pushing his paws deep into the folds of his woolly blue blanket, before jumping nimbly onto a girder from which he surveyed the scene in the warehouse. Jumping to the concrete floor, oblivious to the nightshift sounds of men and machinery creaking into action, he might begin the night by trotting past racks of accessories, to a pile of wooden pallets. There, as usual, a warm portion

of chips would await him. The chips eaten, Unipart, still only a youngster, would willingly be lured into a game. Jinking and whirling he would pursue balls of chip-greasy paper which workmen threw for his entertainment and theirs. When tired of this sport, he would trot on from rack to rack. At secret corners he would inspect cracked saucers of milk, little caches of sandwich crusts, a cold sausage—all left by his shop-floor admirers. Then, unnoticed, he would slip from the neon dusk of the factory into the darkness outside.

Having left the warehouse, Unipart would wend his way through the industrial complex, braving the busy Cowley traffic at a point where the dual carriageway runs below a glass-sided bridge, through which he, and any motorists taking their eyes off the road, could see vehicle chassis moving along a conveyor belt over their heads. Following these husks of cars, Unipart moved into the assembly plant where he spent some time amongst embryonic Austin Maxis. It was in the grounds of the assembly plant that disaster struck. We received a telephone message from the factory that a fox had been injured. We found the casualty inside some ventilation pipes in the roof of the warehouse, with a smashed leg. From his numbered eartags we knew it was Unipart. Malcolm took him home, and the University's vet, Ramsay Hovell, ministered to him. For five days the fox convalesced in Malcolm's garden shed, before we took him back to the factory, equipped with a radio-collar and with his broken leg beginning to set. Unipart returned to his old ways, and could be seen hobbling through Cowley.

Unipart's recovery was remarkably swift. Soon he retained only the faintest limp. The car factories seemed to have lost some of their allure, and increasingly he took to the streets of Cowley where he developed an extraordinary habit of chasing bicycles. As some weary traveller pedalled homeward down the dimly lit street in the small hours, it was indeed a remarkable sight to see a fox dash into the road and canter amiably along behind the oblivious cyclist. In a street of semi-detached houses Malcolm and I spent one especially memorable night with Unipart. He was foraging through the pocket handkerchief-sized gardens as we followed on foot with the radio-

tracking equipment. Every so often he would appear through one wrought-iron gate, trot along the pavement before going through the next gate. At one point he paused, hopped onto a brick wall, and sat staring at us. A cat appeared in the garden and, sitting itself on the front doorstep, mewed loudly. Unipart jumped from the wall, trotted over to sniff the cat and sat down within paw's reach of it. As we peered over the wall, we saw a curtain flicker at the window above the fox: the excited faces of a clutch of children and their parents peered out at their nocturnal visitors. There, within arms' length of each other, were fox, cat and householder—a forceful reminder of our brief from the Nature Conservancy Council: to discover how great was the risk of infection between fox, pets and people in the event of an urban rabies outbreak. There, in that delightful scene, the answer could scarcely have been given more lucidly.

The obvious question in terms of the risk of urban rabies is how many foxes live in cities? This is a very difficult question to answer (*see* Box 29, p. 192). We have made two estimates for the 48 square kilometres of Oxford City bounded by the urban by-pass. These estimates are 130–350 adult foxes in the town. Great Britain is a heavily urbanized country, with towns densely packed with people, dogs, cats and foxes: circumstances which could be uniquely disastrous in an outbreak of rabies. However, Britain is currently free of rabies and, as an island, has a good chance of remaining so if people respect the quarantine laws. Under present circumstances in Britain there is no need to take action against city (or rural) foxes on the grounds that rabies may come one day—an open-ended commitment to reducing fox numbers in anticipation of something that may never happen would be ridiculous (and all the more so considering that even where rabies exists, killing foxes has shown little promise as a method of halting the disease, *see* Box 30, p. 195). On the other hand, it is important to know as much as possible about fox habits, and to use that information to combat fox rabies around the world and also to refine a plan in case the disease does arrive in the UK. In Great Britain, in the meantime, the highest priority is to keep rabies out, and to enforce strictly the regulation that all incoming dogs and cats spend six months in quarantine. Those who flout this law often claim

that the risk of a fine (up to £2,000 and risk of a year in prison) was outweighed by the prospect of prolonged separation from their much-loved pet. Yet such people jeopardize the wildlife and domestic animals (not to mention the people) of a nation. Perhaps they would think twice if the penalty for smuggling was the mandatory destruction of the pet.

Having discovered that the city-dwelling foxes lived in family groups (albeit apparently loose-knit ones), the question arose of whether they too followed the Boar's Hill practice of birth control. The story of the Pullens Lane foxes (one of the six city groups we knew well), sheds some light on this question. Our first acquaintance with the Pullens Lane group came in the spring of 1978. Malcolm and I were in an overgrown garden fitting a radio-collar to a lactating vixen when, to our surprise, we noticed that she was glaring at us through only one eye. Her left eye was missing. With this disability, we did not expect One Eye to last for long, but she raised her cubs and remained in the district as the year progressed. The following spring she gave birth to another litter of cubs, this time in the garden of a nurses' hostel. Another radio-vixen had her cubs in the same earth, and the two reared their 11 offspring communally. Both mothers seemed to suckle all the cubs indiscriminately. What was more, a third radio-vixen shared their home range too. This last vixen also had cubs at the same time, but hers were in an earth some 400 metres distant, in the grounds of Pergamon Press—a good choice of venue considering that they published my book on radio-tracking that year!

It was early summer of 1979 when Malcolm met One Eye again at close quarters. To his astonishment, the pupil of her remaining eye was opaque. How long she had been blind we did not know, but we were not surprised when, a month later, she was killed while crossing a road. However, One Eye's fate was hardly different from that of many of her sighted companions. Indeed, she was amongst our longer-lived city foxes at four years old. The vixen with whom she had shared a den had been run over in almost exactly the same spot six weeks earlier, and in February 1980 the eartags from the third vixen were posted anonymously through our letterbox. It was the same story in the neighbouring

Warneford Group, where Malcolm spent much of 1979 skulking in the grounds of a hospital in order to piece together the story of six foxes radio-collared there. Two vixens bore cubs in the Warneford range that spring, and of their daughters, two remained as adults to breed the following year. Of these two, one reared her litter in the very same earth in which she had been born, whereas the other gave birth in a nearby garden shed. Both these vixens were killed by cars before their second year. There was much about these two groups on Headington Hill that was typical of foxes in Oxford City and, in some respects, markedly different from those on nearby Boar's Hill. There were groups of one dog fox and several vixens in both areas, but in the town overlap was imperfect. Furthermore, in contrast to Boar's Hill, where most resident vixens were barren, in the city more than three-quarters of the vixens bred. So, after five years of studying Oxford City's foxes two new questions seemed to be critically important. Why was the pattern of home ranges within and between groups so vaguely defined, and why were there so few barren vixens in each social group?

Of the 80 urban foxes that we have radio-collared in Oxford to date, the one who contributed most to answering these questions was Oedipus—a most unusual fox. But remarkable although Oedipus was, he was no more so than Patrick Doncaster who gathered a staggering 3,427 radio fixes on his movements. Patrick joined the Foxlot as a graduate student in 1980 on a grant from the RSPCA, and brought with him a quietly disarming brilliance that revolutionized our city fox project. The first inkling of the four years of unorthodoxy that lay in store came on the very first night that I went radio tracking with Patrick, when he arrived with a squeal of brakes and the unwieldy tracking antenna perched incongruously atop his Triumph Spitfire.

With Patrick's two-metre beanpole frame folded into the driver's seat, we charged up and down the Cowley Road, putting to the test Patrick's opening gambit that it was possible to improve upon the speed at which we took successive fixes. However, radio tracking from a Spitfire proved to be too conspicuous from the constabulary's perspective, so it was superseded by the famous Foxlot Taxi. This aged London Hackney carriage had a hole drilled in its roof

Patrick Doncaster with the Foxlot taxi.

to accommodate an elegant series of bearings, needles, and protractors which told the direction in which the antenna overhead was pointing. The yellow light that had once illuminated the word 'TAXI', now glowed invitingly as 'FOXLOT'. Despite these conspicuous alterations, an extraordinary number of would-be customers used to hail that taxi, and Patrick's highly selective response provided a continuous supply of new female acquaintances.

Of Patrick's star subject, Oedipus, we know that he was born in Oriel College sports ground in the spring of 1980. There, on the 30th April, he and his sister, Yellow-Yellow, were caught and ear-tagged. That autumn, Oedipus and Yellow-Yellow were recaptured and, at seven months old, were equipped with radio collars. Oedipus' range had moved to the Pullens Lane group range on Headington Hill, about one kilometre from his birthplace. As Patrick tracked him over the following weeks, it soon became clear that something was amiss with this fox. He was unusually easy to observe, although he seemed

to be acutely sensitive to sounds and smells. Once, as Patrick stood silently downwind at the roadside, Oedipus trotted down the path towards him. Patrick's pleasure at this close sighting turned to dismay as the dog fox approached closer and closer, so that at any instant he must surely notice his observer and be spooked. Astonishingly, Oedipus trotted on unconcerned, until he barged straight into Patrick's legs, and only then dashed off in panic. There was no other conclusion—Oedipus was going blind. Later on he was seen colliding with tree trunks, and getting himself entangled in shrubbery and fencing. Oddest of all was the time when he ran straight into another fox. Oedipus would surely be a most interesting fox, if he could survive without the use of his eyes. However, his transmitter was beginning to lose power and needed replacing. One evening the opportunity arose to recapture him. He was lying up among thick brambles in a back garden. Patrick crept stealthily up to a bramble thicket which the radio signal indicated was the one containing Oedipus, and

leapt in to grab the fox. Alas, our interpretation of the radio bleeps was not always completely accurate and Patrick's brave tackle fell some two paces short of Oedipus, who promptly made his escape. Undaunted, Patrick gave chase, and fox and student raced through two gardens and across a football pitch before Oedipus' visual handicap got the better of him as he plunged into the goal mouth at the far end. Catching him between the goal posts, Patrick's outstretched fingers plucked a saving hold on his fox—but never so firm a grip as that with which Oedipus then proceeded to impale his captor's hand.

There ensued much wriggling from both parties during this painful stalemate, until Patrick could at last prise open Oedipus' locked jaws with his remaining free hand. A new radio-collar was quickly fitted, and Oedipus was allowed to trot away savouring, no doubt, the salty taste of victory in his mouth. From Patrick's examination of Oedipus it was clear that he was oblivious to shape and movement, but had some residual sensitivity to the difference between light and

29. WHAT IS RABIES?

More than a millennium ago in ancient Greece, Acteon the hunter chanced upon the goddess Diana and her nymphs as they bathed naked. In her fury at Acteon's voyeurism Diana magically made his hounds rabid, whereupon they savaged their hapless master. Thus the ancients explained the origin of rabies, a viral disease which kills some 15,000 people annually. Only a few countries, mostly islands, are free of rabies—notably Britain, Scandinavia, Australia, New Zealand and Japan.

Rabies is, for practical purposes invariably fatal in man (in whom, uniquely, it induces the dreadful symptom of hydrophobia—fear of water). The numbers of people dying from rabies vary regionally. In the 1970s, 2,755 peope died of rabies in 21 Latin American countries, while 17 died in 11 European countries and 1 died in Canada. Therefore, as far as people are concerned, rabies is a serious threat to life in undeveloped countries, and a threat to peace of mind in developed countries—it is very expensive in both. As far as wildlife is concerned it is a scourge throughout the world. In the Northern Hemisphere, red foxes are the principal vectors and victims of the disease. Although foxes are particularly susceptible, all species of mammals can contract rabies and the principal wildlife hosts vary regionally—vampire bats in South America, mongooses in the Caribbean and South Africa, striped skunk in parts of the USA, jackals in East Africa, Arctic foxes and wolves in the far north, even an antelope, the kudu, in Namibia.

The rabies virus is generally spread in saliva (occasionally in urine or tissue) which is injected into a susceptible animal when it is bitten by an infected one. Foxes succumb when exposed to 1/10,000th the dose of virus required to infect humans. Once infected most foxes incubate the disease for 19 to 20 days during which the virus travels up their nerves to the brain, where it proliferates. At this stage the fox is infected but not infectious. The virus then travels to the fox's salivary glands where it exists in such concentrations that 1ml of fox saliva could theoretically infect 34 million other foxes. The fox then sheds the virus and is infectious for up to six days, after which it begins to show symptoms for the first time. Thereafter it dies within four days (often within 24 hours). About 11 per cent of foxes show the notorious 'furious' symptoms of blind rage; the remainder suffer progressive paralysis and may lose their fear of humans.

Rabies has swept Europe periodically throughout recorded history. The 20th-century outbreak erupted in 1939 in Poland, and has spread westward across 1,400km at between 20 and 60km per year, at an average speed of 4.8km per month. It reached West Germany in 1950, France in 1968 and Italy in 1977. Almost 90 per cent of the diagnosed Western European cases are in wildlife (75 per cent in foxes), where about 1,400 foxes are reported as rabid from 11 countries annually (average figures of 0.044 to 0.065 cases per sq km). An estimated minimum of 2 per cent of rabid foxes are found, so the total number dying of the disease may be about 700,000 annually. There tends to be a 30 per cent increase in cases and in the speed of the front line during the winter. Rabies is invariably fatal in foxes and their populations are decimated by the disease. Therefore, after an initial peak in numbers of cases, some two or three years may pass in a 'silent' phase, before numbers of foxes build up again to sufficiently sustain a further outbreak. Thereafter secondary peaks in disease incidence recur at four to five year intervals.

In North America the situation is more complex since several species are involved. In the Eastern USA, red foxes, grey foxes, raccoons, and striped skunks are all involved, whereas in Florida 77 per cent of wildlife rabies is in raccoons. Throughout the central plains the striped skunk is the principal vector while in California, bats are important. At the same time as rabies broke out in Europe it also entered Canada from Alaska in wolves and Arctic foxes. It spread over 700 miles in eight months, and averaged over 100km per month thereafter. Now some 2,000 cases are diagnosed annually in Ontario. Of these, 20 per cent are in cattle, while of wildlife cases, 72 per cent are in red foxes and 25 per cent in skunks.

Britain's back garden fox cubs would be less welcome if rabies crossed the channel.

darkness. During the 26 months of his life, Oedipus was recaptured five times to replace the spent batteries of his radio. It was the opportunity to monitor the lifestyle of this fox so continuously for so long that first sparked an idea in Patrick's mind, thus changing our understanding of Oxford's city foxes.

Patrick's association with Oedipus spanned some 560 days, during which time the fox not only survived a broken leg when hit by a car, but lived an effectively normal life despite his blindness. Indeed, he successfully mated and sired cubs in an old air-raid shelter. Oedipus' social ties were normal: he was seen playing with other adults, even indulging in a game that involved him and his mate taking turns to climb two metres up the vertical trunk of a large tree. He was capable, too, of taking on tough competition. Once, at the end of March 1981, Patrick followed him as he trotted up the London Road on an excursion well beyond the border of his normal home range. An unidentified fox appeared in the road, blocking Oedipus' path. But the blind fox was oblivious to its presence and he unwittingly closed in. Perhaps his lack of reaction to what was probably a challenge demoralized the other fox, for it turned tail and loped away. As Oedipus continued up the road, two more unknown foxes appeared, one of which rushed up and snapped at his haunches. Oedipus and his unseen assail-

ant gekkered aggressively, rising on their hind legs and grappling with their forepaws. Despite being off his home ground, Oedipus showed no sign of shirking this contest, and eventually it was the other fox who disengaged and loped off in the direction he had come. Oedipus turned left up Hedley Way and for the rest of the night continued to explore the grounds of the John Radcliffe Hospital half a kilometre beyond his normal range.

Patrick also radio-tracked Oedipus's mate, Lopsie, and found that the two of them shared the same range. It was quite a coincidence—Lopsie was probably a descendant of One Eye Vixen's family, the blind vixen whom we had first met in that range five years earlier; now she was a blind fox's mate. As the history of their lives filled out with months of radio tracking, Patrick began to have the dizzy impression that their shared range was wavering in size and shape. It was, in fact, drifting slowly across Headington. Although Oedipus covered about 40 hectares in the early weeks of 1981, his range had expanded to 50 hectares by the summer, and had shrunk again to half that size by the following spring. For the next month or so, into May 1982, the size of his territory was stable, but its location was not. In fact, as Oedipus's range shuffled around the town it eventually turned full circle to re-embrace areas that had lain outside its border

A radio fox attracted by the mouse-like squeak of its signal in the headphones.

Left overs in a yoghurt pot appeals to an urban fox's sweet tooth.

for an entire year. Until the point in June 1982 when Oedipus was killed by a car, his home range was in continual motion, but a motion that became obvious only because of the length of time for which he was tracked and the intensity of Patrick's radio-tracking effort.

With this discovery in mind, Patrick re-analysed the movements of all 28 city foxes he had tracked, and discovered that their ranges also behaved like amoebae—constantly changing shape and location, drifting around in an area that totalled about three times the size of the range used at any given period of weeks. Then he looked again at the overlap between neighbours, but this time considering only short periods of about six weeks at a time. On this short-term time scale, the overlap between adjacent groups largely disappeared.

At any given moment the fox groups were maintaining effectively exclusive territories. The apparent overlap between them had arisen mainly as an artefact due to studying them over different periods (largely because of radio failure) during which home ranges had been in continual drifting motion. Of course, the obvious question was why should this drifting happen? The question was all the more pertinent considering that the ranges on nearby Boar's Hill were so stable, despite the fact that the foxes in both areas were eating similar foods (*see* Box 17, p. 118) and travelling comparably-sized ranges. Our hunch is that the answer lies partly in the heavy traffic mortality in town. Two-thirds of town fox deaths were in road traffic accidents, and these accidents were all too frequent.

There was no doubt that Oxford's foxes were very adept at crossing roads: we would often see them sitting in a central reservation or on a pavement waiting for a safe moment to cross. Despite this skill, with a lifetime on the streets, it is hardly surprising that sooner or later they almost all made a mistake. Many of them survived broken bones, but nonetheless the average age of the foxes we examined *post mortem* was only 12 months, and the oldest was under five years (remember that on Boar's Hill 60 per cent of a similar sample was five years or older). Of course, such figures are subject to many biases

30. CAN WILDLIFE RABIES BE CONTROLLED?

The fundamental tenet of rabies control, and epidemiology in general, is that an epidemic will occur if each infected individual, on average, meets and infects more than one susceptible individual. In this case the frequency of cases increases faster and faster until the supply of susceptibles begins to run out, and eventually limits the disease. The rate at which infectious animals infect susceptibles is called the 'contact rate' of the disease.

Philip Bacon and I ran a computer simulation of a fox population in which we explored the consequences of varying the contact rate for rabies. When each infectious fox infected 1.9 others the population crashed to about 20 per cent of its carrying capacity, at which point the disease declined and the fox population began to recover until there were once again sufficient foxes to sustain another outbreak. As this process was repeated the simulated population of foxes suffered a crash every three to four years. This was similar to the situation observed over most of Europe (see Box 29, p.192). When we repeated the simulation with a higher contact rate (e.g. 2.9) then the impact of the disease on the foxes was so severe that rabies drove them (and itself) to extinction. When the contact rate was less (say 0.5) the virus soon died out, leaving a healthy fox population. Thinking about contact rate therefore highlights two vital aspects of controlling rabies in foxes. First the spread of disease reflects the nature of fox society, since it is their social behaviour that determines their opportunities to meet and infect other foxes. Second, to control the disease the contact rate must somehow be reduced. This is why government health authorities have tried to control rabies through massive campaigns of slaughtering foxes—the idea has been to reduce the fox numbers to such a low level that most rabid foxes die before they encounter a susceptible to which they can pass on the infection.

In Europe it has been widely held that rabies will die out in an area if the number of foxes killed annually during 'routine' foxhunting falls below 0.3 per sq km, the rather shaky assumption being that the tallies of foxes killed by hunters gave an index of the numbers of foxes in the population. However, in Canada, perhaps because of a reservoir in skunks, rabies persists where fur trappers can catch no more than 0.01 to 0.1 foxes per sq km. In Europe, hundreds of thousands of foxes have been poisoned, shot or gassed in the attempt to halt the spread of rabies, but the disease has nevertheless advanced at a constant pace, although the numbers of cases may have been reduced.

This failure is probably because there are two problems with trying to control rabies by killing foxes. First, fox populations are very resilient to control (see Box 31, p 207). Second, killing foxes may increase the contact rate: the survivors meeting more frequently (and aggressively) in the social chaos arising from the fox control campaign.

Another approach to reducing the contact rate for rabies among foxes is to vaccinate them. In this way the number of susceptibles in the population would be reduced without killing them—they would instead be made immune. This has the great advantage of leaving the foxes' social system intact (and is also much cheaper than the very labour intensive task of killing them). In Switzerland pilot studies have involved monitoring the progress of rabies as it spread up the stalks of Y-shaped valleys. At the entrance to one arm of each Y every effort was made to kill foxes, while at the other arm chicken heads loaded with oral rabies vaccine were scattered—the foxes ate the chicken heads and thereby inoculated themselves. In these trials rabies progressed up the valleys until the junction where it met the two types of 'barrier'. There, the disease continued up the arm of the valley where foxes had been killed, but was stopped in its tracks by the barrier of healthy inoculated foxes. This exciting result was only blemished by worries that the 'attenuated live virus' vaccine employed might be too dangerous for general use.

This difficulty may have been solved by the discovery, in 1986, by French scientists of a new and much safer type of rabies vaccine. The new vaccine is the product of genetic engineering. A relatively innocuous virus called Vaccinia (used successfully as a vaccine against smallpox) has its genetic composition manipulated to incorporate elements of the rabies virus. In the laboratory the modified, 'recombinant' Vaccinia virus can be fed to foxes and is sufficiently similar to a rabies virus that it stimulates immunity to the disease. Thereafter the orally vaccinated foxes are resistant to rabies.

If this vaccine works in the field it could herald the end of the scourge of wildlife rabies. Each fox immunized by the recombinant Vaccinia must actually eat a bait loaded with the vaccine (trials show that chicken heads dropped by aircraft may be eaten by about 80 per cent of foxes). It would be even better, but perhaps a pipe dream, if the same trick of genetic engineering could involve a virus that naturally infects foxes (which Vaccinia does not). If that could be achieved the modified fox virus might be passed from fox to fox (like a common cold) without human interference—they would, so to speak, infect each other with rabies immunity.

(and the section of the population dying may have different qualities to the section surviving). Discounting the infant mortality and considering only those foxes that survived to at least six months old, even they had an average life expectancy of only 19 months—only one breeding season. According to our sample, 88 per cent of Oxford City's foxes were destined to die before their second birthday. This turnover may so disrupt the social *status quo* that relationships between neighbouring groups are in perpetual flux and borders constantly being rearranged. I suspect also that social ties within groups are similarly disrupted, and consequently that the rungs on the social ladder are less clearly separated.

This state of affairs may hold the answer to the question of why the majority of vixens in the city groups bred. In the state of social flux wrought by the heavy death toll dominant animals may be less able to exert influence over subordinates. Another relevant factor might be the instability of some urban food patches. In contrast, Boar's Hill foxes are born into a social and territorial structure that lasts a lifetime and will go on to outlive them.

Road traffic certainly affected the nightly lives of individual foxes. Many foxes lived within earshot of major roads, and their nightly activities were timed to miss the worst of the traffic—they even tended to take a break at pub closing time! Indeed, it is possible that they were using the subsiding roar of traffic as a cue for when to set out for the night. Changes in human activity and traffic density affected the foxes' options during their travels: for instance, when Oxford United were playing football at home in the evening, Old Head the local dog fox interrupted his normal routine to lie up in the seclusion of a nearby churchyard until 10.30pm, by which time the increased traffic of departing fans within his home range had died down again. Other foxes became blasé about cars: Plum, another of Patrick's foxes, could be seen regularly on the grass verge beside the Ring Road, or sitting beneath a flyover watching the cars go by. At least once she spent the day sleeping on the central reservation, sandwiched between the passage of some 3,000 cars per hour.

Several foxes learnt to recognize the engine notes of our various dilapidated tracking vehicles, and ignored our close approach while remaining flighty of strange cars. In particular, the urban vixen Awen would allow the noisy diesel taxi to stay close on her heels whereas she invariably dodged into nearby gardens if any other traffic passed. One night, while Patrick was chugging along just behind Awen, absorbed in her adventures, the fox suddenly shied away and there came a startling rap at the taxi's window. Patrick stopped and patiently wound down the window to be greeted with the terse enquiry 'Ere, are you on Dog Watch?' Countering this attack with a laconic enquiry of his own, Patrick learned that the pet lover's fears had been aroused when night after night he had wondered why he was seeing a taxi creeping along the darkened streets in pursuit of small dogs. He was not easily convinced that it had been Awen the urban fox!

Motor cars were not the only source of human inconvenience to the foxes. One dozing radio-tagged vixen was rudely awoken and forced to decamp when a tramp flopped down to sleep in her sheltered nook. A more direct threat came from people determined to kill foxes. Long vigils listening to inactive radio signals were always tinged with the fear that the ostensibly sleeping fox might actually be in dire straits just out of view. More than one long night has led to a fox hanging in a sack, and an irate farmer or householder waiting in ambush to demand why we had 'sent' our foxes onto his property. Indeed, on one occasion Malcolm and Nick found themselves parked in Southfield Road as a fox called Tipsy moved in a nearby garden. The garden in question was the property of a well-known fox-hater. They were alerted to the possibility that something might be amiss when the radio signal indicated that Tipsy was highly active, yet remaining in exactly the same spot. At last they could sit it out no longer, and crept along the pavement to the house behind which the fox was located. To their astonishment they heard the bangings and rattlings typical of a fox caught in a trap. Sure enough, from the vantage point of a neighbour's garden wall, Tipsy could be seen in a large cage-trap, well on his way to becoming a statistic in the pelt trade. We had invested far too much effort in this fox to endure his premature demise, so rescue plans were laid. Nick was to stand guard at the front of the house, while Malcolm stole into the back garden to

rescue Tipsy. For his part, Tipsy failed to appreciate his saviour's good intentions, so it was at
some peril to his fingers, and amid a din of
rattling and snirking, that Malcolm struggled in
the darkness to feel for the mechanism to unlatch
the trap's door. At last he managed to get the
door open, crawled round to the back of the trap
and tried, with anxious whispers of encourage-
ment, to cajole Tipsy towards freedom. By this
time, however, Tipsy thought he knew all he
wanted to know about trap doors and had not the
tiniest intention of passing through this one,
open or otherwise.

Meanwhile, Nick, attempting to lounge with
inconspicuous nonchalance in the street outside,
heard the fearsome rattlings from within and,
unable to control his curiosity, threw caution to
the wind and rushed, with torch ablaze, to
Malcolm's aid. Malcolm, blinded by the on-
coming torchlight and believing that the householder was on the attack, mustered the Hercu-
lean strength to lift the trap clean off the ground
and shake Tipsy from it. After this heroic and
noisy gesture he flung the trap aside and attempted to vault the garden wall, on top of which he
was painfully straddled before recognition of
Nick's anxious voice penetrated his adrenaline-
drenched consciousness.

Of course, the animosity shown by some
people to the city foxes arose because they saw
them as pests. Urban foxes got a bad press. One
outraged correspondent to the *Cambridge Evening
News* called upon local government to 'curtail the
activities of the fox' and went on to bemoan the
'incipient dangers arising from these animals . . .
that have become urban predators'. A headline in
the *Oxford Star* declared 'Starving foxes close in'
and quoted the view that foxes were 'coming into
Oxford because there is insufficient food for them
in the countryside'. Is the urban fox a pest? It was
with a remit to answer that question that the
RSPCA sponsored Patrick's studentship. Our
answers are summarized in Box 28 (*see* p. 180).

In short, we found that significant nuisance
was rare, and sufficiently isolated that blanket
action against urban foxes would be unwarranted. In fact, we were flabbergasted by the
triviality of many complaints, and saddened by
others. One complainant was outraged because a
fox had 'invaded the privacy' of her garden,
another protested that her daughter could not

sleep because of foxes barking, another complained of a golf ball stolen from the lawn
(doubtless for cubs to play with), another that the
fox had infected their pet rabbit with myxo-
matosis (an impossibility), and several were enraged because playing cubs had scattered neat
piles of lawn-mowings. Others were offended by
foxes drowning in their swimming pools, and
there was the man who demanded the destruction of a family of cubs (the delight of his
neighbour's children) lest they urinate on the
lawn where his daughter did handstands.
Certainly, there were genuine grievances too; for
instance, there was the grief of the little girl
whose cherished guinea-pig fell prey to a fox.
It is not to belittle that grief to suggest that rather
than killing the fox, building a robust hutch is
often a more effective and ethically preferable
solution.

Our interest in long-term patterns of city fox
behaviour was bedevilled by the premature failure of transmitters, a difficulty exacerbated by the
recurring problem of recapturing our subjects to
replace the worn batteries. To catch a fox at all is
difficult enough, but to recapture a particular
individual is even more testing. The vixen Pretty
One was a case in point. She was among a group
of foxes who struck up an unusual relationship
with a couple who wandered Southfield's golf
course by night to exercise their three enormous
Alsatian guard dogs. We had been puzzled by
the large amount of time Pretty One spent on a
particular fairway and it was quite by chance that
Patrick met the couple one night and discovered
that they were feeding the foxes there. Patrick
arranged to accompany them to meet the foxes.
The dogs were kept on leashes for his sake,
although one lunged at him so fiercely that it
pulled its owner clean off his feet.

Despite this nerve-racking distraction, Pretty
One and two other foxes nonchalantly circled the
dogs, trotting back and forth to cache food as it
was thrown to them. This was quite a contrast to
Niff's terror of dogs, and was the strangest fox–
dog story I knew until January 1987 when I was
called to meet a stray bitch which had been living
wild among the foxes on Putney Common on the
outskirts of London. For two years she had been
seen in the company of foxes on nightly visits for
food hand-outs from well-wishers, who had
watched her eating and playing with the foxes,

and had concluded that she was a fox–dog hybrid (*see* Box 1, p. 10).

Returning to Pretty One, her story was reaching an intriguing point when the pulsings of her radio collar developed the tell-tale signs of terminal arrhythmia. This was the opportunity to test Patrick's latest, and highly characteristic, brainchild: 100 metres of specially manufactured netting! Patrick traced Pretty One's failing signal to her sleeping place in a patch of rough brambles bordering the first hole at Southfield's Golf Course. Then, an hour before darkness, he took the massed forces of the Foxlot down to a neighbouring pub and plied them with advance payment for their forthcoming efforts. Finally, as dusk fell, he led us to the site, full of bonhomie, laden with the massive net, dozens of bamboo canes, 200 iron tent pegs and other obscure accoutrements to his plan. With some be-musement we tiptoed behind Patrick and fol-lowed his commands as he orchestrated the positioning of the net.

With grave whispers and emphatic gesticula-tions he impelled us to crawl with the net through a two-metre swathe of stinging nettles. Our goodwill towards Patrick's whims was be-coming a bit less jovial by the time the web had been spun around 100 metres of nettles and brambles. Just as we were set to beat through the scrub and drive the vixen into the net, the full mastery of Patrick's plan was revealed: a barrage of fireworks exploded behind us, from a cassette player hidden in the undergrowth, singer Patti Smith belted out an album called *Waves*, and we surged forward with much hullabaloo. Jolted from her slumbers, Pretty One took the point. Her startled head appeared above the tall grass for the split second required to get a measure of the opposition, and then she belted for the net. With a whoop of victory, Patrick galloped for-ward, only to see Pretty One hit the net with such vigour that it catapulted her to the safety of a clump of nettles. With the coordination of a de-cerebrated frog, Patrick's astonishingly long limbs flailed amongst the nettles as he pounced in after her. There was a ripple on the net as Pretty One slipped neatly beneath it, and then all was still as we watched her canter off to freedom across the adjoining fairway.

Stung, torn and dishevelled we straggled back to the far side of the circle of netting where we found that we had successfully entwined a passer-by and his dog in the fine mesh. Although Pretty One was never recaptured, a week later the Foxlot and Patti Smith were out again, em-ploying the very same method at a site close by, this time catching an enormous dog fox, Hand-some. He later turned out to be Pretty One's mate, and so her story continued to unfold.

Handsome was a magnificent specimen and, like many others of Oxford's foxes, hard to reconcile with the image of moth-eaten town foxes. In 1965, before urban foxes had really caught the public eye, a book called *Town Fox, Country Fox* portrayed city-dwelling foxes as un-healthy degenerates in comparison to their coun-try cousins. This has always struck me as a very odd judgement—on the contrary it seems to be an extraordinary feat of adaptability for a sizeable wild mammal to thrive in our cities. Perhaps the demoralized image of city foxes grew out of an unwarranted parallel drawn between country folk and their flabbier counterparts in the town. Anyway, the idea that city foxes are second-class or unhealthy *émigrés* from the countryside is rife. Is it correct? The answer is no. According to our studies Oxford's urban foxes are neither shorter nor longer, lighter nor heavier than rural foxes. They breed readily in the town, and live at higher population densities and often live longer than many farmland foxes. By these criteria the fox flourishes on city life. What of the idea that they are mangy? Sarcoptic mange (known as scabies in man) is caused by a mite and can debilitate foxes. The mite burrow into the skin, hair falls out, and scratched, suppurating bald patches appear; the fox wastes away and may die from cold or secondary infection. Certainly mange affects some urban fox populations—it almost wiped out the foxes of South Harrow, a London suburb, in the early 1970s and also decimated foxes (and the fur trade) in the Scandinavian wilderness dur-ing the seventies. But is it particularly a disease of urban foxes? The answer seems to be no.

We kept a keen lookout for it in Oxford. Many of the foxes reported as mangy were merely moulting for from April till June they shed fur successively from their feet, tail, rump and progressively forwards until they look very moth-eaten—the shorter summer coat grows to its prime by November. In fact, of the first 94 foxes we handled in the town, only one vixen had mange. She recovered completely and when she was shot by a publican 11 months later he got a good price for her pelt. Mange certainly merits further study, but at present there is no evidence that city foxes are any more, or less, mangy than rural ones.

The prejudice that city foxes are different to (and worse than) country ones is finally dispelled by the fact that individual foxes may move back and forth between town and country. Indeed, several of the cubs that we ear-tagged in the town eventually set up home after dispersing to the countryside. Other foxes spent their days on farmland and commuted into town at night, or vice versa. A typical case was a dog fox known by the unmemorable name of D13, who was born in 1978 in a home range where leafy suburban gardens blended into farmland at the western edge of the city. When he was radio-collared that September, his range was scarcely 100 hectares, but nevertheless spanned three worlds: he meandered between large detached houses and gardens and the adjoining overgrown valley where a shooting syndicate released upwards of 1,000 pheasants annually, and then crossed the city by-pass to explore amongst more urban surroundings. Then, on the night of 22nd September, he took off and cut across country to a spot eight kilometres to the west, near the village of Cumnor, not returning home until 3.30am. Soon afterwards he took to spending the day in the more urban quarter of his group's range. Since the adult members of that group tended to rest by day in the wooded valley, it may have been that D13 was avoiding their company. Indeed, it is a general ploy of young dog foxes to dodge conflict by restricting their movements to a small section of their family's territory.

In early November, D13 set off on another lengthy excursion to Cumnor village. There, he began to focus his exploits in the vicinity of the churchyard adjoining John Gee's farm. For the next two months, D13 became an almost nightly commuter. By day, he lay up in the urban surroundings of his parents' city beat, and by night he crossed the city limits and loped to Cumnor where he donned the guise of a rural fox. Then, in early January, he took the plunge and left the city once and for all. Soon after, while continuing to operate around Cumnor by night, he began to sleep by day in another village,

Appleton, a further four kilometres to the south, and it was there that he was shot just before his first birthday.

Despite their very different landscapes, I gradually came to the conclusion that from the foxes' viewpoint there was much in common between the 'rural suburbia' of Boar's Hill and Oxford City. The major difference seemed to lie in the greater death rate in the city. Thinking back over the foxes from Cumnor's farmland, Cumbria's fells, Israel's feeding sites and others, it was clear that both food (its abundance and dispersion) and mortality affect the ingredients of fox behaviour (namely their numbers, travels, group sizes, age structures and reproduction). The whole Foxlot saga focused into one question: how do food supply and mortality interact to fashion fox society? As one step towards unravelling this interaction I returned, in 1981, to two old stamping grounds: Wytham Woods and the adjacent Cumnor farmland. It was agreed locally that, barring serious damage, fox control would cease while I studied them. So, two very different rural environments with minimal mortality: how would fox society adapt?

11 | BEHIND THE MASK

RASPING CRIES SHATTERED the dawn and, for a moment, silenced the chatter of woodland birds. Stopping the van, I peered through the rising mist that still cloaked that April morning. A second stuttering volley of shrieks cast my drowsiness aside and told that foxes were battling nearby. I let the van freewheel down the gravel track towards the sounds. That spring night had been passed like hundreds before, but now, as I headed wearily for bed, the quarry was closer at hand.

Not 50 metres ahead of me a fox streaked across the track, fiercely pursued by another, both oblivious of my vehicle in their frenzy. The two foxes wheeled across a field of sprouting wheat, met and tumbled in combat before rising together shrieking, and rearing on their hind legs with red coats streaking dark with the moisture of the dewy morning. The two stood like bookends, facing each other, heads thrown back, mouths agape and ears pinned back flush against the contours of their heads as each stabbed at the other's shoulders with its forepaws. Moments later the combatants—both of them vixens—dropped to all fours and another furious tumble ensued. They thrashed together, parted, chased and fought again for a full five minutes until, at last, one broke free and sped away. But the victor was not satisfied, and twice overhauled her adversary in punishing attacks before the beaten vixen, dodging and feinting as she fled, was chased from view.

Almost eight minutes passed before the victorious animal re-appeared on the brow of the hill. Mud-streaked and exhausted, she plodded between the furrows, her sodden brush trailing heavily on the clay and her head hung so low that the protruding pink tongue almost touched the

ground. Nevertheless, she summoned the energy to consolidate her victory by cocking her leg on five different clods of mud in the next couple of minutes. The battleground had been at the junction of the ranges of two families in Wytham Woods—the very same woods where, ten years before, I had taken my first inept steps to launch the Oxford fox project. It was a difficult habitat, far too difficult for me then, but early in 1981, with a decade's worth of fox lore behind me, I was determined to try again.

Judging by the fight I had just witnessed, it seemed likely that Wytham's foxes would turn out to be territorial and my hope in taking on another study area was to disentangle further the effects of differences in food supply and death rate on fox behaviour. The plan was to radio track foxes throughout Wytham Woods and south across Denman's Farm, a 30 sq km block of land which abutted Oxford City on one side, and curled towards Boar's Hill on the other.

Three months later I had ten foxes bleeping around Wytham, and a picture of their social lives began to take shape. The strangest goings on were in Mrs Gardiner's garden, which adjoined a secluded spinney beside Wytham Abbey. At least four, possibly five, adult foxes frequented that garden, three of which were equipped with radios. A radio-tagged vixen, Bramble, reared cubs that spring, as probably did a second vixen, Podge, who was not radio tagged until that November. It was the other two adults that surprised us, for both were dog foxes. Gasper was a big-boned, lean and rangy fox in late middle age; Kobuk was medium sized and unexceptional in appearance, and probably entering his second year. They shared almost identical ranges, spanning the Marley Plantations in

Wytham and both focusing on Mrs Gardiner's garden and the neighbouring farmyard, where they pilfered milk from the storage tank. In dozens of other fox territories, in a variety of habitats, the rule had been one adult dog fox per group. Yet these two not only shared the same range, they were also regularly seen hunting for worms side by side without any sign of animosity. What circumstances lead to adult male foxes sharing a territory, and what are the consequences of their cohabitation? In this case it was more than likely that Gasper and Kobuk had cohabited in that territory during the previous mating season, and it was certain that they were both there during March when Bramble's cubs were born. From our studies in Enclosure III (Chapter 8) I knew that in captivity it can happen that two males carry food to one litter of cubs. Whether Kobuk was Gasper's son, and what their respective roles had been in the siring and tending of the two litters of cubs born that Spring, I do not know. But the prospect of following their careers into the next breeding season was exciting.

Outside the wood, Gasper and Kobuk were relatively easy to watch, largely because they concentrated their worm-hunting in one old pasture. In contrast, once in the woods they were almost invisible.

However, one of the joys of Wytham was that even when the foxes were elusive, the woodland abounded with wildlife. Badgers wad-

dled down the rides, owls glided silently overhead, and broad-antlered fallow bucks sniffed gustily and flicked their tails in agitation as they strained to catch a whiff of danger.

Amongst this nocturnal community, the dog fox Gasper once led me to an intriguing encounter. I was radio tracking on foot, struggling to catch a glimpse of him in the dense undergrowth. He was already at the furthest extreme of his territory when I crept so close that the signal was deafening in my headphones. Ahead of me, I thought I spotted Gasper moving in the tall grass beside the ride, but through the infra-red binoculars I saw that it was not him after all, but a muntjac deer. The muntjac was standing defiant, and stamped its forefoot. Fifteen paces away another adult muntjac fidgetted in and out of bushy undergrowth. Both deer were clearly excited, but although the signal told that he was very close, Gasper was nowhere to be seen. Then, Gasper appeared in the eerie light of the hot-eye, head up and high-stepping like a dressage horse, passing only two metres from the doe muntjac. Following his gaze to her feet, I saw the smallest imaginable muntjac fawn. The doe stamped again, the fawn tottered back and forth beneath her, Gasper whirled around and trotted

past again. The second muntjac emerged from the bushes and moved anxiously towards the doe. Fox and deer stood staring at each other through darkness that hummed with the tension. Gasper wheeled about and jogged off down the ride and out of sight.

The local farmer killed Gasper and Kobuk in the early winter of 1981 while they pilfered from his milk tank and before the next breeding season. So, how their amiable relationship would have weathered the strains of rivalry in the rut remains unknown. But what of the original question: what causes two male foxes to share a range? Although I do not know the answer, it is a fact that over the years I have found four instances of two adult males cohabiting, and in each case they were members of rather large groups, containing five or more adults.

In 1981, Heribert Hofer exploded upon the scene. Heribert had been studying zoology in Germany when he was smitten with a desire to become a postgraduate at Oxford. With an exuberant unorthodoxy that became his hallmark, he assuaged this desire by flying immediately to England, and found his way, unannounced, to my office. At our first meeting he knew only a few English words, but he deployed them in various mystifying combinations and at great speed. I cannot have been the only one to succumb to this whirlwind delivery, in which every protest was disarmed by a beatific smile, because when I next saw him, six months later, Heribert had secured a clutch of prestigious scholarships to enable him to join the Foxlot. Within 24 hours of his arrival he had mastered the Gay Gordon, danced with every girl at our village barn dance, and was already hot on the trail of a radio fox. Five years later, Heribert's thesis, bound, with characteristic flair, in bright yellow, analysed the movements of these and other Wytham foxes and won him the fifth doctorate to come out of our fox studies.

Of those foxes we studied in Wytham Mrs Gardiner's group was exceptional because of its association with the village. Elsewhere in the wood, human dwellings were a much less significant feature of the foxes' lives. Some, like the vixens Old Mahogany and Grizzle, actually had no houses in their territories. Others, like K'boom Vixen and Old Sabre Dog, had a more agricultural existence, dividing their efforts between the wood and the neighbouring farmland. The first step to understand their behaviour was to ask what did the woodland foxes eat?

Between us, Heribert and I found 2,030 fox droppings in the wood. From this hefty sample, rabbits emerged as the single most important prey of these foxes (a quarter of the droppings contained rabbit fur). They also ate lots of earthworms and, in the autumn, blackberries. Indeed, blackberries are such a favourite of foxes everywhere that I suspect foxes are a significant dispersal agent for their seeds. In July beetles and rodents peaked in the diet. As has been the general rule in our studies, the foxes in neighbouring ranges sometimes ate rather different foods. For instance, Old Sabre's range encircled Woodend Farm, where his group feasted on the cleansings of newborn calves. On the other hand, his neighbour, Boots (so named from the time he bit clean through my boot, his canine teeth locking steadfastly in the gap between two toes) occupied a range particularly well endowed with rabbits. For the main part, however, to judge by the contents of their droppings, all the Wytham foxes dined frequently on rabbits, and catching these is a more challenging proposition than overwhelming an earthworm, so how did they do it? I sought out vantage points in the hope of witnessing such kills.

The majestic, broad-leaved trees of Wytham Woods arc in a horseshoe palisade around the grassy flanks of a valley that forms the Great Park. At the foot of the valley, beneath a skyline pierced by Oxford's spires, shaggy-headed highland cattle complete the gothic scene as they graze beside a 19th century abbey. The park is dotted with immense oak trees, once youthful contemporaries of the first abbot, now survivors of the last. Towards the head of the valley, facing each other with a symmetry echoing their belligerence, are the setts of the two clans of badgers that partition this rich worming ground. It was from a vantage point at the top of this valley that I took to lying in wait at dawn and dusk. Hidden behind a gorse bush, I waited for foxes to appear, and took light relief in the antics of rabbits whose warren lay some 50 paces downhill from me.

The sun was already well up, and I was preparing to leave my vantage point, when I spotted a vixen way down the valley, trotting fast from the Marley plantation towards the duck-

pond. Even at that distance I knew it was Old Mahogany, a vixen whose pelt was such a deep chestnut brown that in the distance she seemed black. She reached the thicket and disappeared from sight. Minutes later I caught a glimpse of her ears gliding behind a ridge. The vixen was using slack ground to move unseen towards me, and towards the rabbits that grazed around the warren below me. Minutes later Old Mahogany reappeared, standing stock-still at the end of the gulley, pointing like a bird-dog at the rabbits, and separated from them by an expanse of inhospitably open ground. Her eyes fixed on the rabbits, she paced slowly forward, half crouching. She made, not directly for them, but for a nearby tree, thereby orienting her approach so that two

further trees now lay in line between herself and the rabbits. At a scuttling crouch she moved swiftly to the next tree, her route hidden from the rabbits by the massive circumference of the trunk. The last lap was almost slithered, her hackles jutting above her back as she tried to hug the ground. And then she was behind the last tree, only 20 paces from the nearest rabbit. Old Mahogany peered carefully around the trunk. She was charging at top speed before the rabbits saw her, and she was amongst them in a trice. Soil scuffed into the air as rabbits fled and vixen swerved, claws left raking gashes in soft mud, and Old Mahogany stood there, alone and unsuccessful. She wheeled about and trotted uphill, passing me without so much as a glance.

Old Mahogany's stealthy approach was one of four methods that I have seen foxes use to hunt rabbits. Another method is to lie in wait beside a warren, just as a cat might do, to pounce on an unwary rabbit as it emerges. Even underground, rabbits are not totally secure, for foxes will dig out the shallow breeding stops where low-ranking, doe rabbits stow their litters on the periphery of the main warren. Lastly, there is the dash and grab, to which the preamble varies from a sauntering pretence at disinterest to a full-throttled charge. At the nonchalant end of this spectrum, the fox trots through a group of rabbits, seemingly oblivious of the succulent predatory temptations to left and right; something in the vulpine demeanour must reassure the prey which continue to graze with no more than a cautionary thump of a foot as their long-tailed visitor passes as close as 20 metres. Occasionally, however, the fox's disinterest is a sham; a buck rabbit, too engrossed in the scent of nearby doe, fails to notice the slight tensing in that jaunty gait that heralds a deadly swerving sprint.

The best dash and grab that I have seen involved one of Old Mahogany's neighbours in Wytham, Pintooth Vixen. Pintooth's territory encompassed a place called Hill End, where a long grassy bank curved beneath a field of wheat. The bank was pitted with warrens, and on this particular morning, not long after sunrise, 30 or more rabbits were in view at the moment when Pintooth Vixen broke cover. She was already running when the nearest rabbits jolted upright in alarm; she was heading into the wind and loping fast, but not at full speed. Ahead of her a wave of alarm spread through the rabbits, and those nearest her sprinted for their burrows, tails flicking a warning to their companions. Suddenly, Pintooth accelerated hard, swerved after a rabbit and missed. She hardly checked her pace, but glided back into a loping stride as she ran on along the slope. Seconds later another sprint at breakneck speed, another flurry of scuffed sand,

and another miss, and on she loped. Already the vixen was two-thirds of the way through the long belt of warrens. Thirty metres below her on the slope, a rabbit scuttled aside, changed its mind and dashed back on its tracks. Pintooth's flame-red body coiled in a tight circling sprint, flinging herself downhill. Again the rabbit faltered, and spun for the sanctuary of yet a different hole. Pintooth flung herself in the new direction, turning so sharply that she skidded off balance and, in the very instant that she somersaulted, she grabbed the rabbit amidst a flurry of sand and fur and piercing squeals.

Rabbits had also been the principal prey of the foxes on the Cumbrian fells, where the home ranges of hill foxes had been vast—1,000 hectares or more—how big were the ranges of Wytham's woodland foxes? We set about answering this question as Heribert monitored their movements (and those of the badgers we were studying at the same time) while I extended the study area onto the adjoining farmland, and found myself, once again, on Denman's Farm. In 1972 it had taken me five months to catch Denman's Vixen. Returning to the area, experience seemed to pay off: it was not long before I had eleven adult foxes bleeping. The first of these was a beautiful long-legged dog fox called Bright Eyes, whom I first met not a stone's throw from the woodland glade to which Denman's Vixen had led me almost ten years before. How would this home range compare with the one she had travelled so long ago? As Bright Eyes led me a nostalgic trip around Denman's Vixen's old haunts it was soon obvious that the borders of his range in 1982 were similar

to the ones she had observed in 1973. Indeed, there was much in the detail of his movements that was identical—he travelled the same paths, lay up in the same cover and foraged in many of the same places. It seemed that the framework of the home range had survived the span of generations of occupants. Our three years of fieldwork in Wytham suggested a similar stability there too. However, the answer to the range size question was distinctly different in the two areas: the group ranges of nine fox families in Wytham Woods averaged 70 hectares, and the biggest was

104 hectares. On the adjoining farmland the majority of ranges were between 100 and 200 hectares. In both areas, the ranges were ordered into rather neatly tessellated territories, but why did woodland foxes cover less ground than their farmland neighbours?

Analysis of a further 981 droppings taught me that the principal food of these farmland foxes was earthworms, followed by fruit and scavenged scraps (largely from the nearby village), with rabbits a long way down the list. Indeed, in the autumn, the foxes on Denman's

Farm spent night after night eating windfall plums, occasionally supplemented when they nabbed a rabbit that strayed into the orchard. However, although there seemed to be abundant food in some places at some times on and around the farms, there were large expanses of effectively barren cereals and temporary leys. I suspect the territory sizes were bigger on the farms, not because there was less food overall, but because it was more spread out. A similar answer largely explains why the rabbit-eating foxes of Wytham Woods travelled territories one tenth the size of those on the Cumbrian fells. Whereas warrens on the fells were separated by expanses largely devoid of prey, a Wytham fox which fumbled the capture of a rabbit could turn to nearby fruit or earthworms. Another difference between the two areas was the intense hunting pressure on the hill foxes, which raises the question of what effect does fox control have on fox movements?

In the early 1970s when I first tracked foxes on and around Denman's Farm, they were subject to moderately intense control. In the early 1980s, however the local farmers and gamekeepers kindly spared the foxes for the sake of our study. I believe there were at least two, and possibly three, consequences of this moratorium in terms of fox behaviour. In 1973 by best estimate was that there were only two or three adult foxes respectively in the two territories I knew on that farmland. By late 1983, Bright Eyes' group numbered at least five adults, and there were at least three adults in each of the four farmland groups. Furthermore, although my samples are perilously small, in the period of intensive control barren vixens were uncommon. In 1983 four of the seven radio-tracked vixens did not rear cubs. I suspect that reduced mortality led to reduced emigration and increased group size. I also suspect that it was as a consequence of a stratified age structure and greater social stability that fewer vixens reared cubs (i.e. overall produc-

31. DO PEOPLE LIMIT THE NUMBERS OF FOXES?

There are basically two groups of people involved in killing foxes, and while their aims are largely separate their effects may be rather similar. There are those who view foxes as a pest, and those who view them as a resource. In general the former try to minimize numbers of foxes, the latter try to maximize yield. Together they add up to one of the largest onslaughts on any mammalian species: in one year rabies controllers in Alberta killed 50,000 red foxes, sheep farmers and gamekeepers in Scotland killed 9,000, fur trappers in the USA killed 356,000. Worldwide the annual toll of foxes is astronomical. Over most of Europe foxes can sustain losses to hunters of two thirds of their past-breeding populations (between 0.7 and 2.0 foxes are killed by European hunters each year per sq km, from fox breeding populations estimated at 0.5 to 1.8 per sq km). The fact that foxes remain widespread and abundant is evidence of their capacity to withstand control.

A widespread motive for killing foxes is the hope of increasing the yield of game quarry. Considering the enormous resilience of fox populations, can game managers kill sufficient foxes to increase significantly their harvest of game? There are circumstances where the answer is clearly yes—for example on major shooting estates patrolled by several gamekeepers professionally dedicated to eradicating foxes. Their success stems, in particular, from an ability to find and kill breeding vixens (analogous, in turn, to the fox's impact on nesting partridges).

In many smaller operations (which may collectively constitute the bulk of shooting land and contribute a greater total of foxes killed) foxes are killed by a volunteer or over-worked or part-time keeper patrolling (sometimes rather casually) a smaller area which may be surrounded by land where there is no keepering. In such a case there are several reasons why one might expect killing foxes to have little impact on the yield of game (or the population of foxes). First, many foxes are killed in winter, and many of them are itinerant males who were simply passing through. Second, killing a territorial fox puts a vacant vulpine property on the market, and it is likely, especially in winter, that this swiftly attracts (the 'vacuum effect') a new tenant (of which the surrounding countryside can offer an effectively inexhaustible supply). Third, if the spring population is reduced, the surviving foxes, either through having a greater share of the food supply and/or through the disruption of their social system, will probably produce young at a faster rate; in other words a reduction in numbers of foxes can increase their productivity. Fourth, on such a small operation the loss of game

harvest due to fox predation may be a relatively small component of the total losses.

In collaboration with the Game Conservancy, I studied the effects of a three year moratorium (1976–78) on killing foxes on just such a small (500 ha) 'shoot' outside Oxford. There sportsmen relied heavily on released pheasants, and 12 to 20 foxes were killed annually. There was no clearcut difference in the percentages of released pheasants that were subsequently shot during the years when foxes were tolerated—any effect the moratorium might have had was swamped by the many other factors affecting the shooting success. I certainly do not put much weight on this one pilot study, but it raises a question: about half a million people shoot 12 million pheasants annually in Britain (they release about 21 million)—how many of them would shoot fewer if they ignored foxes?

The same limitations apply to other methods of control which are scattered and sporadic. When I surveyed over 800 English farmers some 30 per cent believed that they suffered significant damage from foxes (many of these were referring to game 'bags' although, interestingly, a slight majority of the sample stated that they disapproved of foxes being killed to increase game shooting, whereas two thirds of them approved of foxes being killed for sport by packs of hounds). 659 of these farmers gave figures for the number of foxes killed on their land during the previous year: the answer was zero on 52 per cent of farms and 2.84 foxes on the average farm (i.e. 2.5 foxes killed per sq km of English farmland annually). This figure, doubtless a rough estimate, embraced farms where game was managed and foxes hunted (the latter accounting for an average of 0.15 foxes killed per sq km of farmland). The analyses are not available to show what affects this level and schedule of control has on fox numbers (and even less is known of how it affects fox damage). However, imagine that an average farmland fox territory is 150 ha (also, as it happens, the size of the average farm). If one vixen breeds per territory and rears four cubs, there will be six foxes there in autumn. If the population is stable, four of these will have to go before the next spring (equivalent to a loss of 2.6 foxes per sq km). In this crude, hypothetical, but not absurd example the just under three foxes killed annually on the average lowland English farm might have no effect on the fox population. The fact that all the control effort is localized on just one third of the farmland increases the plausibility of this general conclusion. Most attempts at fox control probably end up, at most, as fox harvests—the attempt to minimize numbers producing an increase in sustainable yield.

32. DO FOXES LIMIT THE NUMBERS OF THEIR PREY?

Whether predators limit the numbers of their prey (by killing them) and whether prey limit the numbers of their predators (by their limited availability to be eaten) are important questions in ecology. It is obvious that the abundance of prey ultimately limits the numbers of their predators since, at a trivial level, if there were no prey to be eaten there could be no predators to eat them. Equally, it is obvious that predators affect the short term numbers of their prey because having eaten one prey, there will be one less, at least for a while. Far less obvious, however, are the circumstances under which predation can be great enough to reduce the breeding population of prey to a lower level than that supported by other factors (such as its food supply).

By analogy, each year the capital sum (breeding stock) of money in your savings account produces interest (offspring); you (or the fox) withdraw money (or prey) without which you starve. Do these withdrawals only consume the interest, or do they erode the capital? The ecological debate has been about whether predators generally eat into the capital (the breeding stock) of their prey populations, or merely cream off the interest (i.e. the 'doomed surplus', see Box 23, p.152). In fact, very few, if any, studies of natural populations have been able to falsify conclusively either hypothesis, but there is mounting evidence that foxes can limit the breeding stock of some of their prey.

For example, in the prairie pot-hole region of North America, Alan Sargeant estimated that predators (including foxes) reduced the fledging success of mallard ducks from 80 per cent to 15 per cent of eggs laid. Similarly, working on two large islands in the Bothnian Gulf, Vidar Marcström and his colleagues exterminated most foxes and martens from one island and not the other, with the result that, over four years, numbers of adult gamebirds increased by 40 per cent on the predator-free island and hares increased too (and the same occurred on the other island when the treatment was reversed).

Islands are rather a special case in this context, and introduced foxes have annihilated seabird colonies on Alaskan islands (see Box 13, p.84).

In parts of Sweden populations of voles, grouse and hares cycle synchronously over four-year periods (see Box 18, p.122). In these areas, voles are the principal prey, but since they continue to cycle in the absence of foxes (and martens) on Marcström's islands, it seems that something other than predation drives the cycles in vole numbers (probably it is some aspect of the voles' food supply). In contrast, on the island where Marcström removed foxes, annual changes in the breeding success and numbers of game birds fell out of synchrony with the vole cycle. A parallel result arose in a different study area where Erik Lindström experimentally provided foxes with food during a year in which voles were declining. The result was that, in the area where foxes were fed, the grouse numbers did not decline with the voles. Since both removing foxes or giving them something else to eat stopped the cycles in the numbers of their secondary prey, it seems fair to conclude that predation had been causing these cycles. The likely interpretation was that normally the foxes respond to the decline in voles by turning their predatory attention to alternative prey, such as grouse and hares – a peak in vole numbers reduces fox predation on breeding populations of grouse and hares, and therefore leads to a peak in their numbers too (similarly, a crash in vole numbers forces the foxes to feed more on this secondary prey).

A similar principle applies to cases where a primary food source supports foxes in numbers that allow them to limit secondary prey insignificant in their diet. For example, the feeding site at Ein Gedi (Chapter 5) supported a high density of foxes, and in the immediate vicinity sand rats were rare, although they were abundant elsewhere. Similarly, foxes are sometimes held responsible for local reductions in some ground-nesting birds, such as terns, golden plover and stone curlew. In conclusion, although many studies support the view that natural prey populations are limited by their food supply, there are circumstances under which fox predation (or other limiting factors) can limit some prey populations to numbers lower than those determined by their food supply.

The possibility that the breeding stocks of natural prey populations are not limited by their predators has spilled over into a confusion regarding the shooting of wild game. A false conclusion would be: if the breeding stocks of pheasants, hares, etc were unaffected by foxes, then the gamekeeper would have no need to kill these predators. Such logic misunderstands the gamekeeper's intention, which is to maximize the sustainable surplus available to be shot – to the extent that the fox eats part of that surplus which would otherwise have been available to the sportsman, they are in direct competition. Indeed, the 'bags' of hares, pheasants and partridges generally increase where fox numbers crash due to rabies, mange or very intensive predator control, presumably demonstrating just such competition (it does not, however, prove that foxes are limiting the breeding populations of these game). However, where mange has greatly reduced fox numbers in Sweden,

Eric Lindström tells me that not only has the autumn bag of hares quadrupled, but also the spring breeding stock has more than doubled. Assessing the losses of game due to predators is not straightforward. It is even more difficult to predict what impact predator control will have on the number of game shot. The complexities are greatly multiplied when wild game stocks are supplemented (or flooded) with stock hatched in incubators.

The fox and the gamekeeper might be thrown into even worse conflict if it is true that foxes also limit the breeding stock of game as well as competing for the surplus. However, the consequences of reducing the breeding stock are very complicated. If you persisted in eating into your capital you would go broke, but this is where the behaviour of animals is more complicated than that of money – if an animal population is reduced below the numbers that could otherwise be sustained in that environment (the carrying capacity), the survivors compensate, at least up to a point, by producing more offspring (just as a fruit tree is pruned to stimulate a richer crop). The result is that foxes (or sportsmen) could diminish the breeding stock (the capital) of their prey below carrying capacity without causing them to go extinct (bankrupt) in so far as the reduced breeding population produces young (interest) at a higher rate.

There are many ways in which this remarkable phenomenon of compensation can occur; an obvious one is that by reducing numbers below carrying capacity more resources are left for the survivors who can therefore rear more young per head. The magnitude of this compensation (and therefore the sustainable yield) varies with the extent to which the population is reduced below carrying capacity. In the long run, to produce the maximum sustainable yield of prey would be ideal for game managers (and would be for foxes too, were it not that their high mortality rates probably give them a Keynesian disinterest in the long run – *see* Box 21, p.144).

Do foxes eat into the breeding stock of their prey? In general, scientific evidence is scarce, but in the case of the partridge they probably do. Partridges nest in rough grass on farmland. The drive for increased crop yields has resulted in the disappearance of suitable habitat so that nesting partridges are confined to strips of grass along field borders – the very same strips along which foxes travel. The fact that foxes travel routes coincide exactly with partridge nesting grounds may explain why Dick Potts found that up to 26 per cent of sitting hen partridges were killed by foxes even on land where gamekeepers were killing foxes. The problem is exacerbated because the foxes' predation on nesting partridges is density dependent – the greater the number of nests squeezed into a strip of grass, the greater the proportion of nesting hens the foxes killed (presumably because some of them 'got their eye in'). In brief, partridge stocks are higher where nest predators are controlled. There is an inverse relationship between mortality due to nest predators and that due to shooting. Dick Potts identified two parts to the partridge's compensatory reaction to shooting: either, (i) predator control reduces nest mortality, creating a surplus of birds which would have to emigrate if they were not shot, or (ii) in the absence of predator control, shooting reduces the nesting stock of birds, which reduces density dependent predation on their nests. From the partridges' point of view, either they are shot, whereupon the survivors suffer less nest predation, or they are not shot, whereupon nest predation will be high. The important difference is that sportsmen pay about £10 for each bird they kill, whereas foxes do not.

The irony is that while nest predation by foxes can be significant to the game manager, the partridges probably constitute an inconsequential element of the foxes' diet. Predation by foxes was only one factor limiting the numbers of partridges and their breeding success (chemical crop sprays, loss of habitat and crow predation on eggs were all more important). However, since in many cases game-shooting is a livelihood (akin to, and run alongside, farming) and the goal is to maximize the harvest (and thus the income), Potts concluded that some predators (notably foxes, rats and crows) were incompatible with this goal. Of course, one can imagine different goals which, for example, allow for both partridges and foxes to be present. In that case, management would emphasize reduction in chemical sprays and restitution of nesting habitat but not fox control. Some 'shoots adopt this policy and, according to Dick Potts' simulations, they can expect a decrease in sustainable yield of partridges from about 43 per cent to about 24 per cent of the population per annum. Traditionally, such a combination has appealed to those who were prepared to pay for both shooting birds and hunting foxes. It could equally well appeal to those who want to photograph foxes, or to harvest their skins, or to spare them unpleasant deaths at human hands. I mention these alternatives not to be disingenuous, but to emphasize that much of the countryside in the developed world, and much of the wildlife people like to think of as 'natural', is already the product of market forces. As in other forms of management, in wildlife management people get what they pay for.

Ewan Macdonald growing up with Blondie.

tivity per female fell). In the case of the three radio-vixens in Bright Eyes' group in 1983, only Fluff, the eldest, reared cubs; neither Dainty (probably three years old) nor Flame Red (a yearling) did so. Finally, there were signs of some territories shrinking, and one splitting in two. However, it would be foolhardy to attribute this change entirely to reduced death rate since some features of the food supply changed too. One way or another it seemed more than likely that fox numbers had increased. In early 1973 the farmers had shot just one vixen on that fateful day when I first accompanied them through the two woods on Denman's Farm. In March 1984, when the moratorium on killing foxes ended, they beat the same woods three times and shot a total of 19 adult foxes. Happily, Bright Eyes and Fluff were amongst those that escaped. Doubtless the farmers tried much harder in 1984, and perhaps the foxes had grown blasé and were easier to shoot, but it would be hard to escape the conclusion that there had been an increase in numbers. This point obviously bears upon the most contentious question of all: what are the effects on foxes and their populations of people killing them, whether for sport, for their pelts, or in the attempt to preserve other game? In purely biological terms such questions are very complex; worse still, in practice they are inseparable from questions of economics and ethics. The result is a perplexing muddle from which no simple answer can emerge. Nonetheless, in Boxes 31 to 32 I will introduce a selection of the issues.

How do these results tie in with our findings in other areas? This book is not the place for a theoretical treatise on the detail of fox society, but perhaps a few generalizations are appropriate. First, fox behaviour is so variable that the only robust generalization is that there is no robust generalization. To make a sensible guess at the territory size, group size and hence approximate population density of foxes in an area probably requires knowing about the abundance and dispersion of their food, and the pattern and rate at which they die. After all this work on fox society, I am prepared to offer a hunch (but definitely not a statement) on how it might work.

In brief, richer food supplies lead to smaller territories and more patchy (heterogeneous) food supplies permit larger groups. A very high death rate leads to smaller groups and a smaller proportion of barren vixens, probably together with larger territories. An intermediate death rate may be insufficient to reduce group size substantially, but nonetheless may disrupt social stability sufficiently to diminish the proportion of barren vixens and thereby increase the overall productivity of cubs. A low death rate facilitates larger groups, lower productivity of cubs per female, and probably smaller territories.

These are just the simplest of tentative generalizations, and even they can interact to produce an intimidating number of outcomes to different sets of circumstances. The task of separating cause from effect is further complicated by the practical difficulty of simultaneously studying foxes, their food and their mortality. There is great scope, and daunting practical difficulty, ahead for challenging experiments on this topic. So, I hope this is not the end of the story. Foxed, but still foxing, I start to know enough to pose some sensible questions.

In the meantime, what of the Foxlot? Nick and Malcolm, street-wise from urban foxing, are now successful businessmen; Patrick, Heribert and Andrew are research scientists in France, Tanzania and Paraguay respectively, while Chris

is a university lecturer in Australia. Pall is Director of the Icelandic government's wildlife service, Ian is a regional advisor for the Game Conservancy and Gill is conservation officer for the Agricultural Training Board. For my part, I write this on the 25th February 1987, a day that has gone rather well; at first light Mike Fenn and I radio-collared Wide Brows the dog fox. Mike is a new member of the Foxlot, busily applying his irrepressibly wry humour to the impact of Wide Brows' predation upon the radio rats we are now tracking over the local farms. A few hours later a knock at the door announced the arrival of White Flash, Blondie and Duff Legs, three 12cm long survivors of an earth crushed by excavations on a building site. Their eyes are firmly sealed, and their white tags are absurdly pronounced. Looking at their high-domed, golf ball sized heads nuzzling into the crevices of my pullover, I found myself laughing aloud at the pleasure of their company. Hopefully, they will grow up to help me with a new generation of questions.

But before closing this chapter let me hark back to one outstanding question. In Chapter 8, I speculated that the social hierarchy provided a mechanism for tailoring group size to food supply. The idea was simple enough—when times are hard the underdogs are evicted—but testing it was far from straightforward. In an attempt to do so I set in train an ambitious plan: the idea was to infiltrate tame spies into the wild fox community. Imagine the possibilities of whistling up a couple of wild foxes who emerged from the undergrowth to enact their social exchanges in full view. This dream had been very firmly in mind when we began to hand-rear the orphaned cubs in the spring of 1975, but it took 18 months of careful preparation before the actors were ready for the role that I had in mind for them. Whitepaws, Big Ears and Wide Eyes had been destined for the second enclosure. Their sisters, the middle-ranking vixens, Sickly and Pseudo-Sickly, were groomed for lives as a biologist's narks. The preparations were absurdly hard work: the two vixens had to be kept tame, and had to be familiarized with their future home range. So, after their three sisters had been moved to the second enclosure, Sickly and Pseudo continued to live in their modified garden shed at Hamels. Everyday they were fed and played with, and often were taken for leash-

Courtship in January: a dog fox (on the left) makes a cautious approach to the vixen. Their postures reveal an uneasy blend of playfulness and aggression.

walks. While I worked in other study areas, these tasks fell increasingly to Jenny.

In terms of scientific results, the lengthy preparations would yield nothing in themselves. It would take, so to speak, 18 months to arrive at Square One. One spring night in 1976 it looked like effort down the drain. Jenny was following her normal routine; the day's school teaching over, she changed into muddy jeans and set out on a tour of the local chicken farms to gather fresh corpses that the farmers kindly left in our regular pick-up places. With the car full of fox food in various stages of decay, she drove to Hamels. Arriving at the vixens' shed she whistled the call-sign. No sound of tails thumping a greeting on the wooden walls welcomed her, no squeals of excitement, no tetchy squabbling in excitement at the impending meal. With her heart in her mouth, Jenny fumbled to unlock the series of padlocks that secured the two safety doors to the shed. Inside, a large pile of soil and the torn edges of the wire floor told all: the vixens had escaped.

The light began to fade, and with it went our hopes of ever finding Sickly and Pseudo-Sickly. Then, from the direction of the burnt timbers of Hamels House, came the faintest suggestion of a whimper. We clambered into the charred wreckage, whistled the call-sign and held our breath as we strained to hear a response. High above us, in the third storey rafters, came a delighted squeal of vulpine greeting. Carefully, we negotiated the burnt staircases until our heads were level with ragged-ended beams which jutted like charred fingers into the open air from the third storey floor cavity. From that space, the two vixens' heads popped out, ears flicking back in their excitement at seeing us. Sickly hopped onto a protruding beam and, to our horror, began to squirm in greeting, rolling on a plank that was barely the width of her body, and suspended some ten metres above the rubble-strewn concrete foundations. The truants hopped nimbly and precariously from beam to beam, then scuttled back into the cavity beneath the floor boards. We could not see how they had got into the floor cavity, and they apparently could not find a way out. They dared not jump the abyss to reach Jenny's outstretched arms. Soon they had worked themselves into a dreadful panic. The only option seemed to be to cut an escape hatch for them in the floor. Armed with a saw, I climbed inside the remnants of the house and onto the floor beneath which I could hear the vixens scrabbling. I selected a spot as far as possible from the open edge, and began to cut through the timbers. At each stroke of the saw the vixens made as if to leap from precarious perches—leaps which we were sure they could not survive. Each cut of the saw was agonizingly

slow, and interspersed with attempts to calm the foxes. At last I cut a fox-sized trap-door opening into the floor, and wide-eyed with fear they emerged, cobweb encrusted, into Jenny's arms. With the painstaking necessity to saw quietly, the rescue had taken more than five hours!

On 16th August 1976 we finally began the planned release of the sisters. Boar's Hill seemed to be divided into contiguous fox territories, with no space for newcomers. If we provided a new food supply, in an area that was not already important for foraging wild foxes, could the sisters create a new territory? Both were equipped with radio-collars. The plan went like clockwork: they continued to visit their shed, and turned up nightly to meet Jenny when she arrived with their food. At first they took up residence together in a long disused and derelict cesspit. Thereafter they moved their daytime harbourage into the charred rafters of the Hamels House. By October they were travelling confidently through a shared home range of 20 hectares, occupying an area that had previously been unimportant for foraging within the White-legged group's territory. What is more, the northern boundary of their newly established range ran almost precisely along the division that had separated the White-legs from Toothypeg's group. Although we provided them with sufficient food each night, their droppings revealed

that they were eating wild caught prey. Indeed, it seemed that Sickly and Pseudo had been successfully infiltrated into the vulpine community, and that we had created a new territory.

Now I could test my expectation that if food was short it would be subordinate vixens in a group that would bear the brunt of the hardship. It had been these thoughts of hierarchy that led me to select Sickly and Pseudo for release. First, they had been of very similar, and middling, status amongst the five sisters. How would this equality change when they were relieved of the oppressive influence of their superiors? Second, due to their position in the hierarchy, neither vixen would have been expected to breed while in the company of their more dominant sisters. Once released from such social suppression, would either or both of them breed? I had opted to release them in the autumn of their second year, since by that age there could be no question that any failure to settle down or to breed was due to adolescence. Prior to their release, the relationship between Sickly and Pseudo had changed very little since their cubhood: Sickly was marginally dominant to Pseudo. Following their release we had the thrill of watching their interactions in the wild. Whistling the call-sign and rattling a tin of chocolate drops, we would watch, enchanted, as two adult vixens bounded across the meadow in flamboyant greeting. With

their sharp noses restlessly stabbing the air for whiffs of news, they epitomized wildness—yet they ran for chocolate drops and sat, with eyes half closed, soliciting a tickle in that special trance-inducing place just behind the ears. In front of us, however, in a wild and different world, changes in the vixens' relationships unfolded.

At first, the majority of their interactions were friendly or playful, and any aggression took the form of only a mild rebuff. By the end of September they took to sleeping apart: Sickly on a mattress in a top storey bedroom, Pseudo in a downstairs hearth. As time wore on, released from the anonymity of middle rank, the two sisters' interactions became polarized: they no longer played, and Sickly repeatedly intimidated Pseudo, sometimes attacking her fiercely. Some of the attacks had nothing to do with food. Sickly

would corner her increasingly demoralized sister and sideways-barge her again and again until Pseudo would break away in tail-lashing flight. However, until 11th October none of these episodes had been more than humiliating for Pseudo Sickly, and the two vixens still fed together. On the night of the 11th it was clear that things had changed: Pseudo threw herself into paroxysms of submission at so much as a glance from Sickly, and did not dare approach the food while her dominant sister ate. A fortnight later, antagonism had reached such a pitch that Pseudo had to grab food surreptitiously when Sickly's back was turned. Once, Sickly turned around to see Pseudo slinking off with a mouthful of food. She gave chase and thrashed Pseudo, drawing blood, retrieving the food, which she cached before continuing her interrupted meal. My hunch was that it was prudent for Sickly to exert her authority even when there was plenty of food—the result was that she had Pseudo well under her thumb just in case she ever needed to pull rank in earnest. One such circumstance arose when it came to courtship.

I was too keen to see how the sisters reacted to potential suitors to leave such observations to chance. Rather, we contrived to ensure that Smudge, Niff's yearling son, met them on his daily jaunts. These engineered encounters were telling: Sickly would approach Smudge whimpering with her brush lashing and ears half back, mouth slightly agape she jigged around him soliciting play. Their rough and tumbles might last for quarter of an hour or more. For her part, Pseudo was besotted with Smudge, and made no pretence at playful flirtation—she was paralysed with excitement at the sight of him. Indeed as she writhed towards Smudge in an ecstasy of squeals, she would often cover the last few feet rolling on her sides, kicking herself in an undignified slither towards him, and squirting little pulses of urine into the air. On these occasions Pseudo's antics with Smudge prompted Sickly to ferociously attack her prone sister as she writhed on her back, stricken between obeisance to the dog fox and terror at Sickly's onslaught. In effect, Sickly's interventions ensured that Pseudo was denied prolonged encounters with Smudge.

Pseudo became increasingly jittery. Was her inferiority brought on by moment-to-moment intimidation by Sickly, or did it indicate a long term change in her character? Bribed with a surfeit of chocolate drops, Sickly was persuaded to spend a night locked up in the shed. That night Pseudo was her old self: calm and friendly, she ate her fill and then methodically set about caching surplus food—a luxury that she had not enjoyed for the previous two weeks.

A few hours of freedom from Sickly's oppression were sufficient to change Pseudo's entire demeanour—the traits of social status seemed to be barely skin deep. Immediately her dominant sister was released, Pseudo's confidence collapsed, but at least for a few of the ensuing nights she escaped the brunt of Sickly's domination by utilizing the caches she had made during the brief respite. So, the situation stabilized: both foxes had enough to eat, but Sickly also secured enough to make caches, and Pseudo obtained her daily fare under duress.

Clearly both were capable foragers in their own right, and could supplement the food we provided. What would happen if food ran short? On the night of the 1st December the two vixens were given a few chocolate drops each, to show good faith, but otherwise they were left to their own devices. I stood by for a long night of radio tracking.

Sickly was unabashed by the failure of her accustomed catering arrangements. As I watched through the hot-eye, she trotted purposefully here and there through the undergrowth, emerging periodically with a mouthful of food retrieved from one of her many caches. Pseudo was in worse straits. She nervously nosed around, picking up occasional scraps that Sickly had dropped, but keeping a low profile. Doubtless she too was hoping to unearth some of Sickly's caches. However, not only was she at the disadvantage of not knowing the hiding places, but she also faced the risk of a thrashing each time Sickly thought she was getting too 'warm' in her search. By midnight, Pseudo had departed markedly from her normal habits. She had made four swift forays into the nearby gardens, normally the preserves of neighbouring foxes and therefore out of bounds to the two sisters. Shortly after midnight she moved into Toothypeg's territory and, trotting through what were almost certainly unknown surroundings, cut west to skirt the top of Dixieland Wood. From there she headed in a wide loop to the north, generally keeping to the houses and gardens of Toothypeg's range until she struck out across the farmland towards Black Agnes' territory. There, she moved swiftly through more large gardens until she reached Dr Stringfellow's garden. This was more than a kilometre from home, and a place where food was provided for the resident foxes. In the small hours of the morning, Pseudo made her way home, again navigating through previously unexplored areas. It is widely believed that one advantage of territoriality lies in knowing an area well. Pseudo's excursion raised the spectre of a corollary to that belief: was she at greater risk of misadventure when travelling unfamiliar ground? By dawn she had reached the border of her own range, and curled up to sleep for the day in an adjacent patch of scrub.

The following evening we provisioned the feeding site with plenty of food, but as soon as darkness fell Pseudo hastily made her way back to the environs of Dr Stringfellow's garden. She did not return home until midnight. It was a frosty night, and the snapping of ice-brittle grass under Pseudo's footfalls was clearly audible to both Sickly and me as we waited at the northern border of their range. Sickly listened intently, then sank to the ground, ready to pounce. As Pseudo padded nonchalantly into view, Sickly rushed her. There was a scuffle and the two bodies rolled into the beech hedgerow. Aside from the snapping of brittle twigs and the rustle of a thousand frozen leaves, there was a surprising silence: neither vixen voiced even a murmur. Whatever passed between them I doubt it was a reconciliation. That night when we provisioned the feeding site, Pseudo was nowhere to be seen but Sickly was in high spirits, frolicking around Jenny, pouncing on her feet and wrestling with her ankles. Suddenly they heard the noise of an animal approaching through the frosty grass: Sickly froze, listening intently, then bolted for cover. A few seconds later Pseudo appeared from the undergrowth and began to eat. The noise of her crunching on rabbit bones was clearly audible, and Sickly emerged and advanced cautiously. Sickly was not favoured by the wind and seemed uncertain of Pseudo's identity. Keeping more than 25 metres off, Sickly circled the feeding site until she cut the wind. She sniffed, stiffened with recognition, and hurtled towards her sister. Pseudo fled to the burnt house, and the two vixens sped upstairs to the attic, whence the sounds of a prolonged and dreadful fight echoed through the charred rooms. Ten minutes later, Sickly reappeared and continued to feed.

It seemed that the one night of disruption to the previously stable food supply had triggered a profound change in Sickly's tolerance of her subordinate sister. Oddly enough, the frequency of aggressive encounters between them fell, but this was because Sickly's attacks had reached such a remorseless pitch that Pseudo now took great pains to be unprovocative, skulking out of sight. On the evening of 4th December, Sickly trotted down from her third floor bedroom when Jenny arrived with the sisters' food. Pseudo appeared from her hiding place, submitting on the run. Writhing, low to the ground, ears plastered back, squealing as she made a dash for the food, Pseudo grabbed a lump of meat and

fled, brush and body convulsed with submission. In a trice, Sickly overtook her and forced her to drop the food. Sickly picked up the meat and carried it off to cache. A few minutes later, Pseudo ran the gauntlet again, and this time after a lengthy chase, was able to keep the food that she had grabbed. Later that night, Sickly permitted her sister to feed, but every attempt to cache food triggered a thorough trouncing. It seemed that a new *status quo* had been reached: Pseudo was tolerated, but strictly on Sickly's terms, and these terms did not include making caches.

Two nights later, Pseudo found no chance to steal scraps from her sister's table, and so she set out on another trek through unfamiliar terrain. She was once again in the Stringfellows' garden when I left her before dawn. The next morning a telephone message called me to Boar's Hill: on a quiet country road a kilometre from her territory I recognized the fine-muzzled face lying on the blood stained asphalt before I was close enough to check the code number of Pseudo's radio.

Following Pseudo-Sickly's death, Sickly continued to flourish in the wild. She seemed to have become a thoroughly dominant wild vixen. In January 1977 she began to token mark for the first time in her life. She also paced aggressively outside Niff's tennis court enclosure and, although she submitted to Niff's mate, she lay in wait to attack Niff during experimental walks. On the other hand, she seemed quite amiable in her interactions with her sisters in Enclosure II and I began to worry that when it came to breeding she would still be under the influence of the dominant females therein. However, on 1st February I surprised a large wild dog fox sleeping with Sickly, and the next day he was once again curled up beside her. Since, in the enclosures, only breeding vixens are favoured with such attentions, I jumped to the conclusion that freed from the oppressive dominance of her sisters Sickly had come on heat. We waited excitedly for the cubs to be born, but there was no sign of them. Indeed, two springs came and went without trace of cubs being born to Sickly. Yet she was completely at home in the wild. Sometimes, when food was abundant, days would pass when Jenny would not see her; anxiety would mount, and then one evening she would come bounding out of the undergrowth and proffer her ear for tickling. Now I could not get closer than 20 paces

to Sickly, and only Jenny could stroke her. In 1978 her radio collar fell off, and shortage of funds prevented me from replacing it. No outward sign remained to distinguish Sickly from her wild companions.

Dawn had just broken on the 6th January 1979 as I patrolled the frost-crisp fields of Boar's Hill. At the time I was trying to radio-collar as many foxes as possible to up-date my picture of the local territories. On this occasion luck was with me: I had caught a fox where a well-trodden trail slipped through the hedge bordering Aubrey's field. It was a powerfully built vixen, with a full red pelt and teeth that had long since lost the pin-sharpness of youth. It began to rain. I was cold, drowsy and, now, wet, as I buckled on her radio collar. Two hazel-brown eyes watched me from a strangely expressionless face. At the instant I released the fox, she swivelled around, gripped the peak of my cap, and dashed off across the field with it firmly in her mouth. Lumbering in pursuit, I followed her tracks across that field and half way over the next, until I found the cap discarded. There was something odd about that vixen's appearance—her muzzle had lacked the dark 'tear-drops' which, to a greater or lesser extent, mark out the typical foxy face. I mused on the fact that I had only known one other fox with these bland markings, Sickly. Suddenly it dawned on me that I had, unwittingly and somewhat unceremoniously, just equipped Sickly with radio-collar and eartags!

That night Jenny toured Hamels, whistling the call sign and rattling the tin of chocolate drops. At last, in the fading light, a fox came running towards her. It was Sickly and, sure enough, she was wearing a new radio-collar. Meanwhile, as March advanced, Sickly's swaying undercarriage left no doubt that she was pregnant. Her intermittent assignations with Jenny became, once again, nightly affairs until 19th March, whereupon she disappeared without trace. Four days later she appeared at the run, with trim flanks and heavy with milk, and grabbed a huge mouthful of food before dashing back to her cubs.

Sickly reared her cubs in a den amidst a tangle of overgrown brush beside the charred remains of Hamels House. Her aggression towards the inmates of the tennis court grew more violent, and well worn paths developed on both sides of the enclosure fence as the would-be protagonists paced back and forth snirking and gaping at each other. Meanwhile, Sickly moved her cubs into the burnt house. There were two of them, and while we could hear them playing in the ruins, they grew up as wild and shy as could be. In late May, Sickly moved them again, this time to the thick scrub adjoining the tennis court—a move devoid of diplomacy considering the animosity between her and the inmates.

Sickly died that summer, from a septic leg wound, but not before she had reared her cubs. For nearly four years she had lived as a wild animal. She had shared the woods and fields with companions whose greatest preoccupation was to avoid people at all costs. By night she had hunted and fought, conceived and born cubs, known snowy winter winds and summer sunshine, and she had slunk silently away from the sound and scent of strange humans. Yet, daily, she had volunteered to shed the mantle of wildness, to swop worlds, and enjoy a few chocolate drops and a tickled ear.

For her three sisters, the years of Sickly's liberty had been passed in the security of Enclosure II. For three breeding seasons, wooed first by Smudge and latterly by Fox, their reproductive entanglements had been laid bare before us (Chapter 8). My voyeurism had convinced me that the notion of social contraception was not whimsical: among these vixens in my fox groups the opportunity to breed was linked to their social standing. But although the behaviour of the inmates closely mirrored what we saw in the wild, the sceptic could nevertheless dismiss the results as artefacts of captivity. There was one acid test: to establish the inmates of Enclosure II in the wild, while continuing to pry into their relationships unfettered by captivity. On the 29th April 1980 we unravelled holes in the chain-link fencing to allow passage into, and out of, the enclosure. The vixens, Wide Eyes, Big Ears and Whitepaws, and the dog fox, Fox, were free to come and go as they pleased.

It worked. The four foxes rapidly adjusted to life in the wild, setting up residence in roughly the same area that had been Sickly's home range previously. The bulk of their food was provided daily, but they soon took to supplementing this through their own foraging activities. Both Fox and Wide Eyes, then the dominant vixen, sprinkled the vicinity with copious token urine marks. The lower status vixens, Big Ears and Whitepaws, also marked but much less frequently. All three vixens continued to submit to Fox, whose surly rebukes to Whitepaws verged upon brutality. Good natured as always, Big Ears continued, on the one hand, to be tolerant of Whitepaws, despite her fallen status, and on the other hand, flicked her ears at Wide Eyes just enough to be respectful, but not obsequious. And all this happened in the wild. We could hardly believe our luck when for six weeks of pollen-laden summer the foxes lived in field and copse as an integrated and tolerably harmonious group, keeping their nightly liaison with Jenny, her food bucket and chocolate drops. Then disaster struck.

It was a warm June evening. With an armful of dead poultry, Jenny made her way towards the *rendez-vous* where Big Ears and Whitepaws seemed unusually excitable, and Wide Eyes was nowhere to be found. Jenny was on the verge of leaving when a faint whimper led her to a tangle of bushes. Wide Eyes looked up and whimpered a greeting before turning back to licking the severed stump of her leg. The remainder of the limb hung by no more than a bloody strand of skin, the bone and muscle had been sliced through. A nearby hayfield had been mown that day, and we could only guess that the flailing blades had caught Wide Eyes unaware as she dozed at the field edge in the sunshine. Jenny gingerly picked up Wide Eyes, her leg dangling hideously on its string of flesh. But it seemed that Fox sensed Wide Eyes' plight and perceived Jenny's interference as an added threat. As Jenny cradled Wide Eyes in her arms, Fox leapt up, grabbing at the injured vixen, trying to pull her free. As Jenny tried to carry Wide Eyes to the car, Fox tried to grab her knee, leaping and scrabbling at her legs at every pace. In his attempt to release Wide Eyes, Fox was clawing at her severed limb.

By now Jenny was shaking with dismay. In desperation she shouted at Fox, trying to shoo him off, but to no avail. It was a dreadful blood-

stained scene: Wide Eyes' tail was swaying in plaintive greeting, Fox was in a protective frenzy trying to bar Jenny's progress. Jenny shrieked at Fox, and pushed him away roughly. Taken aback by this first rebuke in his hand-reared lifetime, Fox jumped aside, but followed close at Jenny's heels as she carried the mutilated vixen to the car. Ramsay Hovell, the vet, could only confirm what was already obvious, and that night Wide Eyes was destroyed. A few hours later, when we returned to Hamels, Fox had gone, never to return, leaving Jenny with a last image of him in the rear-view mirror, standing forlorn in the track as she had driven away with his mate.

Wide Eyes' death gave rise to an intriguing observation: the next day Big Ears was busying herself with some food at a cache; when she picked up a mouthful and ran off with it. As she ran she whimpered in the way that foxes do when they are giving food to cubs. It was more than a year since Big Ears had made that call. Now she carried the food to the blood-stained hollow that marked the spot where Wide Eyes had lain. There, Big Ears whimpered the food-giving call, then she cached the food beneath the very blades of grass on which her injured sister had lain. Much agitated, Big Ears and Whitepaws trotted up and down the web of fox paths, sniffing continually. They seemed to be greatly vexed. Could Big Ears have been trying to give food to her injured group mate? Another observation adds weight to my suspicion that she was. The case in point involved two other free-ranging, tame foxes. In that case a dog fox was lamed by a thorn in his paw, and badly debilitated by the resulting septicaemia. The dominant vixen of his group carried food to him and gave it to him. We only saw her do this once, and the dog fox soon recovered, but that one observation is all the more notable considering the possessiveness adult foxes generally show amongst themselves over food.

Big Ears and Whitepaws settled down to a new life. Within a week they were being seen in the company of a wild dog fox, whose red radio collar (sadly defunct) identified him as a tenant of the adjoining territory. What would happen to the social standing of the surviving vixens with Wide Eyes' death? As number two in the hierarchy, Big Ears was the heir apparent, but would her second place guarantee her inheritance.

Almost immediately Big Ears again stepped into dominant pads. The most conspicuous sign of her status was an immediate increase in her rate of token marking. Whitepaws' lowly position remained unchanged, which may explain why, that autumn, she quit the territory.

Big Ears was completely at home in the wild by the winter of 1980-81, and days might pass without her coming for food. Her self-assured status was evidenced by the urine marks that she sprinkled throughout her territory, and by her antagonism towards intruders. This was amply illustrated when, in mid-November, Sandy Vixen and Friendly Male devised a way to escape from the nearby Enclosure III. Big Ears was already in the habit of patrolling the outside of this enclosure, glaring threateningly at the inmates while she token-marked more than once a minute. Sandy Vixen was the first inmate to climb a large sycamore tree, pick a route to the extremity of a bough, and catapult herself to freedom. We did not see their first encounter, but to judge by Big Ears' high dudgeon and the tufts of fur missing from Sandy's coat, it had been unfriendly. Having learned the trick, Sandy tried it repeatedly, despite my efforts to block her escape routes. A territorial dispute in microcosm developed. Big Ears spent more and more time lying in wait to attack Sandy as she plummeted from the tree. Sandy always seemed happy to be rescued from this treatment and returned to her enclosure, and would often be waiting at the door when we arrived.

Later in the month, Friendly Male followed Sandy over the fence. By the time we arrived, Sandy had been driven off by Big Ears. Meanwhile, Big Ears and Friendly were excitedly chasing each other through the undergrowth, their flirtatious antics accompanied by much squealing. Eventually Jenny intervened in what seemed to be a budding romance picking up Friendly and returning him to the enclosure. I spent a further hour up the tree, modifying the barrage of wiremesh nailed across all the major branches. Meanwhile, Big Ears patrolled nearby, still marking at a high rate. A week later Sandy, the truant, came home and having run the gauntlet of Big Ears' teeth, was returned to her enclosure.

As the winter of 1980 closed in, we watched Big Ears, freed from the yoke of Wide Eyes dominance, and completely at home in the wild, with one question in mind: would she breed? Her appearances at the feeding site became increasingly irregular and in early December she arrived with a badly gashed and possibly broken hind leg. The wound was slow to heal, and having accepted an antibiotic pill coated in margarine on Christmas Eve, she disappeared. Eventually we were forced to the painful conclusion that the infection had claimed her.

On the evening of 11th August 1981, I was languishing in a discouragingly long cinema queue that stretched between me and James Bond in *For Your Eyes Only*. I was meditating on the disadvantages of abandoning our place in the queue in order to search for Jenny, who was already late for our meeting, when she arrived in a great fluster. On the principle that it never rains but it pours, it seemed that Friendly Male had again scaled the plum tree to escape from Enclosure III, that the new owner of Hamels had bulldozed the screen of shrubbery that hid the tennis court, and that Big Ears had come home after an eight month absence. As we sped off towards Hamels, Jenny described how she had arrived there to find Big Ears waiting for her beside the customary parking place. Despite her prolonged sojourn in the wild, the vixen had greeted her warmly. She was slightly worn and torn—her brush was broken near the root and so hung at a garish angle, and she was a bit lame—but the real problem was that she looked thin and drawn. Was it illness that had brought her home from the wild and a private life in which, as I later discovered, she had indeed born cubs?

Big Ears was there to greet us when we arrived at Hamels, and once the jollity of the reunion was over it was clear just how haggard and lack-lustre she looked. Her weakness for chocolate drops was unabated, and with this lure she was persuaded to hop into the cat basket in which, six years before, we had collected her from Mr Spring as a four day old orphan. At this point, Friendly Male trotted up. While he was distracted in greeting Big Ears through the walls of the basket, we were able to grab him and return him to his enclosure, and I worked up the tree until midnight trying to pre-empt further escape attempts with yet more wire barracades. Then we took Big Ears home to a shed in our garden. That night she was not well and by sunrise she was gravely ill; during the next two days her strength ebbed away. On the evening of the 13th, I sat beside her motionless form, as she lay stupified by the toxins that leaked from her failing kidneys. Suddenly she looked very small. She stood up and took two wobbly paces before collapsing and falling asleep. Time passed, and at last she lifted her head a little. I slipped one hand under her chin for support, and edged a margarine tub of sweetened, fortified milk to her lips. Big Ears hesitated, and began to lap. I was swept with a surge of hope—not only was she drinking, she was drinking while cradled by hands that had barely touched her for two years. What a strange life she had led, and how consistent had been her sprightly good nature towards both other foxes and ourselves. As she lapped, I remembered the three hourly feeds day and night of her cubhood, the milk drawn in an eyedropper from a mug bearing an owl design, which has remained my special coffee mug to this day. I remembered her early struggles for dominance over Whitepaws, her second accession after Wide Eyes' death, and their three quite different characters. I remembered her running free along the fox paths at Hamels, along the very same paths where, long before she was born, I had first watched Blackfringe and Downwhite. Now she was exhausted. Her eyes were sunken, her breathing fast. Her fur, long and bleached tawny, fell open in interweaving runnels that exposed the dark underfur beneath. Over her temples, and at the side of her shoulders, it faded to a burnt cream. Her thin figure carried the trophies of age—the disjointed brush, the long-since broken toe healed askew, the heavily scarred muzzle, the lower incisors worn to stubs, one canine smashed, another gone. Slowly she lapped, her chin resting heavily on my hand. During ten laboured minutes she drank. Too ill to even lick her milky lips, her head sunk onto her forepaws and she fell asleep. A little later, as I stared at her lying dead, I found myself noticing, as if for the first time, that she had very big ears.

E N D

The Oxford Foxlot in 1981—Bottom row (lft to rt) Gill Kerby, Jenny Macdonald, David Macdonald, Patrick Doncaster, Malcolm Newdick. Back row (lft to rt) Heribert Hofer, Pall Hersteinsson, Emilio Herrera.

INDEX